CONNECTING WITH THE
ONE CONSCIOUSNESS

Connecting with the One Consciousness

Spiritual Awakening, Mystical Sufism, and the Lessons of Mohammad Ali Taheri

Sheida White

Minneapolis

Also by Sheida White

Taking off from Tehran: An Iranian Immigrant's Memoir of Leaving Behind Gender Expectations and Succeeding in America

Most of the proceeds from this book's sales will go toward a scholarship fund. This fund will support anyone who is enthused and ready to facilitate the awakening of the One Consciousness in others.

ISBN 13: 978-1-63489-565-1

Library of Congress Catalog Number has been applied for.
Printed in the United States of America
First Printing: 2023

27 26 25 24 23   5 4 3 2 1

Chapters 1 and 2 have been adapted from previously published work *Taking off from Tehran: An Iranian Immigrant's Memoir of Leaving Behind Gender Expectations and Succeeding in America* © copyright 2022 by Sheida White.

Cover design by Nupoor Gordon
Interior design by Patrick Maloney

Wise Ink Creative Publishing
807 Broadway St. NE
Suite 46
Minneapolis, MN 55413

To learn more, visit www.sheidawhite.com

I dedicate this book to Mohammad Ali Taheri,
whose teachings awakened me to the purpose of my creation:
to know my true self, beneath the thinker,
as the immortal One Consciousness.

Contents

Author's Note

OST OF THE poems in this book are translations of medieval Persian poets, such as Rumi, which I've gathered from various sources. Deeply rooted in Persian culture, the poems remind us how spiritual profundity combined with artful expression can be a sustaining part of everyday life. They bring the sacred and the earthly together in startling ways. Growing up in Tehran, I, like everyone else, used poems as a tool for persuasion. A key axiom of my native culture is this: "If the poet said it, it must be true." I know of very few Persians who do not know some poems by Rumi and Hafez, which they recite on various occasions. Rumi, as the most widely sold poet in America, has also become a part of contemporary Western literature.

Taheri tells us that no human being is separate from all the others. Rather, in our essence, we are one. Thus, a change in one of us, however slight, reverberates throughout all of us, either uplifting or degrading humanity. As more and more people practice and share this timeless principle, which is in line with ancient Persian Sufism, compassion for others and healing in our world will naturally follow. Therein lies the pathway to a more peaceful and unified planet.

Acknowledgments

MY DEEPEST GRATITUDE goes to Sheila McEntee and Abbie Phelps, my editors, for their astute comments and for bringing this book to its final form. Carla McClure, my devoted first reader, was meticulous in offering her editorial and substantive comments.

Thanks to Alyssa Bluhm, Patrick Maloney, and Hanna Kjeldbjerg of Wise Ink Creative Publishing for their invaluable guidance throughout the publication process.

Discussions with Maryam, a close friend and a trained instructor of Taheri's teachings, catalyzed my spirituality. This book wouldn't have been written without her encouragement and multiple reviews.

My warmest thanks to Dr. Stephen Kercel, a friend and scholar of quantum physics, for helping me understand technical concepts outside my profession.

I would like to express my enduring respect and gratitude for the people in every part of the world who are nurturing what is deepest and best in us all—our collective consciousness.

Finally, this book would be unfinished without blessings from that unseen force that lights our way—the infinitely good and merciful God, the "face" of the One Consciousness.

Introduction

TODAY OUR WORLD is experiencing great upheaval. Unprecedented political and racial division exists, particularly in America, while a recent global pandemic and war have ravaged families and economies. In response, social and mainstream media pummel us with a continuous barrage of anger and angst, amplifying and, to a great extent, contributing to the upheaval. Now, more than ever, we need a different kind of energy—strong, positive energy—to release us from the grip of these highly negative thought streams.

Strong, positive energy emanates from a certain vibrational frequency, indeed, a divine power. To help end the struggles afflicting our world today and bring the light of our true essence, or what I call the *One Consciousness*, into the world, we must begin with ourselves. As the One Consciousness emerges, our ego diminishes and the spiritual dimension expands, creating a kinder, more peaceful, and more unified world.

In the fall of 2019, I joined a small group, led by a Persian friend, to study the teachings of Mohammad Ali Taheri, an Iranian spiritual leader who escaped death in Iran and now lives and teaches in Canada. Over a period of months, I experienced a spiritual awakening so profound that I was drawn to write about it and share my insights. I feel I have been called to this sharing the way I was called to fulfill earlier aspirations in my life: with great enthusiasm, curiosity, focus, positivity, and gratitude.

My main exposure to Taheri's school of thought has been through transcriptions of his lectures, which he gave in Farsi prior to his imprisonment in Iran in 2010. Though I've studied his teachings for two years, I feel that I have been preparing to experience and share my awakening since childhood. A divine energy with incredible power guided the writing of this text. This intelligence, which emanates from God, is using me as a vehicle to create a manifestation that has the potential to send positive energy into our world.

The insights that have come from my understanding of Taheri's teachings arrived suddenly as gifts from the realm of consciousness. That's where our real power lies. Indeed, my enthusiasm and creative flow for writing were so intense that I completed the first draft of this book in just two weeks. On more than one occasion, I sat in front of my computer wrapped in a towel after taking a shower, fearing the solution to a problem I was working on might evaporate in the short time it would take me to get dressed.

To confirm that my insights were inspired by something greater—something divine—I asked myself whether I would still write this text if I were to publish it anonymously, with no expectations of praise. The answer was yes. Then I asked myself the next question: Would I still write it if I didn't enjoy the process? The answer was a decisive no. When sudden insights come from an epiphany—that is, a manifestation of the divine—the journey of creating has its own inherent joy, which stems from being fully present. The outcome becomes irrelevant. Even obstacles are transformed and become playful and helpful.

As a scientist in the field of literacy (reading and writing), I enjoyed the quality of full Presence in the form of intense enthusiasm, curiosity, and rapt attention, which I applied to solving conceptual problems. As a researcher, I strove to uncover aspects of reading and writing that hinder children who experience the toughest conditions for learning. I called these aspects *Task Inhibitors*. Interestingly, I am experiencing that same quality of full Presence now as I try to unmask aspects of the mind that function as Task Inhibitors, hindering us from being fully present in our lives. I am convinced that my experience with both types of Presence—*focused mind* to reach scientific solutions and *still mind* to reach God—has been guided by the Divine Intelligence. I am simply an "assembled vehicle" for this intelligence to delight in expressing itself.

This book's main purpose is to illuminate the teachings of Taheri and thereby draw attention to our collective consciousness, the sacred essence of who we are. It exists in each of us, waiting to be awakened by those who are enthused and ready. Many are. The momentum to seek collective consciousness is growing around the world. We need only let the goodness that is already within us emerge. That goodness wants to be aligned with a universal intelligence—the Divine Intelligence.

Those with open minds and hearts, who have no prejudgment or bias toward new information (افراد بدون پیش داوری), will benefit most from the concepts in this book. They will admit, with courage, what they do not know, and stay open to information that may be foreign to their own thinking and experience. Most important, this book will appeal to individuals who have great enthusiasm for connecting with their inner selves.

The spiritual ideas in this book, in and of themselves, do not have the power to determine who you truly are. They can, however, help guide you in realizing your true identity as the One Consciousness. Indeed, discovering this identity is the purpose of our existence in this world. We can only feel the One Consciousness when we let go of our thoughts. In so doing, we quiet the ego, which consists purely of thought.

As you come closer to knowing your true self, the One Consciousness, you may notice, as I have, that you are more peaceful and less reactive to unsettling circumstances—political unrest, or people whose values and aspirations differ sharply from yours. Instead of listening to divisive commentaries on cable news, I began writing this book, and in so doing began to feel connected to others, my readers. If I can enrich lives, no matter how few, with my experience of spiritual awakening, I will have also enriched the universe. I have allowed myself to become an opening that positive energy flows through for the benefit of all.

I hope that the concepts in this book will offer the same transformative power to you as they have to me. Whether or not they are read widely, I believe my expressing them will naturally affect the underlying consciousness of humanity in a positive way.

Ultimately, our life on Earth is a dance between the two dimensions that make up our reality: the secular and the sacred, or the focused thoughts and the zero thoughts (stillness of the mind). The two are deeply intertwined. Neither is sufficient by itself. Earlier in my life, as a competitive ballroom dancer, I delighted in using long-practiced dance techniques to become the embodiment of rhythm—to become at one with the music. In much the same way, using Taheri's concepts, we can come to know our true selves and become the One Consciousness, harmonized and at one with the Divine Intelligence.

As noted earlier, it was during a time of worldly upheaval that I turned to focused thinking—that is, to writing this book. Because the book is based on theories that help us grow spiritually while living in the world's uncompromising realities, it is a melding of focused and zero thought.

In truth, I've spent much of my life pursuing worldly goals through focused thought. Indeed, chapters 1 and 2 describe my journey to self-actualization, from a childhood with little hope in Iran to education and a dream-come-true career in America. Rejecting the restrictive values of my native culture and pursuing my dream in America would not have been possible without my abiding faith in God, which began in childhood. More recently, as I describe in chapter 3, my faith inspired me to delve more deeply into my relationship with God and to seek and practice the principles that unite us all in the collective consciousness. That seeking led to the spiritual discoveries I relay in the subsequent chapters of this book.

I invite you to share the dance between those two dimensions, secular and sacred, with me. In joy and enthusiasm, I hope you will open yourself to the emerging One Consciousness, thereby living in unity, grace, and alignment with the Divine Intelligence—that which connects all things. Therein, I believe, lies the pathway to a more peaceful, kind, and just world.

PART ONE

A Quest to Know God

1

Claiming My Life

Today, like every other day, we wake up empty
and frightened. Don't open the door to the study
and begin reading. Take down a musical instrument.
Let the beauty we love be what we do.
There are hundreds of ways to kneel and kiss the ground.

~Rumi

IN THE SPRING of 1962, I was barely fifteen years old and living with my family in Tehran, Iran. One day, my parents announced that I was to marry a handsome, successful, thirty-year-old dentist. If I did not, they said, I would miss the opportunity of a lifetime.

At fifteen, I was shy and reserved. I didn't talk back, or talk much at all. When a man looked at me, I flushed and lowered my eyes at once. I was not only timid, I was afraid—of almost everything, but especially of the dark.

Even so, I already had my own ideas about how I wanted to live my life. I wanted to go to college and make something of myself. I fantasized about becoming a doctor and finding a way to beat cancer, despite my parents' belief that a woman's place was in the home. I didn't completely grasp how difficult my desired path might be for a girl growing up in the pre-revolutionary days of 1960s Tehran. I just knew it was the path I wished to walk.

My desires to learn and to make a difference were strong, even in a society where external values, such as physical beauty, the prestige of your family, and the amount of money you had, were prized over core values like education, honesty, and service to others. Quitting school at ninth grade to marry and have babies didn't make sense to me. I did not want to live like my mother, who, at sixteen, quit school to marry my father, who was twenty-three. Like all Iranian marriages in the 1930s, theirs was arranged by older members of their families. By age seventeen, my mother already had the first of her three children.

A month or so after my parents announced my engagement to the dentist, I sat on the edge of my bed in tears, staring at the tall, brown cardboard box of china that loomed in a corner of the room. Just a few days earlier, the dentist and I had selected and purchased the china set for twelve from the bazaar in Tehran. I turned my attention from the box of china and looked around my little room, which was in a fifth-floor apartment on a noisy street. Though it was sparsely furnished and the walls were bare, I cried to think it would soon become only a memory.

A few days earlier, through the closed living room door, I had overheard a conversation between my mother and the dentist's father, who said I didn't need to go to school beyond ninth grade. My mother agreed, especially when the man reminded her that a high-society family was trying to grab his son for their own daughter.

As I replayed this conversation in my head, my brother, who was six years older than me and a friend of the dentist, walked into my room. Seeing the tears streaming down my face, he asked, "What on earth is the matter with you?" I told him that while the dentist had no obvious faults, I was confused and afraid. Being married at barely fifteen, I confided in him, was not the way I wanted to live. I knew that marriage to the dentist would shatter my aspirations.

As I told the truth to my brother, my heart hammered against my chest. When I finished, there was a heavy pause. We sat quietly for a little while, then exchanged a few more words, mostly about why I hadn't spoken up before. Then he gently left. That night, I buried my face in my pillow and cried silently, surrendering myself to God.

The next day, my brother approached me, grinning.

"I've talked to the dentist," he said. "You are now free."

His words hung in the air for a moment before I grasped their meaning. Then I hugged him and thanked him again and again. I could hardly believe it. I was free! My life had been given back to me.

Rejecting the dentist and the lifestyle my native culture expected me to embrace was a major turning point in my life. It meant I could still pursue my dreams, but I had also rejected my parents' plans for me. In holding on to my dreams, I knew I would be on my own. I could not be fearful. I would have to be determined and strong.

Perhaps, when my deepest desires for agency and fulfillment were wrenched away from me and then miraculously returned, there rose up a gratitude so strong that it fueled an unstoppable motivation to succeed. Looking back on this painful time, I see that the vision I had created for my future—and my faith that this vision could become reality—unleashed the all-important energy of enthusiasm, excitement, and joyfulness. To make my vision a reality, I learned how to sacrifice, work hard, and focus my thinking. These actions ultimately sustained me through more difficult times to come, providing the foundation upon which I began to build my dreams.

Earlier Struggles

NOT LONG AFTER MY breakup with the dentist, my parents separated. Their life together, and my life with them, had been filled with struggle. While I was growing up in the 1940s and 1950s, we moved many times so my father could pursue employment; we even spent several years in a small village in the newly established state of Israel, where he worked on a farm. Being Jewish, my family settled comfortably there, yet my father missed his homeland and became depressed. His health also suffered, as he developed asthma. Wretchedly unhappy, he released his frustrations by abusing my mother, my two brothers, and me.

My father eventually returned to Iran, leaving the four of us in Israel until he could get his health back and find a job. By all measures, we lived in poverty. To support us, my mother worked in a peanut factory in a nearby town, walking a long distance to and from her job each day. My oldest brother, who was then seventeen, earned money as a rifle-carrying guard on a nearby farm, where he protected melons from nighttime raids by Arab intruders.

Two long years later, my mother, my brothers, and I left Israel and flew back to Iran. My father had found a good job in Khorramshahr, an Iranian city that lies on the banks of the Karun River. We were given a house, a full-time servant, and a chauffeur. Unfortunately, the job in Khorramshahr lasted only a year. When it ended, we moved back to Tehran for a year, then to Tabriz for two years.

It may have been my father's increasingly abusive behavior, or perhaps the continual upheaval I experienced, that led me, as a twelve-year-old in Tabriz, to develop a strong sense of responsibility and accountability to God. I did this on my own. I rarely attended a synagogue or read the Torah—in fact, my family concealed our

Jewish heritage because of the strong Islamic sentiment in that city. Yet I saw God as a divine power within me, a part of who I was, a friend who was concerned with my every thought and action, my "musical instrument" that went beyond my thoughts (my interpretation of Rumi's poem above). I felt that God was capable of answering my prayers, if only to give me extra strength to deal with the challenges in my little world.

After Tabriz, we moved back to Khorramshahr for a year. Then, in 1961, we moved back to Tehran when my father took a job in Babolsar, a town on the coast of the Caspian Sea.

Perhaps my parents' separation, when it came, should not have been a surprise. Though he was loving and encouraging to me at times, my father had continued to be violent. Several times, we took shelter in the home of my mother's older brother for weeks or even months. My father was also unfaithful to my mother. Still, despite all this, separation was highly unusual in those days in Iran. It revealed to everyone the severity of my family's situation.

Making a Plan

AFTER MY PARENTS' SEPARATION, my mother and I moved into a more modest apartment. My mother, who worked as a backstage manager at a performing arts complex, did not have the means to support our earlier lifestyle, and my father provided no assistance. Once I was free from my engagement to the dentist at age fifteen, I was, without question, in charge of my own life. My mother had learned that she could not dictate my future against my will, and my father was no longer in the picture.

At this point, I came to accept that if I was going to sit in a university classroom someday, I would have to take certain risks and learn to rely on my own secret strength. I would also have to rely on God, who I believed was behind my strength, listening to my desires, supporting me, and guiding me. As much as I could, I avoided negative thinking about my family and my oppressive native culture. I knew that succumbing to that would only hold me back.

Yet even with God's grace, I knew that to make my dreams come true, I needed a plan. I had no money or skills. Fortunately, my aunt was the director of a three-year vocational school for girls. I asked her if I could go to the school to learn secretarial work. I told her I had decided to quit regular schooling at the end of ninth grade and instead try to learn skills that would make me employable. I did not tell her that my real goal was to make money and save it for college in America.

My mother's oldest brother was already living in America. Reading and hearing about the country, I liked its emphasis on individualism. American culture valued self-reliance, intelligence, compassion for others, hard work, education, and accomplishment. I compared that to the Iran of the 1960s, when what mattered most was being born into wealth or a "good" family. Though America was still only a faraway dream, when I was accepted at my aunt's school, my hope and enthusiasm began to grow. I saw a pathway to my dream, one I could actually walk.

Still, there were obstacles. The vocational school didn't offer math and science classes, which I would need to get into college in America. Then it occurred to me that I could take these classes at night. Now fully focused, and with growing hope and determination, I found the classes and enrolled myself. I didn't mention them to my vocational school classmates, my teachers, or even my aunt, however—I didn't want anyone to know that, for me, secretarial skills weren't enough. In my plan, they were only stepping-stones.

I went to school six days a week. Every morning I took two

different public buses to get to the vocational school. Then I took the same buses back home, burst through the door, grabbed a few bites to eat, and caught a different bus to the night school, which began at six in the evening and ended at nine.

In those days, my biggest challenge was finding time to study. I would unroll a light mattress on the carpet in our living room, set the alarm for four in the morning, get up in the pitch darkness, and study for a couple of hours before getting ready for vocational school. This was my life for three years, from age fifteen to eighteen. I didn't miss a single night class, even during the harsh winter months, when snow piled up high in the streets and made walking nearly impossible.

Upon graduation from both schools, I got a job as a chief secretary in a company that manufactured agricultural pesticides. I worked eight hours a day, six days a week. Though the work was not stimulating, my focus and determination never wavered.

After three years, I had saved enough money for a one-way plane ticket to the United States and one year of college tuition. I figured that once I got there, I'd find some way to continue my education beyond the first year. I was twenty-one years old.

Lacking a guidance counselor or any friends or family members who knew about colleges in America, I went to the American Embassy in Tehran and asked for some catalogues. The kindly American woman behind the counter gestured to a room that contained hundreds of them. I was immediately overwhelmed. How could I study and evaluate hundreds of colleges in a country I knew little about?

Instead, I asked the woman for a map of the United States. When she unfolded it and laid it on the counter, I pointed directly at the middle. Wouldn't a college located at the center of the nation be representative of colleges throughout the country?

My finger had landed on Springfield, Missouri. I asked for a catalogue from a college in that town. With that, Southwest Missouri State College became my choice for a school. I had my transcripts translated from Farsi to English and sent them to the college for review.

A few months later, a letter arrived in our mailbox offering me admission to the college. No one celebrated, though I was thrilled and full of pride! I had defied the cultural norm of remaining in my "proper place" inside the home. As author and scholar Farzaneh Milani, a close friend, would often say, the privilege of self-directed movement has been generally recognized as a male-only prerogative in Iran. Yet with great eagerness, focused thought, determination, and God's help, I had claimed it.

2

Overcoming Obstacles in America

Enthusiasm surfaces when you strive with dedication toward worthy goals.
And it is enthusiasm that frees the energy and the power.

~Woodrow Wilson

WHEN I ARRIVED in Springfield, Missouri, I was very excited to start a new chapter in my life. Once classes began, however, I quickly realized that, while I had passed proficiency exams in written English in Tehran, my listening skills were not developed enough to understand lectures given by American professors. I could not keep up with their rapid dialogues with other students or make sense of their idiomatic expressions. I began to lose confidence.

I knew I needed a strategy. I decided to drop my social studies classes and replace them with chemistry and math. I thought that understanding formulas would be easier than understanding spoken English. Although I was not passionate about learning chemistry and math, I ended up with almost a 4.0 grade average—unusual, I was told, for an international student in the first year of college.

In the spring of 1969, I was told that my dormitory would be closing for the summer. Not only did I have no other place to go, but I had no funds to continue my college education beyond that semester. I had to fight feelings of hopelessness. I deeply feared being deported, because my visa was only good as long as I was a student.

I explained my circumstances to the dean of women; soon thereafter, a kind and generous host family in the community opened their doors to me for the summer. They drove me to and from a bookkeeping job I had found that paid $1.50 an hour. The job was boring, and I made only $500 for the whole summer, but I was profoundly grateful for the safety net it and the family provided.

At the same time, a Korean student from the University of Mississippi, whom I had befriended earlier at an international student event, sent me an application for a scholarship to his school. I completed the application and was later delighted to receive a letter from the university's international student advisor, offering me not only a full scholarship due to my high grades but a part-time job on campus. Relief flooded me. I could stay in school, and I could stay in America! My Korean friend even drove from Oxford, Mississippi, to Springfield to help me pack, and then drove me back to my new school, where I would study for the next three years.

I look back on this period in my life, when all I had hoped for and worked for might have been taken away from me, and feel certain that God intervened on my behalf. Through the Divine Intelligence, God supplied a host family, insights about how to navigate challenges, and even a friend with an application for a scholarship to a new school—rewards for my enthusiasm and vision (see chapter 7).

Family and Forgiveness

BY 1970, I HAD settled fairly well into my life as a college student at the University of Mississippi. I was studying ultra-hard to maintain a grade point average high enough to keep my full scholarship, and I was also working part-time on campus to cover my basic needs. In addition, I was busy fulfilling my obligations as the president of the international student organization on campus and enjoying an active social life.

Then, in August of that year, I received a surprise call from my oldest brother, who said that he, his family, and my mother were in New York City. They urged me and my second-oldest brother, the one who had saved me from marrying the dentist and who now lived in Canada, to join them for an impromptu reunion. I was flabbergasted, but I hopped on a plane and flew to the city. We enjoyed a whirlwind few days visiting together and seeing the sights. Then, my mother returned to Oxford with me so she could see the university and visit a while. Two weeks into her stay, when I offered to make her return flight reservations, my mother told me she had left Iran for good and did not intend to go back.

I adored my mother and had always felt extreme sorrow for all that she had endured in her marriage and her life. Yet she was only fifty-one years old! Was I, in an instant, becoming her guardian at age twenty-three? I was more than shocked. With this news, my life was suddenly turned upside down.

There were myriad questions to answer: Where would she live? How could I support her financially? She spoke no English—how would she make friends? Could she get a job in a small university town? What if she got sick? Who could I ask for help? I felt stuck, shackled, and helpless.

And there was still another painful question I struggled with long after my mother's announcement. It felt as if I had been tricked into taking responsibility for her under the pretext of a joyful family reunion. How could I shake off my resentment? How could I not be bitter? In the ensuing weeks, I had frequent nightmares; for the first time, I was overcome by dark moods of despair.

Eventually, however, I pulled myself together. I became determined that my despair would not defeat me. After all, I had come up against many other roadblocks in my quest for a life of freedom, and I had persevered.

The first step was to start the process of forgiving my family, as I had done in the past. I remembered how my oldest brother had helped us financially for several years after my mother separated from my father. I figured that if I put my efforts, uncontaminated by anger, into finding logical solutions to the unanticipated responsibilities before me, I would feel calmer and be more effective. After all, I knew I was responsible for the way I felt. There was nothing in this world that could not be solved with a proper attitude, patience, and belief in God.

As in the past, the Divine Intelligence intervened, and solutions materialized. I found a good living arrangement for my mother: a room to rent in the home of a local woman her own age. The international student advisor and I brainstormed about the types of work my mother could do. After much thought, we zeroed in on her sewing skills. Through his network, the advisor referred several clients to my mother; she purchased a secondhand sewing machine, which she set up in her room. As for her temporary visa status, my mother's oldest brother, a longtime citizen of the United States, sponsored her citizenship.

There is something else I see as a miracle born of forgiveness and determination: along the way, I began to deeply admire my mother. I admired her zest for learning English, her willingness to help herself, and her sense of humor. These qualities helped sustain us both, and thus we coped and thrived for the next three years.

It was then that my mother's youngest brother, an orthopedic surgeon living in Providence, Rhode Island, and his gracious American wife, Linda, invited her to live with them until she could become independent. My mother accepted. While living with my aunt and uncle, she learned to be a hairdresser. After a few years, she established a new career and was able to move into her own apartment and support herself. My aunt and uncle were, quite literally, godsends to my mother and me. They welcomed my mother and gave me space to focus on my own life at a critical juncture.

Dreams Come True

EARLIER, A LITTLE OVER a year after my mother came to America, I had met the love of my life at an off-campus party. His name was Tom White, a first-year graduate student in psychology. At the time, I was a junior majoring in chemistry. Not long after the party, we began dating. Unlike other men I had dated, Tom talked to me about ideas and the human mind. We found we were intellectually similar and complemented each other in the ways that mattered to us both. After a year, he proposed to me, and I accepted immediately. We were married on April 21, 1973, in the beautifully landscaped backyard of the mayor of Oxford, Mississippi, and his wife, who offered their lovely venue and paid most of the expenses. It was at our wedding that my uncle extended his invitation to my mother to come live with him and his family.

Five years after our wedding, in a judge's chamber in the town of Riverhead on Long Island, New York, I took the Oath of Allegiance to the United States, pledging that I would support and defend the Constitution and laws of the United States of America. When the judge declared that I was now a naturalized US citizen, I felt a rush of emotion much as I had when the university chaplain had pronounced Tom and me husband and wife.

The next several years were exciting and intellectually stimulating for both of us. Tom received his doctoral degree in developmental psychology from the State University of New York at Stony Brook. Later, I earned a PhD in linguistics from Georgetown University, under the guidance of Dr. Deborah Tannen, who would later write the bestseller *You Just Don't Understand: Women and Men in Conversation* and other books on language and relationships. Together, Tom and I served as reading researchers at the Center for Development of Early Education in Honolulu, Hawaii.

While in Hawaii, I developed an instructional procedure for teaching volunteers in the community how to read with children. The concept, called "Guided Paired Reading" for nonfluent minority children, was based on my own research findings. A few years later, the method was adopted widely in the state of Hawaii; in 1993, it was commended by the governor and President Bill Clinton. Though we'd left Hawaii by then, I was invited to return to Honolulu to be honored as the founder of the program and to see it being practiced in some schools. That was a proud moment.

Meanwhile, a new opportunity had unfolded stateside, and from it my career blossomed. From 1991 to 2018, I was blessed with a dream job at the National Center for Education Statistics (NCES), the main research and statistical agency within the US Department of Education. It gave me the chance to do meaningful and highly visible research that focused on improving the literacy of those of the global majority who have been historically disadvantaged in American society. I held my teams to high standards of research design and analysis, and together we worked to uncover what matters most in successful reading and writing. I knew from personal experience that education represented the surest way out of bad circumstances. I wanted to see that my research findings had a direct impact on those experiencing the toughest conditions for learning. My commitment led me to develop an original theory of literacy and produce over fifty publications that have received nearly six thousand citations.

Although I retired in 2018, I continue to act as a consultant to NCES on projects related to improving literacy for children, particularly those with low socioeconomic status. In this way, I continue to reap the many personal rewards of meaningful focused thinking, while opening my mind further to the realm of zero thought and spiritual seeking.

Reflection

I NEVER RETURNED TO Iran. I have sometimes longed for certain aspects of my native land—the courtyards with high brick walls that surrounded beds of roses and jasmine, the hawkers who brought cherries, peaches, rose-perfumed apples, and apricots on carts pulled by donkeys. These sweet memories still live in my heart. Yet it was America that gave me a life consistent with what I value most: personal responsibility and the freedom to pursue self-defined happiness.

There were several forces that, alone or in combination, might have derailed me in my pursuit of my dreams. An arranged marriage at barely fifteen; my parents' deeply rooted belief that a woman's place is in the home; financial constraints; extreme shyness; a dysfunctional family; lack of college entrance credentials; lack of a mentor to guide my way to college; inadequate English comprehension skills that limited my ability to understand college lectures; and, finally, taking on the responsibility of providing for my mother at age twenty-three—all could have kept me from my full potential. Yet at each roadblock, I received a helping hand—a home, a job, a scholarship, an insight, encouragement, another chance. I persevered with the help of the Divine Intelligence, which honored my enthusiasm and provided these things. At the same time, I was prompted to tap more deeply into my inner strength—that is, my belief in God, my optimism, and my determination—in order to adapt to new realities and, ultimately, recover from crises.

The journey hasn't ended. I will always be evolving toward a better self. I know that when I pass from this life, there will be nothing left for my family and friends but fond memories and photos that will be unrecognizable to the next generation. My professional accomplishments—national literacy assessments I directed and articles and books I authored—may live a bit longer. In either case, nothing truly important will survive long after I die. Yet the light of my inner consciousness—that which is one with God—will live on and on. It is that aspect of my life, and all human life, that I explore in the following pages.

3

Seeking Spiritual Community

Give up searching and you will find.
Suspend your mind and all will bind.
The deeper you dive the surface hides.
The surface you seek the depth confides.
The core and shell are all but one,
so, rest your soles, for here you're found,
in His presence, safe and sound.

~Rumi

FOR MOST OF my seventy-four years, I was focused on achievement and success, both personal and professional. As a young girl, my considerable energy was devoted to finding a way to leave a life in Iran that held no potential for me. Then, as a young woman in America, I worked hard to obtain the higher education that ultimately paved the way for a fulfilling career as an internationally recognized scientist in the field of literacy. Along the way, I also became a ballroom dance champion, all the while growing in partnership with my husband of now forty-eight years.

Through the years, as I have faced challenges and overcome obstacles, my faith in God has been a mainstay. As a child, my perception of God as a loving, caring being helped me through the pain of growing up in a dysfunctional family. Later, as a young adult, it gave me the strength to leave Iran and pursue my dream of education and a career in America.

When I was a child in Iran, my Jewish family never kept Kosher, never observed Shabbat, and attended synagogue only on Yom Kippur (the day of fasting). We hardly ever discussed God or religion. Now that I reflect on it, I realize that my relationship with God deepened as I navigated painful challenges as a child and young adult. Some of these challenges were beyond my control, including my abusive father and my parents' eventual divorce. Others were voluntary: studying, working hard, and saving to come to America and make my dreams come true.

Growing up, most of what I knew of my Jewish religion was about Abraham. I knew that the main idea he gave to the world was that there is one and only one God. He also suggested that the only way to know God is to discover Him within ourselves. Abraham taught that God speaks to every person who yearns and surrenders to Him, rather than hanging on to external earthly matters. These ideas served me well throughout my life.

As my life circumstances changed and professional responsibilities were no longer my main focus, however, I found that I wanted to delve more deeply into my relationship with God. I wanted to understand and strengthen the bond that had always existed between us from the earliest moments of youth. I craved to do this in a community, a group of people who shared the same desire to know God more intimately through the transcendence dimension.

A Return to Judaism

AFTER RETIRING IN 2018, I once more returned my full attention to my quest to know God more intimately, this time through religious community. I first turned to Judaism, the faith of my birth. I gravitated to the only Jewish temple in town. The unpretentiousness of the small white building appealed to me. I paid the required annual membership and attended my first Shabbat service in November 2018.

While I did not know the words and could not sing along, I found the traditional Hebrew prayer songs beautiful. I stood up and sat down several times, as instructed by the rabbi, but I did not know why. I kissed the large Torah as it was passed around and listened to the Torah reading in Hebrew, but I didn't understand it. In English, the rabbi announced some upcoming Jewish holidays and historical events that might have interested me, had I had more background to appreciate them.

In the end, I was puzzled by all the "doings" in the service and disappointed in my ignorance about Jewish history, language, and song. I felt I needed some encouragement and advice, so I asked our young, very personable rabbi if we might have lunch together. He graciously agreed to meet me.

During our lunch at a Thai restaurant, I fully displayed my naivete and bluntly asked the rabbi what I should be getting out of my attendance at the Shabbat services. He paused for a second or two, then recommended that I read a book on the Reconstructionist approach to Judaism. The rabbi later described himself to me as a Reconstructionist Jew and a progressive. He explained, however, that the temple itself was nondenominational.

I read the book he recommended, and while I appreciated its focus on responsibility to community and cultural observances, there were parts that did not resonate with me. To clear up some of my questions, I asked the rabbi if we could meet again. Once again, he graciously agreed.

At our second meeting, I told the rabbi that I found Reconstructionist Judaism's view of God to be radically different from mine, and that I thought it strange for a book on religion to get into the politics of the day. Specifically, I explained to him that, in a theological context, I view "social justice" as a core value that governs my personal behavior toward others in society. This includes showing compassion for those with whom I disagree. But I do not equate compassion with expression of my political views about past or present wrongdoings, creation of victim identities, or demonization of perpetrators. I told the rabbi that to water the seeds of compassion, we needed to first wake up to our own divine essence and then move forward to make positive changes.

The rabbi, a warm and considerate individual, simply listened. Perhaps he was just as puzzled to hear my reaction to his recommended book as I was to read its contents. After a long pause, he suggested that I start reading the entire Torah, also known as the Five Books of Moses, and join the weekly Torah study group. I thanked him for allowing me to be honest about my reaction to the Reconstructionist book. Then I went home and began my latest assignment. Later, I patted myself on the back for completing two of the five books, Genesis and Exodus, on my own. By then I had begun faithfully attending the study group every Thursday morning.

In the study group, it felt good to be part of an extended Jewish family with a shared history. I liked the discussions about traditions inherited over the course of three thousand years, what they meant to our ancestors, and how we could interpret their underlying importance and wisdom for our lives. I could see how learning some of the ethics revealed by our inherited traditions and holidays could enrich my appreciation of Jewish heritage and potentially improve my own sense of morality.

Yet, while certainly necessary, improving morality was not sufficient for the kind of spiritual development I was seeking. My purpose for attending the temple and study group went beyond serving others or understanding Jewish history. I wanted to get closer to the "rock" upon which my lifetime achievements had rested, to know my invisible self, with whom I had conversed many times since I was a little girl.

Though I hoped we could find some common meeting ground, my Torah study group did not seem to share my interest in forging a deeper personal connection with God (akin to the One Consciousness). Nor did we agree on certain interpretations of passages in the Torah. For example, I thought some major events in the Torah could be symbolic,[1] representing something that has greater meaning for those seeking God, whereas the group believed they were cultural myths.

The ancient Persian poet Hafez often wrote artfully about wine and *saghi* (someone who pours wine and serves it). In Persian poetry, wine is traditionally considered to be a symbol for Awareness and *saghi* a symbol for the Creator. Surely, I thought, as in poetry, there must be a kernel of deeper meaning about God waiting to be unlocked in the Torah, if we only approached our seeking from our nonconceptual intelligence, rather than solely from our analytical mind and limited vocabulary. In one discussion, I suggested that God's order of the killing of firstborn Egyptian sons in Genesis could be a symbol of His existence as a mighty power. Yet another member of the group interpreted this quite literally as an example of God being a "jerk."

I was told in the study group that your perception of "God" can be anything you want it to be. And, indeed, everyone constructed their own meaning based on their personal ideologies and experiences. I had difficulty relating to some of the statements made in the group regarding God, including that God was not One. This contradicted Abraham's belief that there is one and only one God. Others said that God is not concerned with our every thought and action, does not answer prayers, and does not "reward" or "punish" us after death. Some said you did not have to believe in God at all to be a Jew.

Leaving the Temple and the Study Group

ULTIMATELY, MY STUDY GROUP experience left me with an empty feeling. While I admired my fellow Jews' commitment to their community and social justice, it seemed to me that their approach created a rift between themselves and God. They were focused on the cultural aspects of what they perceived as myths in the Torah, not on their inner dimension, which was my main interest.

Regardless of whether the stories in the text were literal, symbolic, or mythical, I knew I did not need to depend on the language in the Torah to find God. Looking at the extraordinary beauty and order of creation, the miraculous chemistry and composition of the human body, and the way my soul's light radiates outward to my body, I cannot help but conclude that there is a superintelligence behind them. Is it not arrogant to think that a supreme intelligence does not exist because the idea does not agree with our limited perception and vocabulary? Do humans have all the knowledge? Does intelligence lie solely in the mind? I do not believe so.

I saw the people at the temple as being Jews largely by virtue of their rituals and holidays—that is, by virtue of being born Jews. The Torah stories they call myths have kept them together as a people. Their cultural events serve the same important function. Without a Jewish community committed to reading and understanding the Torah, the Torah could lose its usefulness in provoking thoughts on meaningful matters. A static Torah without human interaction could cause Jews to lose their identity—a process that might lead to the gradual disappearance of the Jewish culture, traditions, and religion.

The chasm I felt between the study group's practice and God continued to concern me. I once asked a temple member why my fellow Jews had become estranged from God. He replied that many Jews became disillusioned in the aftermath of the Holocaust. They felt their God had died along with the six million Jews in the concentration camps.

Deep down, I began to realize that the Torah study group was not the kind of spiritual oasis I was searching for. I had discovered that my most strongly held values and perspectives were not shared there.[2] For me, there was no point in engaging in conversations about the existence, semiexistence, or nonexistence of God. While I still felt strong compassion for these members of my "extended Jewish family," there was no place for me in their community. After four months, I stopped attending.

Even though I left the group, my participation had served an important purpose, as the questions raised there fueled my continued search for answers: Could God be intrinsically fair and yet not have intervened in the brutal victimization of Jews by the Nazis, or in the bloody eleventh-century persecution of European Jews who declined converting to Christianity? What are we to make of a God who allowed Jews in the Middle Ages to be placed in ghettos, made to wear yellow emblems on their clothes by the ruling Christians and Muslims? Isn't Abraham the root of our common heritage? If so, how could any religious leader believe that they and only they have the right answers? How could they pave the way for the machines of anti-Judaism to turn against the children of Abraham? Aren't we all one, deep inside?

4

Lifting up Humanity

Discovering Mohammad Ali Taheri

IN THE MIDST of my renewed searching and questioning, God offered direction, as He has throughout my life. In November of 2019, I invited the six Iranian women who live in my little town for a luncheon at my house. I had met only one of them before. At this gathering, I learned that one of my guests, Maryam, was also an expert in the teachings of Mohammad Ali Taheri, an Iranian spiritual leader. Maryam told us she was interested in forming a group to study Taheri's teachings.

She explained that Taheri had been imprisoned in Iran in 2010. Iranian authorities reportedly didn't like the content of his teachings, so he was sentenced to death twice, in 2015 and 2017. Fortunately, with help from the United Nations Commission for Human Rights and others, Taheri was freed and granted asylum in Toronto, Canada, in March of 2020.

Along with myself, two others at the luncheon that day expressed interest in starting a study group. Roya epitomizes Persian social grace and elegance; her mother was the sixth generation from the eldest son of Fath-Ali Shah Qajar, the second Shah of the Qajar dynasty, dating to around 1800. Farrokh is a Pakistani woman of Iranian origin who is also a lover of poetry, a musician, and a lifelong spiritual seeker. Many significant factors already unified us, including a common native language, country, cuisine, and culture, yet we also seemed to be cut from the same spiritual fabric. We formed an immediate bond sealed with a comfortable ease and empathy for each other's desires and experiences. Soon thereafter, we came together like a cosmic force as Maryam took us tirelessly through Taheri's voluminous, transcribed lecture notes, which she had fully internalized.

I was intrigued to learn that Taheri views the human being holistically. He teaches that we are all connected to a universal consciousness that governs the universe through multiple channels, which I call *Links of Grace* (حلقه های رحمانیت). Activating these links enhances the flow of intelligence between the human and the divine. Each divine link has a specific purpose, ranging from supporting physical and psychological wellness to establishing harmony with self, others, and the universe. The Links' ultimate purpose is to deepen our Awareness of who we are, where we came from, and where we are going—questions humans have asked since the beginning of time. The answers we provide ourselves for these basic questions determine how we choose to live in this world—how we act, how we think, and how we develop the latent potentialities within us. Moreover, they have consequences beyond the life of this world.

The theological root of Taheri's philosophy is the mystical tradition of Sufism, ancient Persian spiritual teachings that both emphasize the inward search for God through direct experience and embrace the universality of all humans as one (see appendix 1 for more details). Sufism has nothing to do with the religion one believes in but everything to do with God. Its key insight is that our thoughts are often marred by a fundamental flaw: our ego. The good news is that it is possible to quiet our thoughts and thereby minimize our ego's control in our journey toward Enlightenment. Sufism has inspired some of the world's most beloved literature, the poems of Rumi, a renowned thirteenth-century poet known simply as Molana, an honorific title meaning "our master" to most Persians. Taheri reintroduces, explains, and expands upon the concepts of Sufism with unmatched specificity and reasoning; and, importantly, he places them in a new context based on his own personal insights and revelations.

Even as a very young child, Taheri had an immense longing for answers to a multitude of questions about his origin, path, and destination. At age twenty, he began perceiving the concepts he teaches today. After experiencing loneliness, hopelessness, and depression as a result of his adversarial stances toward the world, he underwent an inner transformation. Having no mentor, he received divine revelations, among them the Links of Grace that are available to all people as an inner resource for purification. He has devoted most of his life to teaching students around the world. His message is new, and his approach is straightforward and practical.

Engagement with the Indefinable

Worshiping ignorantly is nothing but temptation.
The ways of enthusiasm are not learned at school.
You never become mystic through logic and geometry,
as the grounds of love can't be found through such spheres.
That silent spot is unutterable.
The first step is to forget all your books and learning.

~Tabrizi

THERE ARE ALWAYS PITFALLS in trying to describe the indescribable, yet our spiritual essence calls to us and challenges us to understand it with our thinking minds. Our task in this earthly life is to interact with what we cannot understand, wrestle with it, stumble, and then stretch our hand forward for divine guidance and revelations.

While they cannot be wholly defined by objective measurements, the divine revelations of Mohammad Ali Taheri and their connection to one another seem, to my thinking mind, reasonable and logical. Throughout this book, we will see how Taheri's teachings intertwine in harmonious ways with many traditions, including the mystical revelations in both West and East (described in Huxley's *The Perennial Philosophy*) and the concepts recorded in the *Bhagavad Gita,* the Gospel of Hinduism, over five thousand years ago. The records left make it abundantly clear that all these ancient traditions were attempting to describe the same indefinable facts, which are viable in the present day, according to their own culturally bound language.

It is virtually impossible to apply scientific methods to the study of abstract spiritual concepts, such as the One Consciousness; the moment the mind becomes involved, access to them disappears. Nonetheless, until the day we are able to explain the unexplainable, Taheri's teachings, some of which I have borrowed for this book, are valuable assets that serve us well.

Taheri's logic starts with the assumption that there is a Divine Intelligence in the universe that creates laws and order. Assuming that the laws of the Divine Intelligence are orderly and logical, any guidance received from the Divine Intelligence must then be orderly and logical as well. Because the Divine Intelligence is limitless, its manifestations are also limitless—as a result, the universe is limitless. Thus, this world, where we spend our earthly life, is likely one of an infinite number of worlds—the others indefinable. This world is perhaps one of many stopovers on our journey toward Enlightenment, where time, space, and opposites gradually lose their meaning.

Our purpose in this world is, essentially, to move from egoic ways to awakening, and then, finally, to Enlightenment, or spiritual perfection, which flows naturally from the core of our being (see discussion on "Enlightenment" in chapter 6). We need guidance from the Divine Intelligence along the way to make that journey and to fulfill that purpose. Later in this book, I will attempt to describe, using my own insights and some of Taheri's revelations, how the Divine Intelligence can guide us not only toward awakening and Enlightenment but also toward actualizing our deepest desires through enthusiasm and focused thought, as they pertain to lifting up humanity, always anchored to our sacred being.

This Book Is a Beginning

I ENCOURAGE MY READERS to refer to Taheri's original lecture notes, books, articles, website, and video recordings on YouTube for complete and original explanations of his theoretical and philosophical intents. This book is not a translation or a condensed version of Taheri's teachings; rather, it's my interpretations of his teachings on humanity's collective consciousness, my integration of those interpretations into a coherent whole, and my thoughts on how we can apply them in our daily life for the betterment of ourselves and our world. I've used plain language addressed directly to the English-speaking seeker, Iranian or otherwise, even if such a person has no previous knowledge of the subject.

In addition to offering an elucidation of Taheri's ideas consistent with centuries-old Persian oral tradition and interspersed with mystical poetry, this book invites readers to "take a tour of the house" and perhaps be inspired by it. I believe that if the concepts presented here are collectively applied, we can begin to transcend divisiveness in our world and move toward the unity of our collective consciousness.

Still, I offer an important caveat: Interaction with and interpretation of any theory carries with it the risk of creating nuances unintended by the theorist. Indeed, my reading of Taheri is naturally influenced by my own insights and personal experience, in addition to some language variations. Although I studied Taheri's teachings in their original language, Farsi, I express his concepts in English. In some instances, I could find no exact match for Farsi words in English, so I used words that match as closely as possible. In some cases, I also include Farsi along with English to honor the original expression of ideas for my Farsi-speaking readers.

I want to emphasize that my writing in no way attempts to complement Taheri's theories with new ones or to manipulate and make alterations to his original concepts. This book simply offers one way to understand, synthesize, coherently present, and apply his essential ideas to my personal experiences as they relate to the concept of consciousness. To my mind, the fact that Taheri's theories inspire personal and universal applications indicates that they are good, sound theories. The overall intention throughout this undertaking is to make Taheri's teachings more comprehensible to English-speaking audiences, and thereby more illuminating. I believe Taheri would agree that it is better to be of the same heart than of the same tongue, serving as testament to Rumi's assertion that "when it comes to love, the pen breaks."

Spiritual Awakening: Your Journey

WHAT YOU'VE READ SO far is my "spiritual memoir." I hope that reading my story has caused you to think about your own story— the parts you've lived and the parts you're writing daily as you go about your earthly life. As I said at the beginning of this book, my life has been a dance between the sacred and the secular, the earthly and that which is beyond earth—I believe the ground of one is needed to see the figure of the other. Just as the context of my life story is needed to trace my personal spiritual journey through the concepts elucidated by the remainder of this book, so too are the events of every person's life intimately tied to their path toward or away from the One Consciousness.

I'm telling my story—how I learned to steer my soul toward "oneness" by knowing where I came from, my life's purpose, and the path I needed to choose to fulfill that purpose. As I approach the end of this phase of my life, I realize that every principle I've learned works in tandem. Now I have a reservoir of timeless spiritual teachings from my own language and culture that I can pass along.[3] There isn't any single path toward changing your own life. The goal isn't to follow some rigid map, but rather to customize your own as you apply Taheri's concepts—guiding you to the divine spark within you.

In the next three chapters, I aim to share "spiritual concepts" gleaned from my encounter with Taheri's teachings. Some of these concepts may be new to you. Others may strike a familiar chord, like a song you once knew but had forgotten. In either case, because the spiritual perspective[4] may be so unlike those you are accustomed to, it takes time and thought for comprehension. As such, these chapters are best read slowly, with pauses to allow for moments of quiet reflection.

If you are reading this book, something has already opened up in you. With that motivation and readiness, you may recognize the concepts in the coming chapters as things you intuitively "know." The insights that come as you read and reflect will prepare you for the final chapters. There you'll find personal stories and specific action steps to help you get in touch with your inner self, the One Consciousness.

Along the way, watch for signs of spiritual awakening, such as a longing to . . .

o   Heal from a sense of separation from others and instead come to the realization that we are all one.

o   Know that every action that comes from a stance deep in oneness, no matter how small, sends positive vibrations into the world—even if there is no visible witness.

o   Identify and tame the ego, or "the antagonist," which keeps us separate from others and from the universe.

o   Experience joy, creativity, inner calm, appreciation of little things around you, less reactivity, and acceptance of unsettling circumstances, all of which flow naturally from a deep connectedness with all beings.

o   Cultivate a deeper understanding of Enlightenment, our life's purpose.

o   Deepen and sustain a close relationship with God.

o   Gain a more expansive awareness of our origin and destination.

o   Obtain a wider acceptance of death.

o   Create a kinder, more unified world by becoming an opening through which positivity flows for the benefit of all.

I do not offer these signs of spiritual awakening as someone who has completed this transition herself. In fact, I'm learning *with* you as I write this. I have not passed through any exceptional hardship,

I don't have extensive spiritual training or experience, and I am not a certified instructor of Taheri's teachings. I am an ordinary student of Taheri trying to inspire my readers to join me on a journey I haven't yet completed. But if my words fulfill their intention, my ordinariness will serve as a facilitator. If I, a novice spiritual seeker, can see the profound transformation of consciousness in a relatively short period of time, we must be almost there. The universe is calling forth our gifts of courage and humble actions.

Unfortunately, the education systems in most modern societies do not encourage young people to answer that call. Increasingly, these systems focus on equipping students for the performance of practical tasks that have a direct function in society—preparing computer scientists to build handy apparatuses, electrical engineers to develop electrical systems for aircrafts, and bioengineers to design artificial joints, for example. While the value of these practical skills to society is unquestionable, the bigger question— who we truly are and what we need to know to live meaningful lives—is being largely ignored. Students are not encouraged to ponder the higher questions of existence and experience the joy of creating for its own sacred sake, not the outcome or their own ego.

A related obstacle to bringing meaning into life is social media. The young generation is rarely alone for introspection. Their world is brimming with an endless supply of distractions, and few walk around without wearing earbuds, directing every ounce of their attention to such preoccupations as unrelenting news alerts and web surfing. Amassing acquaintances and followers on social media has become an alternative to what matters most—connecting to that sacred space within—because it takes less work to focus on the physical than on our souls. But how can we learn about the treasure box within each of us if we refuse to look inward? In the following poem, Rumi guides us toward our inner treasure over distractions that abound in our world.

> *Why seek pilgrimage at some distant shore,*
> *When the Beloved [God] is right next door.*
>
> ~Rumi

It appears the young generation also doesn't realize that they have become, in a sense, worshippers of idols—in this case technological tools, which millions of children use to derive their philosophy of life. As a piece of technological advancement, a smartphone is admirable. Its only defect is its addictive and distractive nature, which allows few opportunities for tranquility of mind and imageless contemplation—necessary conditions for all-around development and effortless insights through divine grace.

That said, there seems to be a new collective hunger for meaning on the part of many young people, without diminishing their need to connect with the world online. There has also been greater attention paid to consciousness in recent years, especially by physicists and cosmologists, though it hasn't become part and parcel of the human life and worldview. I am highly optimistic that we will find a new path to help us get through the current state of the world.

PART TWO

The One Consciousness

5

What Is the One Consciousness?

On the face you are the microcosm.
But in essence, you are the macrocosm.

~Rumi

Our Sacred Essence

THIS BOOK'S PRIMARY PERSPECTIVE is the principle that everything else is by some degree subordinate to: the concept of oneness. Oneness, or what I call the One Consciousness, has as its starting point the belief that in essence, we are entirely one and undivided. All except the One Consciousness—that is, our sacred essence—is contingent and will inevitably decay. While primal and permanent, the One Consciousness is in dynamic relation with the physical universe, which originated from it.

We humans are not merely individuals, made of flesh, bone, particular knowledge, and personal history. As Taheri reminds us, while we may seem finite and small in our physical form, we are, in our essence, as vast as the whole universe. Persian mystics like Rumi have told us across the centuries that the consciousness[5] within our bodies (microcosm), once tapped into, brings us to a higher level of consciousness, which is as vast as the universe (macrocosm).

We are each an expression of one entity, the One Consciousness (شعور کل). Our existence begins with the One Consciousness, which has no temporal beginning. That is, the One Consciousness didn't emerge from anything. Everything emerged from it. All beings are birthed from the One Consciousness, exist in consciousness, and into consciousness eventually dissolve. Thus, the One Consciousness is our sacred essence and that of all existence. Once we discover who we are in a spiritual sense, we gain an insight into the mystery of the One Consciousness. We also come to realize that our physical attributes, such as our race, gender, intellect, and our five senses don't really define us, and that what we call "I" has its true existence in a deeper reality. As we travel upon this road of self-knowledge, we gain new perspectives. We learn how our earthly life began its journey and where we shall go after the end of this journey.

The sense-organs and the intellect,
Are instruments only.
He who knows himself other than the instrument,
His heart grows pure.

~Bhagavad Gita

The One Consciousness is not detectable through thinking. Indeed, experiencing it requires letting go of thoughts. We don't have the perception, technique, or language to describe the One Consciousness because it is absolute, meaning that it exists independently beyond our planet. Let me correct what I just said: The One Consciousness cannot be said to exist. It is existence itself.

Because the One Consciousness cannot be derived from or explained in terms of something else, it is not subject to the dualities[6] that characterize our bipolar universe. Because there are no distinctions or differences that can be compared and correlated (the processes of scientific measurement), instantaneous knowing, love, and insights arising from the One Consciousness are unmeasurable. As such, we cannot define the One Consciousness, in the same way that we couldn't define nighttime if its opposite, daytime, did not exist. It is a primal form of existence out of which everything else arises. Thus, it cannot become an object of thought. Any attempt to make the One Consciousness explicit through intellectual analysis wouldn't make it easier to understand. It would merely mean that we understand something other than what we are seeking to know.[7] Yet, while invisible, the One Consciousness has certain attributes that can be experienced directly.[8]

There is one single consciousness, and matter, which makes up our bodies and the whole universe, is its derivative. We never experience multiple consciousnesses—ours and that of somebody else—although the One Consciousness may be experienced at a different level of unfolding by different individuals depending on their level of spiritual awakening. In a way, we're like the twisted strands of a single piece of thread. How the cosmos shares its most fundamental identity with our very selves had until recently been a topic described mainly by the thirteenth-century Persian mystics and Sufis, including Sufi poet Rumi.

The One Consciousness is not generated by an entity outside itself. It is always complete and grounded in the eternal "now." That is, it exists in the pre-created state of the universe, where there is no time, space, matter, and energy. Therefore, nothing can be measured scientifically. There are no data to collect, no mathematical formulas to be written, and no comparisons to be made. Moreover, the standard scientific criterion of replication cannot be applied. The third-person representation cannot be a replica of a complete first-person experience, because experience cannot be reduced for convenient methods of understanding.

Thus, it is impossible to coherently articulate the One Consciousness. This failure to fully explain the One Consciousness is the result of our own limitations. How can qualities that can only be experienced directly—such as the warmth of love, the astringent taste of persimmon, or the scent of a beach rose—be explained in terms of quantities and the properties of matter? It will have to be open to a variety of meanings validated from first-person perspectives.[9]

While the One Consciousness is indescribable, it is within each of us in its totality, waiting to reveal itself when we are ready and enthused. If we are, we can experience this absolute reality that is behind the scenes. Enabling that reality to shine through is the purpose and destiny of all of us.

While we have neither the perception nor the tools to fully de-scribe this reality, it is a more authentic story about who we are and where we are headed. What gives it significance is our own inner experiences. The way I understand Taheri's notion of this pre-creation state is as the source of true Awareness, the womb of reality, a stream of consciousness at its deepest level: an irreducible and fundamental speck of quantum vacuum that contains no phys-ical properties but has the energy of a billion suns and is the source of an infinite number of possible universes. One of these is ours, the Big Bang, where, by general agreement, time (زمان), space (فضا), dualities (تضاد بنیادی), matter (ماده), and energy emerged.

To illustrate this concept, Taheri uses a metaphor[10] in his teach-ings: Imagine you are an ocean. The surface moves in waves (sym-bolizing your physical form, thoughts, fantasies, and emotions). As you go deeper, these movements subside into a steady current. Deeper still, the current slows. At its very bottom, there is no current at all. That silent awareness is what I call the "One Consciousness." Our entire story in life is accomplished within that Awareness, which contains the story's beginning, middle, and end. That Awareness is not abstract, intellectual knowledge—it is the aim of our spiritual journey, a state of consciousness that must be experienced directly. Defining the One Consciousness as the sole primary entity in which all Awareness resides seems fair enough for our discussion purposes in this book.[11]

Though we as humans are limited in our abilities to perceive, we can, through reasoning, draw some conclusions about the qualities of the One Consciousness. According to Taheri, the first such quality we can deduce is that it is *one and only* (واحديت), because, as noted earlier, there are no opposites to describe or evaluate it against. The second quality is that it is *whole* (فردانيت); it cannot be reduced to simpler parts. Finally, it is *limitless* (احديت)[12]; that is, there isn't a place in the universe that is void of consciousness,[13] despite its appearance as nothingness.[14]

These qualities of the One Consciousness are interrelated such that if we know one of them, we can deduce the rest. For example, knowing that the One Consciousness is one and only, we can reason that it must be everywhere; and if it is everywhere, we can glean that it must be in its complete unity.

The One Consciousness is the highest form of consciousness. It is the origin of everything—beyond the creation of macrocosm (universe) that, in my interpretation, the thirteenth-century Persian poet Rumi alludes to in the poem above. And it is the deepest focus of this book.

When we succeed in connecting with the One Consciousness, which is our sacred essence, we know life at its deepest and fullest. Out of the One Consciousness springs not only divine Awareness, but also empathy, compassion, tolerance, forgiveness, gratitude, and humility—all of which are forms of *love*.[15] When there is love, we see ourselves in one another—not through our eyes, but through our hearts. Love is in the very nature of the One Consciousness; where we find love, we find the divine gift. As Rumi promises,

With love, bitter turns sweet and copper turns gold,
With love, pain becomes healing manifold.

~Rumi

The love that emerges from connection with the One Consciousness is not the same as romantic love, which is the sublime human emotion and experience.[16] The love that emerges from the One Consciousness refers to the recognition of absolute oneness, that feeling deep within ourselves of interconnectedness with other human beings, and the universe. Another distinguishing mark of such love is that, unlike other forms of love, it is not an emotion, but rather a purely spiritual Awareness. Love of emotions does not unite in essence. It may even have the effect of eclipsing it when there is fear, fault-finding, coercion, hatred, envy, craving for power, and other forms of ego.[17] The divine love that arises when oneness is recognized is unconditional and impersonal. It is beauty, creativity, and pure love. What is loved here is not someone's thoughts and behaviors, good or bad, but rather the person's true self, which is the same as our own true self, the One Consciousness.[18] In the following poem, Hafez states that even if the person is a "drooling mess," all he perceives is their divine worth, which is what you'll see in others as you connect to the power of the One Consciousness.

When you sit before a master like me,
Even if you are a drooling mess,
My eyes sing with excitement,
They see your divine worth.

~Hafez

We, humans, are unique among all living beings in our ability to bring out and reveal the divine love, the One Consciousness, that lies behind what we feel for one another. Without the divine love, we are incapable of experiencing earthly love.

Love comes this way or that way.
Either way, it leads us toward Him in the end.
It was God's theosophy and destiny
that we are enamored of each other.

~Rumi

Compassion and love for all human beings give evidence of our oneness. Think of the sense of connectedness that emerged all around the world during the COVID-19 pandemic. On every continent, millions came together in common grief, sensing that what was happening to people elsewhere was in some way also happening to them. Complete strangers, shaken out of their isolation, reached out to whomever they could help and reassured each other. Our One Consciousness spawns an ocean of compassion when there is a mass shooting, terrorist attack, war, hurricane, famine, earthquake, flood, or forest fire, wherever it occurs on the planet. We reach out to one another not only on the collective level, but also on the individual level, out of concern for our fellow humans, even though we may not know them personally. When one human suffers, we all to some degree feel the pain.[19]

Think of the One Consciousness as our collective, innermost self; that is, the sacred essence of who we are. This collective consciousness is already complete and whole. It is the "we" that encompasses all space and time—from conception to death in this life and in the myriad other worlds through which we may travel seeking Enlightenment. The collective "we" can be experienced deep within ourselves, though it is concealed beneath our physical bodies and individual personalities.

We might also think of the One Consciousness as a divine treasure box of Awareness that lives within each of us. This box contains infinite qualities, including nonattachment, forgiveness, and generosity—forms of love for all human beings. Within us, these divine qualities are waiting to be fully realized through connection with the inner self, the One Consciousness. When connection with the true self becomes a natural state of being, we begin experiencing these qualities; that is, we begin accessing the treasure box of Awareness that is within all of us. The Persian poet Attar speaks of recognition of the inner treasure in the following poem:

> *You are hidden from yourself.*
> *If you finally become visible,*
> *the hidden treasure inside your soul will appear.*
>
> -Attar

Yet, while we have access to this treasure box at all times, full realization of its contents requires that we learn lessons about our origin, our destination, our true identity, and our life's purpose. Taheri's teachings can help us on this path to Awareness. In the moments that we journey beyond our earthly lives toward greater knowledge of ourselves, the limitations of time[20] and space[21] and the dualities of the human world disappear one by one.

As we are in closer touch with the One Consciousness, our actions and thoughts reflect our oneness with all of life more and more. In that state of connectedness with the One Consciousness, we experience true love and joy. We are able to recognize the divine essence in others and stop reacting to their egoic words and actions. In that place of connectedness, we perceive God's majesty in everything. We become keenly aware of the sacredness of seabirds riding the wind, the holiness of a fragrant spruce forest. We are in awe of the vastness of the universe not only in a quantitative sense (no matter how many zeros it adds to distances in galactic space), but in the grandeur of the One Consciousness.

As soon as we sense our underlying harmony with others and with the universe, we realize we are not separate from them. We become realigned with the wholeness of life. When we listen to birds singing in the early hours before sunrise and others join the dawn chorus, something within us resonates with the songs, as if in recognition. That recognition of oneness is quite joyful.

When we are in alignment with the One Consciousness, it means that we are in alignment with whatever happens. Instead of judging every event as good or bad, blaming, defending, or resisting what is or isn't happening, we accept it. When we relinquish resistance and accept what is, we are not at the mercy of what happens. Then, any action that we take from this deeper dimension to address a problem or resolve an issue becomes empowered by the collective consciousness.

> *When a man goes astray from the path to Brahman*
> *(the One Consciousness),*
> *he has missed both lives, the worldly and the spiritual.*
> *He has no support anywhere.*
> *No one who seeks Brahman ever comes to an evil end.*
> ~Bhagavad Gita

Everything else, including our age, health, wealth, name, profession, gender, physical appearance, beliefs, and societal role, is relatively unimportant in comparison to the One Consciousness, because it is all transient and fleeting. Taheri calls these short-lived external dimensions of ours واقعیت. This Farsi term means that these dimensions have only occurred—they are like our reflection in a mirror, which we can see but are misperceptions of who we truly are (حقیقت), or radio waves used for long-distance communication, which we can't see and are an imperfect record of speech. Our true nature is not captured in our appearance. However beautiful, attractive, or powerful that appearance might be, it is only a fleeting aspect of who we truly are—nearly all "empty" space giving the appearance of softness or solidity by the motion of electrons around the nuclei of atoms in our body.[22]

A similar analysis has been offered by Arthur Schopenhauer, a German philosopher of the nineteenth century. He called this outer appearance of the physical world representation because of the ways it presents itself to both our five senses (like color and flavor) and our conceptual reasoning that organizes those sense data into comprehension. Our inner essence, which he called will, is prior to and independent of our senses and perceptions. It refers to the "one being" or the "kernel" of every phenomenon—the One Consciousness, using our own language. Grasping that inner essence could radically change our life for the better. We'll begin to see ourselves as eternal spiritual beings having a human experience, rather than human beings having an occasional spiritual experience, as the mid-twentieth century French theologian Pierre Teilhard de Chardin reminded us.

There is nothing more fundamental than the One Consciousness. This sacred essence is all that is left after we set aside all representations, including the physical universe. The One Consciousness is self-luminous, and we, a physical representation, are the reflecting body. This cognitive mirror, our individuality, is a transitory experience arising from and dissipating in the physical universe. Our sacred essence reintegrates with the One Consciousness after death because death does away with the illusion that separates our essence from that of the rest. That essence, the One Consciousness, is whole and undivided even though we have idiosyncratic points of view about the physical world surrounding us. The primordial objective of this absolute reality is self-knowledge. Its purpose in unfolding is for humans to self-reflect and contemplate eternal life through direct experience.

It is astonishing to me that we can directly experience the One Consciousness in an immediate manner (see chapter 7), even though it can't be known because it is rooted outside space and time. As I describe in the next topic of this chapter, "Working Principles of Consciousness," the One Consciousness enters space-time as universal "consciousness" and presents itself just enough to give us a hint of its existence and nature. This ineluctable force, which acts on consciousness to form the world, bypasses the intellectual operation of the mind so that we can experience it directly. This is the way the noumenal reality we call the One Consciousness is known to us.

Albert Einstein, who understood the nature of the universe more deeply than most, once encountered a grieving father who had just lost his young son to polio. He told the father that at the deepest level, we are woven into the whole web of the universe—yet we tend to experience ourselves as separate from the universe. This delusion, Einstein said, restricts our compassion to the few persons to whom we feel most connected. Our task, then, is to widen our circle of compassion to embrace all living beings, including ourselves. That Einstein, a great physicist, spoke of the delusion of separateness and of the wholeness of the universe is very telling. His advice to the heartbroken father was to seek comfort by including himself in his circle of compassion. Einstein understood the need to guard against the suffering that stems from seeing ourselves as separate and to cultivate compassion for all, especially ourselves because treating others with love automatically follows love of self. Self-love in our darkest moments is not only a healer but an indication of knowing who we are in our essence, the One Consciousness.

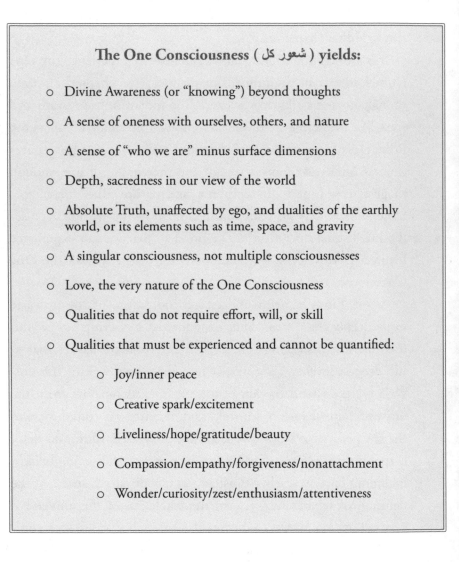

The One Consciousness (شعور کل) yields:

o Divine Awareness (or "knowing") beyond thoughts

o A sense of oneness with ourselves, others, and nature

o A sense of "who we are" minus surface dimensions

o Depth, sacredness in our view of the world

o Absolute Truth, unaffected by ego, and dualities of the earthly world, or its elements such as time, space, and gravity

o A singular consciousness, not multiple consciousnesses

o Love, the very nature of the One Consciousness

o Qualities that do not require effort, will, or skill

o Qualities that must be experienced and cannot be quantified:

    o Joy/inner peace

    o Creative spark/excitement

    o Liveliness/hope/gratitude/beauty

    o Compassion/empathy/forgiveness/nonattachment

    o Wonder/curiosity/zest/enthusiasm/attentiveness

Other scientists have also tried to weave together knowledge and "knowing" that can't necessarily be explained. When the astronaut Dr. Edgar Mitchell viewed Earth from space during his return trip from the moon on Apollo 14 in 1971, he was struck by a profound sense of universal connectedness—a mystical experience in which the ego vanishes when confronted with the immensity of the universe. This transformative experience that the Earth and its atmosphere together constitute a single living organism, shaped his life's work. He established the Institute of Noetic Sciences, still active today, with the sole mission of revealing the interconnected nature of the universe. The first sentence on the Institute's website says this: "Through modern scientific inquiry, we seek to better understand a timeless truth—humanity is deeply interconnected."

In a poem published in his collection *Leaves of Grass*, Walt Whitman, one of America's most influential poets and essayists, describes his awareness that "all things are part of a vast similitude. All suns, planets, human beings, animals, plants, all of the future and the past, and all of space are essentially one and the same." Whitman was highly inspired by Rumi, the Persian Sufi mystic. In another poem called "A Persian Essay," he divides himself between the "I" that involves itself in everyday matters like politics and fashion and the "Soul" that represents his deepest and most universal essence.

And here is a quote from Ralph Waldo Emerson, another influential American poet and essayist of the nineteenth century, who too was an admirer of Persian Sufi poets: "We live in succession, in division, in parts, in particles. Meantime within man is the soul of the whole; the wise silence; the universal beauty, to which every part and particle is equally related, the eternal ONE." And again from Martin Luther King, perhaps the greatest civil rights leader in American history: "It really boils down to this: that all life is interrelated. We are all caught in an inescapable network of mutuality, tied into a single garment of destiny. Whatever affects one destiny, affects all indirectly."

All these illuminated individuals agree that beyond our mundane, physical world is a transcendent realm, which is distant from our descriptions. The fact that they all came to that view independently lends a certain sense that it might be right.

Working Principles of Consciousness

You are the mirror reflecting His magnificence,
and your reflection is indeed all the universe.

~Attar

SCIENCE TELLS US THAT all things in our universe, including our bodies, the food we eat, the trees, the rocks, and our possessions, are constantly in motion. All are composed of molecules, atoms, and electrons, which are always in motion at different frequencies. The high-velocity motion of the electrons around the nucleus of an atom creates the feeling of solidity. These seemingly solid objects are not solid at all. An apt analogy is the blades of a fan—as they rotate increasingly quickly, eventually we see just a still, round disk.

My fingers, for example, which at this moment are processing these words on my keyboard, are made up of molecules composed of atoms. These atoms include electrons that constantly vibrate at certain frequencies (or speeds), creating various energy fields, including electrical and magnetic fields.[23]

If we each lost the volume inside our bodies created by the motion of electrons, the entire human race, along with everything else that exists in the universe, would probably fit into the volume of a sugar cube. That sugar cube would likely be the collection of atomic nuclei in our bodies and all things, which would transform into an absolute unity with the energy of a billion suns to create another universe with new stars and planets.[24]

Thus, if the existence of the universe is dependent on motion, then the universe itself may be viewed as a mental abstraction (مجاز), despite the fact that it has an appearance (واقعیت) and we can see it. Whatever exists in the universe is a reflection of a truth (حقیقت) behind the scenes, called consciousness,[25] emerging from the One Consciousness—recognizing, as noted earlier, that its existence can neither be proven nor disproved by logic.

As the Persian poet Rumi tells us, the particles that make up our world give meaning to the universe through the language of "dance," that is, motion:

> *Every particle of the universe is bursting to speak out and groan.*
> *Without a tongue, what can it do?*
> *The language of the particle is "dance."*
> *It can't express itself but through an elegant dance.*

> ~Rumi

Taheri teaches that every matter in the universe, including the "dancing electrons" on which the universe depends, is influenced by what we might think of as "consciousness" (شعور) infused with exquisite inherent intelligence, which emerges from the One Consciousness discussed earlier. This one universal life is what animates every molecule of our physical bodies and permeates every life form in the universe.

The teachings of Taheri echo those of the *Bhagavad Gita*, a five-thousand-year-old epic that provides key philosophical principles of Hinduism (its Gospel, one may say). When seen in that light, Taheri's teachings become even more meaningful and full of understanding. The *Gita* views the concept of the One Consciousness, discussed earlier in this chapter, as an ontological truth, the ultimate reality, *Perusa,* known in the world as *Brahman.* It is endless, everlasting, and invisible. When our inner self (the soul or *Atman*) is connected to *Brahman,* there is spiritual oneness in all existence.

The *Gita* differentiates between the One Consciousness (*Brahman*) and "consciousness" (*Prakriti*), the topic of this section. Consciousness is said to emanate from the One Consciousness. It exists in every living being, and everything, including inanimate objects, exists in the all-pervading consciousness. The One Consciousness (the knower of the field) and consciousness (the field) are neither independent of each other nor possessed of beginning, time, or space; rather, they are *superior* and *inferior* forms of the same source. What seems to be superior about the One Consciousness (*Brahman*) is that it is the pure consciousness—the origin and base of everything prior to the creation of the universe, the absolute truth. Consciousness (*Prakriti*), on the other hand, is inferior because it isn't the absolute truth, but rather flows from it. All evolution (including our bodies, senses, perceptions, and emotions) comes forth from Prakriti. However, our three broad innate personality attributes, Gunas, such as enthusiasm [rajas], calmness [sattva], and laziness [tamas], come forth from beyond evolution.

Consciousness is neither matter nor energy. While it can interact with matter and energy, consciousness itself is nonlocal[26]— that is, its influence is seemingly everywhere at once because it is not characterized by the dimensions of space or time. Yet it is fundamental to any true understanding of the universe, how we got here, and key topics such as Awareness and death.

We cannot see consciousness with our eyes, but we can experience its effects. Experience itself is the primary datum of reality; everything else is provisional. Experience can be validated or falsified by comparison to the observations of other individuals. One of the ways we experience the effects of consciousness is through vibrations. The nature of these vibrations, which are similar in structure to the vibrations of an event in the material world, is beyond our understanding. Have you ever questioned why you are subconsciously attracted to someone, and yet repelled by another? Can you sense the mood of a room when you first walk in? These days, I tend to pay more attention to how people, places, and objects intuitively feel to me.

A simple act of kindness will send positive vibrations across the infinite net, touching every person in existence. When the feeling of connectedness becomes part of our natural state of being, we are no longer under the misperception that we are all separate beings. When we break such egoic patterns, which get in the way of our perception of the unified consciousness, or when we engage in anything else that is aligned with our true self, we can sense a flow of positive vibration that carries us. Life takes on a positive quality. We now experience inner peace, love, and joy. We may find that we are more attentive to nature, that we enjoy art and music more intensely than before, that we are more mindful of the quality of our work, and that we are more likely to understand and forgive others, even those with whom we disagree.

The positive stream of vibrations flowing from our natural state of connectedness to the One Consciousness can help heal the divisions in our world today. Imagine the universe as a vast net, its intricacy much like that of a spider's web, stretching out infinitely in all directions. As Chief Seattle, an esteemed Native American leader, explained in 1887 when describing humankind, whatever we do to one strand of the spider's web affects the entire web. If we damage one strand, we injure the whole. Similarly, Shabestari, a Persian poet, reminds us that every single cell in our body is meaningful in the context of other cells:

> *If you remove a single particle from its place,*
> *the entire world will be damaged.*

> ~Shabestari

This mystery can be explained by the working of a divine form of intelligence, which existed before the birth of the universe, when time and space did not exist.

Just as loving, compassionate acts affect the entire net, so too do destructive acts. Negative vibrations can be produced by our reactions to even minor irritations, such as snarled traffic, missed flights, or rude people. These negative vibrations can impact us and others. If we sit around a dinner table with friends gossiping, making sarcastic remarks, ridiculing others, or arguing disrespectfully about others' political or religious views, we instantly generate negative vibrations.

If I were to resent writing this book, the resentment could seep through the manuscript and rub readers not just the wrong way, but away from my book. After negative vibrations have been emitted, we may feel low on energy and become unmotivated, lethargic, and irritable. These negative feelings are likely to be expressed in subsequent toxic behaviors, such as preoccupation with negative media, using a demeaning tone, worrying about the future, or assuming the worst about people. It is not only what a person says, but the level of consciousness from which they speak

(محور وجودی) that influences others. Many people say they can literally feel the vibrational difference between positive and negative thoughts.

Taheri teaches that any creation, be it a painting, a song, a book, a poem—even a slice of pizza—is influenced by the consciousness of its creator. The space where the object is created is influenced as well. Was the room used to uplift some aspect of humanity, or to degrade it? Was a book written to enhance its readers' consciousness, or just to make money for the author? Was the use of hydrogen inspired by a therapeutic purpose, or to make a bomb? Depending on the creator's state of consciousness, different vibrational fields will be released, and the receivers of the creation will react differently. Transformative books emerge from the writer's authentic state of being carried through the words. Whether it is lightness of being or a heaviness weighing them down, the recipients experience the sensations and pass them on to others. Similarly, if we see that our neighbor is not physically apart from us, the ensuing sense of oneness can produce a profound sense of peace—a worldview that brings us together more closely than could be achieved by any peace treaty among governments.

There is always more to a thought, feeling, action, or creation than is visible. They have the power to influence others positively or negatively, depending on the consciousness behind them. This has everything to do with whether they flow from our deep connection with the universe and all beings, or are trapped in the ego (a sense of self that works against us, such as arrogance).

In summary, we emit either positive or negative vibrations through our thoughts, emotions, words, and actions. In turn, the universe responds. We act to influence the universe, and the universe, in turn, acts to influence us. Then we, again, reflect that influence back into the world.

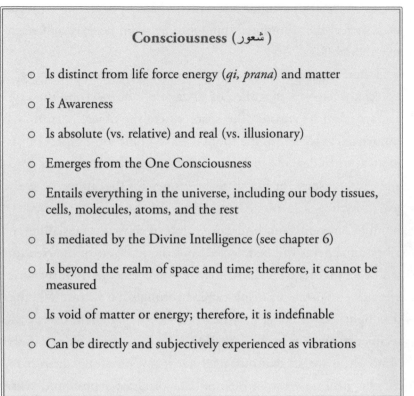

Consciousness (شعور)

o Is distinct from life force energy (*qi, prana*) and matter

o Is Awareness

o Is absolute (vs. relative) and real (vs. illusionary)

o Emerges from the One Consciousness

o Entails everything in the universe, including our body tissues, cells, molecules, atoms, and the rest

o Is mediated by the Divine Intelligence (see chapter 6)

o Is beyond the realm of space and time; therefore, it cannot be measured

o Is void of matter or energy; therefore, it is indefinable

o Can be directly and subjectively experienced as vibrations

6

Connectivity of the One Consciousness

The nightingale noted a sweet singing over the cypress tree.
It was the spiritual mediators' lesson last night.
It meant come and see how the fire of Moses transformed into a flower,
and listen to the monotheism that the tree speaks of.

~Hafez

An Integrative Theory of the One Consciousness

IN THE PRECEDING chapter, I said that the One Consciousness is the core concept for this book. That idea, which coincides with the ancient Persian teachings of the Sufis, is what has resonated most deeply with me in all my studies of the spiritual. It is also, in my mind, what is most in need of attention today in light of the division and separateness the world is experiencing, especially in America. It is a reminder that, while on the surface we may differ in our backgrounds and political viewpoints, in our deepest essence we are all expressions of one entity, the One Consciousness.

In this chapter, I explain how I connected the threads to the One Consciousness to create a harmonious and thematic whole. In reality, these threads are not as distinct and discernible as presented here. Nevertheless, the way they've been brought together is useful for the purposes of our understanding and discussion.

Once I decided to make the One Consciousness the focal point and target construct of this book, I then culled Taheri's other ideas by carefully following thematic threads and weaving them around that concept. Creating a coherent whole with a new overall theme, distilled from 2,250 pages of transcribed lecture notes in Farsi, was a labor of love. It was not an easy task. Apart from the sheer magnitude of the material and the translation issues, I had to wade through lengthy transcripts of constant questioning by Taheri's classroom students. Though some noteworthy ideas emerged, the questions at times derailed the topic at hand, lessening the thematic and sequential coherence of the lectures.[27]

Yet after many weeks of review, a thematic whole did emerge. Seeing that whole, I created two broad categories, which I named *Facilitators* and *Inhibitors*, to explain the concepts of divine Links of Grace (which pave the way to Presence) and egoic thoughts (which hinder Presence). Within these two overarching categories, I included other concepts scattered throughout Taheri's lecture notes that either facilitate or inhibit connection with the One Consciousness. In short, the hope was to learn from and be inspired by Taheri without being so unduly limited to him that I abandoned my own unique creative signature.

The graphic representation that follows shows the connections among all the various threads I pulled together and their relation to the concept at center stage, the One Consciousness. To be clear, Taheri's teachings are reflected in each individual concept represented in the graphic. However, the centrality of the One Consciousness and the convergence of the other elements, as shown on the graphic representation, are my contribution. This way of perceiving the One Consciousness and its connectivity to relevant concepts is not only reasonable to my thinking mind, but has transformed me in ways I couldn't have imagined earlier in my life. I have more compassion for my fellow human beings, more wonder at the beauty of nature and my surroundings, and more Awareness of my true self as the immortal One Consciousness. This transformation has nothing to do with my political views, the number of professional journal articles or books I publish, how much is in my bank account, or how I look on the outside.

The graphic illustrates the complex interdependence of several elements surrounding the One Consciousness, that implacable eternity into which we are born and in which we live and die. The circle depicts the universe as an infinite web of connections, none of which exist as a separate entity apart from the others.

Thus, the One Consciousness is necessarily central to other concepts, primarily God, the Divine Intelligence, and the Laws of the Universe. God directs the Divine Intelligence but not vice versa, as shown by the arrow. The Divine Intelligence, in turn, determines, among other things, what laws need to be created to meet God's demands for continuous creation and infinite abundance. The dotted arrow indicates that the influence of God on the required laws is indirect, mediated by the Divine Intelligence. (The triangle within the circle is explained in the next chapter.)

CONNECTIVITY OF THE ONE CONSCIOUSNESS

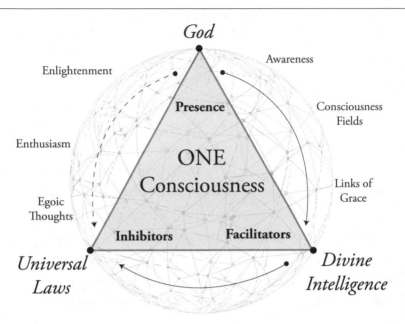

God

There is a breath of God in each of us human beings.

~Rumi

EVERY CULTURE, IN EVERY language, has a slightly different use for the word "God." Moreover, the essence of the word is often lost in the ineffability of any language. There is a preconceived notion among many that God is a closed concept—possessing some sort of image, a male gender, an emotionally volatile tyrant, instilling fear of hell, allowing people to suffer, hating sinners, requiring a life of rules and rituals, and so on.

These preconceptions seeped into the religious texts, perhaps as the result of incomplete information or the bias of those who wrote them, and were fostered over the centuries by religious believers of all stripes. Many young people are turning away from God because they associate Him with religious texts, which they view in terms of *dogmatism* ("Anyone who doesn't believe in our truth is going to hell"), *moralism* ("Don't do this and that"), or *favoritism* ("We are singled out by God for special treatment").

Unfortunately, these images and personifications of God get in the way of deeper understanding of who we are and the path that binds us directly to Him. Any image or object we create in our mind, however good, will be a barrier between us and the Divine. When we view religious ceremonials, elaborate rituals, and the letters of time-bound words as being intrinsically sacred, the inner truth (the divine essence) cannot arise.

Religious experience is generally interpreted in terms of an idea of God derived from *other sources*. The tenet of this book is that the presence and wisdom of God need to be experienced, *firsthand*, in order for God to be known. The truth is that God is not a concept we can understand on an intellectual level because we don't have the intellectual capacity or wisdom to understand Him.

The God that I speak of in this book is void of all forms. He is not merely of power, but of goodness and wisdom. He never says that an action is "right" or "wrong" because to do so would be to strip us of our greatest gift—the opportunity to experience the results of our free will and to create ourselves anew. He is a universal force that resonates in the core of everyone's soul if they aspire to intimacy with Him while still in this world. God is known by many names, and there are countless paths that can lead us to Him. Even though God is unseen, we can *feel* His force pulsating through our body when we are willing to step outside the grandiosity of our limited self and express an honest and humble desire to know Him. It is in this higher state of being that we know we are guided and deeply loved. God invites us, the beloved, to come to union with Him through a channel of grace, which I call the Links of Grace (discussed in chapter 7).

For our purposes, a helpful approach to understanding God might be to turn to the Persian mystics of the Middle Ages as the major sources of insight. I don't profess to be a scholar of any spiritual philosophy, let alone one as rich and profound as Sufism and, by extension, Taheri's. Nor do I come from the purely intellectual discipline of philosophy. But I do know that in the spiritual discipline of Taheri, God is not reduced to a personalized characterization or tied to space, time, and dualism. In these respects, we might say that the One Consciousness manifests itself as God, akin to, or identical with, the individual soul.

The language of the One Consciousness described earlier (see chapter 5) further permits the following view: When the One Consciousness is considered in relation to this universe, it is regarded as God with attributes. God expresses the infinite attributes and qualities of the One Consciousness, such as generosity, knowing, love, goodness, perfection, and compassion, in ways that we can understand through our physical mind and experience through our senses. We each perceive, experience, and emulate these qualities when we are in touch with our true essence, the absolute truth I call the One Consciousness, though our perceptions and experiences are different depending on our Awareness's level of unfolding.

We see God's creations all around us and appreciate the Laws of the Universe that govern them. This is why God is referred to as the Lord of the Worlds in Farsi (رب العالمين). The One Consciousness is beyond all action. Therefore, it cannot be said to create. It is God, the "face" of the One Consciousness, Who creates the universe, preserves it, and dissolves it. When at the end of its life cycle the universe is dissolved, it goes into a phase of potentiality (بالقوه), like a seed of all lives, and awaits its next creation. That is, the universe merely returns to the One Consciousness which sent it forth, and remains there in an unmanifested state until it is recreated.

Metaphorically speaking, we may think of God as the rays of the sun reflecting their Source concealed under all-natural light, the "unseen and unseen" (غيب الغيوب) in the nonpolar world, the One Consciousness. Just as the sun and its rays, crudely speaking, are the same in essence, so are the One Consciousness and God. God reflects the qualities and attributes of the One Consciousness in the same way that the sun's rays reflect the qualities and attributes of the sun, which lifts our mood, warms us up, and brightens our surroundings.

In this sense, we can say that God is the light with which we see all things—a reflection to our five senses of the primitive and fundamental process underlying all of reality, so that we can see our true nature as the nature of God, the One Consciousness—always pure, complete, unattached, and nonperishable. When our true nature becomes illuminated with the light of God, it gladly accepts whatever happens, knowing that events come and go but are not the absolute truth, though they've happened to us.

God embraces both "pre-universe" and "universe." He is the author of this world, the unmoved (pre-universe) and the moving (the universe). He is both immanent (manifested in the material world) and transcendent (surpasses the merely physical experience). There cannot be two independent entities: the Creator God and the indefinable Source. That would ultimately involve dualism, thereby negation of oneness. Everything that exists is the manifestation of God[28] rooted in a pre-existential reality I call the One Consciousness. Meister Eckhart, a German mystic of the Middle Ages, spoke of the inseparable God that is both *absolute* and *creator*.

I am aware that the inseparability of God and the One

Consciousness can be an obstacle to some who prefer to think of the One Consciousness as a less personal thing—not realizing that God, too, is devoid of "personality." For persons who have been brought up to think of God by means of explicit and visible piety and so little on the "experience of God," it is hard to think of Him in terms of anything else other than "the Word of God." That is why many authors of spiritual books are too conscious of being ecumenical to use a strongly connotative word like "God."

My worldview is God. This makes me, among my intellectual friends and colleagues, an anomaly, hopelessly dated. While I respect their view as well as the principle of devotional practices within the religious life, I find the notion of the One Consciousness to come the closest to capturing God's essence without clothing Him in concepts or practices that conceal Him. God is quite beyond conceptualization. Human thought can only limit or negate Him. My view of God is not from religious or philosophical descriptions, but rather from direct experience. The unbiased reader can see far down into God's grace, glimpse at His nature, and say that "all is well."

> *You cannot see me with human eyes.*
> *Therefore, I give you divine eyes.*
> *I am the soul that dwells in the heart of every mortal creature.*
> *I am the beginning, the life span, and the end of all.*
> *Great in soul are they who become what is Godlike.*
> *They alone know me, the origin, the deathless.*
>
> ~Bhagavad Gita

In God's "residence," which Taheri calls the unipolar world,[29] our true selves, the selves connected to the One Consciousness, were imbued with God's Soul (روح الله) and we were given the divine treasure box of Awareness. This happened long before we evolved as *Homo sapiens* in the bipolar world. Characterized by space, time, and dualities, the bipolar world is not a single world. It consists of many worlds, one of which is Earth, where life unfolded from the series of events that began with the Big Bang (discussed in chapter 11).

We will never know God by our thinking minds or reason. Rather, we sense God by all that exists, known and yet unknown. Evidence for God is literally all around us. When we contemplate the incomprehensible enormity of the stars, planets, and galaxies, for example, we are essentially looking at the manifestations or the "outside images" of God. Analogously, we are looking at aspects of our own physical body and experiences. These external properties of us and the universe are those that science can capture and describe in terms of laws and relationships. The internal aspect is the intrinsic essence: the reality that is not easily expressible or measurable in the language of relations.

While we humans are like one another in our essence, God is incomparable. Our collective essence resonates with God, the One from whom we derive our life force. As we pass through this temporary world and continue our journey through the cycle of lives (چرخه ی انا لله وانا اليه راجعون)[30], we understand more deeply and maturely, with each new context, that whatever we experience comes from God. We become more and more aware that for the true self, there are ultimately no limitations of time, space, and dualities.

God is waiting to be revealed to those who seek Him. The continual challenge is to bring forth great enthusiasm, abandon our stumbling thoughts, experience Presence, and thereby connect with our sacred self, the timeless One Consciousness. Gradually, the curtain will be opened and we will realize that God has been within us all along. We just didn't know how to access Him.

In the following poem, Attar, a highly esteemed Persian poet who had a great influence on Sufism, points out that all we see with our eyes is virtual. The main world will appear only after we pull down the curtain of our virtual world.

> *Your eyes cannot see anything*
> *but an imagination from the world.*
> *Leave all these imaginations behind,*
> *so that the true world could appear before your sight.*

> ~Attar

God lies not only within us but everywhere, in all things. Yet perceiving God as being present everywhere is difficult for some people. They might imagine Him as a supernatural being who resides in the heavens. Because of this incomplete perception of God, they have been unable to find a satisfying answer to their relationship to Him. Some see God either exclusively within themselves or entirely outside themselves, not understanding that God cannot be divided into pieces. Yet, if God is seen as a whole, belonging to every time and place, it is easier to find Him everywhere. The whole of the universe is His presence. His presence, then, is within us.

Unfortunately, we often call upon God only when we are unhappy or in need rather than acknowledge Him as part of our inner selves at any moment in the beauty before our eyes. God is not the "complaint department." One of the greatest ways to revere God is to acknowledge the miracles of His creations—the graceful sway of a tree in the wind, the ant valiantly carrying a seed, or the softness and comfort of morning fog on a river.

I perceive God in the transcendent sense, not the traditional sense of a controlling authority figure in the skies who instills fear. I do not associate any gender (God or Goddess) with the

Divine, recognizing that imposing a gender on an all-encompassing Creator limits our idea of Who and What God is. However, the faith of my ancestors, Judaism, describes God as a father. As a child, that's how I saw God too. Though my thinking has since evolved, I use the masculine pronoun "Him" in this book because the usage will be familiar to many readers, not because I view the Creator as a male.

I also don't search for or try to understand God. As I noted earlier, the feeling of God, which lies beyond what can be expressed in words, began to manifest in me early in my life, though I had no parental direction or religious community. As a child, I sometimes referred to God as my rock, or the divine power within me that gave me strength in those difficult years. I believe there exists a link that binds us directly to God, and a path to reach Him for those who aspire to intimacy with Him while still in this world. As Rumi said:

> *There is a link, without asking how, without analogy.*
> *Between the Lord of man and the soul of man.*

> ~Rumi

While it is impossible to form a mental image of God, He is accessible to all of us. In Farsi, the meaning of the word *God*, or خدا (pronounced "khoda"), is, appropriately, "know yourself." God has already granted His qualities to us as part of our treasure box of Awareness. We experience some of these qualities, such as love, compassion, and forgiveness, when we are in touch with our true self. As the Persian poet Hafez says, the starting step of creation was based on love. All that followed had the same impetus, and the human being became the messenger of love.

On the first day of eternity, when the ray of God's beauty was manifested,
love was created and forged the entire world.
The sky could not accept the responsibility,
and the lot fell upon me, the madman of His love.

~Hafez

God (خدا) is:

o All that is and all that is not (seen and unseen)

o One and only one

o The collective attributes of the One Consciousness

o The unipolar world where we were imbued with His soul

o Not visible or known by the mind

o The owner of the Divine Intelligence

o Revealed in the lawful harmony of all that exists

o Not a controlling authority in the skies that instills fear

o Generous by granting us free will[31]

o Accessible to those who avail themselves of Him

o The one we turn to for help

o Love (the only reality in our experience that is nearest to God)

o Revealed in the world of experience

Divine Intelligence

AT ANY GIVEN MOMENT, according to Taheri, there are three types of elements in the universe: matter, energy, and consciousness (شعور). The former two have emerged from and are contained in the latter, as noted earlier. Matter consists of the atoms that make up human beings and every other visible object in the universe, including the stars and galaxies we see in the cosmos. Energy, a property of matter, exists around us all the time in a multitude of different forms, including electrical, chemical, and thermal. Consciousness, on the other hand, cannot be explained through physical concepts and equations, because it is made up of primordial Awareness emerging from the One Consciousness unconstrained by space and time.

The effects of consciousness can be revealed as fundamental vibrations[32] (ارتعاشات بنیادی) in a variety of consciousness fields[33] (میدانهای شعوری) mediated always by the Divine Intelligence (هوشمندی). It is with this understanding that the secret of the Divine Intelligence is unveiled. The Divine Intelligence is responsible for creating the universe—that is, its architectural design to meet intended goals, its stock of resources such as matter and energy, its implementation, and its overall management.

According to Taheri, after creating matter and energy, the Divine Intelligence created both the natural laws of the universe, such as the Law of Gravity, and spiritual laws, such as the Law of Enthusiasm. Discovery of the natural laws gives us an understanding of the principles that govern the physical world around us, while revelations about the spiritual laws give us a sense of the principles that go beyond the scope of the mind in an attempt to make some sense of God's perspective. Spiritual laws are to the One Consciousness as the laws of nature are to the physical universe. Our lives aren't only about practical applications, but also about meaning and purpose. Unlocking both the natural and the spiritual mysteries of the universe is mankind's pursuit.

Here is an example of how these natural and spiritual mysteries intertwine in our lives. During the COVID-19 global pandemic, a catastrophic outbreak that took many lives, an intense enthusiasm manifested in scientists from around the globe to develop effective vaccines. At this writing, their extraordinary efforts using a new technology have led to remarkably safe coronavirus vaccines in a very short amount of time. Scientists' rare and rapid success is miraculous, given that the development of vaccines is a complex process that usually lasts many years.

Very possibly, this is evidence of the Divine Intelligence activating the Law of Enthusiasm to reward the highly enthused scientists unified in their collective will. It is amazing and affirming to see how the divine power can flow through scientists committed to saving defenseless bodies exposed to an unpredictable virus. Said differently, the "unseen hand" of the Creator is triggering a spiritual law to help those with intense enthusiasm unlock the Creator's own natural laws. In other words, the natural law and the spiritual law seem to act in harmony for the benefit of mankind. There is a vast network of interconnected laws that, once unlocked, can impact every aspect of our lives.[34]

The Divine Intelligence creates these universal laws in response to God's will, which scientists endeavor to unravel. Yet the Divine Intelligence is not separate from God. Rather, it might be described as God's determination (اراده الهی), serving as His deliverer (کارگزار الهی). It is somewhat analogous to the Holy Spirit in Christianity.

The Divine Intelligence also sustains our physical bodies by coordinating our fifty trillion molecular geniuses, each cell with its own DNA structure, through our *Sacred Cognitive Dimension* or the "mind" (كالبد ذهن), which is both invisible and indefinable (see chapter 11 for more details). Note here the power of a divine entity to affect a physical entity in the universe (the cells in our bodies). Assuming that Divine Intelligence's Laws of the Universe are orderly and logical, we can infer that its coordination of our complex cellular system is orderly and logical as well.

There is tremendous intelligence within our bodies, but we are unaware of most of it. Indeed, only a tiny fraction of this intelligence, such as the capacity of the human body to store five million terabytes of information in its twenty-three grams of DNA, is understood by scientists. How humbling this is when I compare that figure to the one terabyte of storage on my Mac! Our immune system is another example of our bodies' vast intelligence. This defense system, under the surveillance of the Divine Intelligence, continually monitors our bodies without having an independent existence. It holds "conversations" among all the trillions of specialized cells, which, in concert with other cells, identify outside invaders and change the body's responses accordingly. Even in the absence of foreign invaders, the Divine Intelligence oversees the continual "conversation" among molecules of the liver, skin, and other organs because they are mutually affected through the network of the immune system. With constant, exquisite elegance, the Divine Intelligence maintains harmony in the body. We are so used to our bodies working that we don't appreciate the mighty intelligence that maintains them but doesn't exist anywhere. This immense intelligence is largely unrecognized by science. I sometimes communicate to my body cells my gratitude for being on duty 24/7, providing me with life-giving energy, even though I don't know their language. I like to think they will pick up the loving attention at the vibrational level.

Human beings also possess vast spiritual intelligence, yet it is virtually impossible to apply scientific methods to the study of divine concepts. We cannot know and understand what our limited minds cannot fully perceive and comprehend. The scientific method is a process of collecting ideas with an open mind, yet the idea that "if we don't see it, it doesn't exist" has unfortunately become a common error. It is perpetuated primarily by *reductionists* (who reduce a complex event into its tiniest parts and then explain the event entirely in terms of the interactions between those parts, without allowing the influence of the whole on the properties of its parts)[35] and by their concrete offspring, *materialists*, who imply that matter is primary.

In addition to creating the laws of the universe and coordinating the extremely complicated functions of our cells, the Divine Intelligence turns on the switches to God's Links of Grace (discussed in chapter 7), which help us to acquire divine Awareness. The activation of the Links of Grace, and consequently our connection with the One Consciousness, depend on our level of enthusiasm for connection and our ability to be present through *witnessing*. Witnessing is the process whereby in stillness, we notice changes in our bodies without judgment. (For a fuller description of witnessing, see "My Spiritual Practice: Visiting with My Sacred Self" in chapter 8.)

Divine Intelligence (هوشمندی الهی) is:

o God's deliverer, determination, or architect

o Designer of dualities (e.g., birth/death, good/evil)

o Creator of the universe (e.g., matter, energy, space, time)

o Creator of the laws of the universe (e.g., relativity, motion)

o Coordinator of body cells

o Coordinator of life force energy (*qi, prana*)

o Activator of the Links of Grace

o Mediator of the consciousness

Laws of the Universe

"IT IS ASTOUNDING TO think that nature operates by rules that we can discover, by trial and error, of course," said Jim Peebles on the day he received the 2019 Nobel Prize in Physics for his discoveries in cosmology.

In the same way that the Divine Intelligence generated the phenomenality of all existence, the laws of the universe generated the unfathomable complexity of today's universe. Taheri teaches that behind the seemingly random and chaotic events in the world and in our individual lives, there lies a higher order and purpose. Often it is difficult for us to imagine or understand the purpose that a particular event has in the tapestry of the whole, yet Taheri asserts that there are no random or isolated events—even the smallest events are connected with the whole universe, as intended in the beginning of creation. We cannot understand this higher order and purpose by thinking about it, because it emanates from the Divine Intelligence, or the realm of consciousness.

What we call the Laws of the Universe are our descriptions of the universe's causal constraints that prevent some events and make other events happen, whether biological or not. These constraints apply to all processes in our universe.[36] Indeed, they are built into its structure. That structure, the causal constraints that go with it, and the laws we use to characterize those constraints are all entailed by consciousness (see "Working Principles of Consciousness" in chapter 5). We can get a glimpse of understanding by aligning ourselves with the One Consciousness.

We know that every natural event in our earthly world follows precise laws. For example, if the speed of light from the sun was even a tiny bit higher or lower than about 190,000 miles a second, life on Earth would either melt or freeze. Earthquakes occur when precise physical conditions, such as volcanic eruptions, are met. We don't know all the reasons for such natural events. Many cannot be explained by the actions of people. Rather, they are workings of the laws of the universe, including the *Law of Cause and Effect*, which Ralph Waldo Emerson called "the law of laws." This law states that every action in the universe produces a reaction. Similarly, as noted in chapter 5, every human thought is capable of setting off a wave of vibrations that passes through the entire cellular structure of the body and out into the universe.

The world is the way it is because it could not be any other way and still exist in the physical form. Natural disasters and the birth-death cycle are part of the polarity of life on Earth. That is why mystic masters remain unshaken in the face of the worse experiences of life. According to Taheri, when we object to events caused by the natural laws of nature, we invoke a moral law against their originator, God. If we accept the fact that the laws of the universe are orderly and inexorable, we may infer that they are also purposeful in ways beyond our current understanding. For example, lava that bubbles up from beneath the earth's crust has helped create some of the most exquisite natural beauty on our planet, like the islands of Hawaii. Though people may fear and dread volcanic eruptions, volcanic ash releases minerals into the soil, enriching it for agriculture. And let us not forget that although natural events occur, life on Earth is still viable.

Like the Earth itself, animals and plants follow their own laws. A hummingbird, instinctively attracted to nectar and the color red, finds the feeder I put outside just moments before, yet a robin shows no interest in it. An apple tree does not get bored with producing apples and suddenly decide to grow oranges. A honeybee cannot produce anything but honey. They all do what they have been programmed to do by the laws of the universe, designed by the Divine Intelligence.

Sometimes conditions are such that charismatic individuals with extreme egos and no conscience or consciousness, like Adolf Hitler and Joseph Stalin, create enemies in their minds, seek to destroy them, and then convince others to engage in heinous activities. These events, amplified by egoic thinking, also follow the laws of the universe, as does the milder suffering that we endure in our daily lives. The collective consciousness of millions who willingly submit to evil acts is capable of producing outcomes of unspeakable ugliness. They too act according to their own laws. Similarly, when a new virus is transmitted from animals to humans or created in research facilities, and the human immune system cannot defend against it, the virus can spread widely and rapidly.

The laws of the universe are finely tuned to sustain complex life. The unfolding of these intricately balanced laws reveals something of the intelligence behind them. That is, we start from the end point. If we understand that fairness and healing aren't always the outcomes of actions in this world, we may stop asking, "Why me?" "Why us?" We learn to embrace life's dualities. In a world full of dualities such as ours, there are myriad opposites: good and evil, light and dark, joy and sorrow. Ultimately, it is these dualities that give our lives meaning. If there were no day, night would be meaningless. If there were no crime, justice would mean nothing.

It took years for Einstein to come up with the relativity theory, but most people attempt to explain why a benevolent God allows evil with what their brain tells them at any given moment. However, in higher states of Awareness, they can see that evil is just one necessary component of the reality. The secret to a peaceful state is to stop the cognitive loops of thought and worry that distract us from the sensory experience of being in the here and now. In the present, it is impossible to get immersed in evil—that is, our attachment to our ego, which creates anger, jealousy, fear, or frustration when it experiences some sort of threat. External enemies and events, however brutal they are, have no power to harm us beyond this lifetime. Our ego, on the other hand, can cause trouble in future lives. It can, in fact, be our worst enemy. When I remember that I'm at one with the universe, the ego loses its power. To experience misery due to a war, global pandemic, or civil disorder may not be a choice, but to suffer is a choice.

The very existence of the universe depends on pairs of opposites. It is a "dance" between the two halves of a single system, or the two sides of a coin. It is this polarity that, for example, gives rise to the motion of electrons, which, in turn, form all the matter in the universe that we see. In so doing, they create balance. Whether it be support and challenge, ease and difficulty, or virtue (خیر) and vice (شر), these dualities ultimately light our pathway to Enlightenment. Through God's Links of Grace, which are Facilitators, we can overcome Inhibitors, which are Facilitators' opposites (including egoic thoughts), and remain spiritually whole rather than splitting up into dissociated parts.

Beyond the understanding that brokenness is just the way of the bipolar world and that fairness and healing aren't always the outcomes of actions, it is helpful to know that if God were to prevent suffering from happening, humans would no longer have free will. All our events would become predictable. This would make voluntary progress toward spiritual growth and Enlightenment meaningless, because we would no longer feel responsible for our actions. If we can accept this, we can live a more peaceful life—we won't be taking an adversarial stance toward God, and we won't find fault with the chief lawmaker, the Divine Intelligence. (See "Perceiving Our Destination" in chapter 11 for relevant discussion.) Rumi reminds us through the following poem that in a dualistic world, joy and sorrow coexist.

Where there are roses, thorns abound,
In the grand bazaar of life, joy without sorrow cannot be found.

-Rumi

Awareness

IN OUR QUEST FOR a spiritual life, connection with the One Consciousness gives us divine Awareness beyond conceptual knowing, although we may not perceive it as such. This primordial Awareness that resides in our unified consciousness doesn't recognize space or time. Because it is not bound by space, it sees all that exists, has existed, and will exist in the future; that is, Awareness knows the truth about all things from our origin to our destination. It is from this source that helpful insight arises—and, because

Awareness is not bound by time, it can arrive in a split second, so we must be poised to catch it immediately as it arrives. These days, I carry a pencil and paper with me on my walks in nature, so that I can capture fleeting insights about the content of this book and other aspects of my life. I do not want to miss them, like packages I don't receive because I'm not home to sign for them.

As I noted before, divine Awareness is not a self-contained phenomenon inside our head, our emotions, the world outside, or our body, or something new to be acquired; therefore, we can't make it into an object. There is *existence,* which results from thinking or reasoning, and there is *being,* which lies deep within ourselves and is equivalent to the vastness of the universe. Awareness inhabits a broad, infinite consciousness that extends beyond the limits of ego, personality, the physical body, and even the empirical universe. Yet it is specific and substantive, and it is experienced as fresh and new. It can come in a variety of forms: a song, a poem, an idea, an insight, an image, a person, a text message—anything, depending on what is most useful to us at the time.[37] Awareness comes as "knowing" that can't necessarily be explained. The guidance coming from our sacred self has the power to transform us in a way that guidance from friends or reading does not. Even relying on our "feelings" is not the same as receiving divine Awareness, because feelings emanate from thoughts rather than from the wisdom of our sacred self. Awareness speaks to us through our bond with the One Consciousness.

Indeed, Awareness not only comes in different forms, it also conveys different messages. If we are open to these messages, which are connected to the Divine Intelligence, we can absorb them and carry them with us to the next life. These messages are separate from human thoughts, emotions, and reactions.[38] Our ego often surfaces and attempts to interpret or control a situation.

But when we witness this happening and are aware of it, we go beyond the ego, beyond our dependency on materialism, fame, and other forms of attachment.

Awareness also reveals to us that in our essence, we are inseparable from other human beings. We understand that there are divine manifestations in the universe that unite us, and that God is present everywhere. We know that everything in the world comes from God, and that aligning and harmonizing ourselves with the world around us paves the way for ultimate Enlightenment. We also come to know our origin, the purpose of our creation, and our ultimate destination.

Connecting with, or, more accurately, returning to the forgotten One Consciousness helps us access the treasure box of Awareness and its insights throughout our life journey. Because the One Consciousness is timeless, it continually propels us from our current state of little Awareness to more mature states of Awareness, and ultimately Enlightenment, as we journey to different worlds. In our quest for Enlightenment, the speed with which we acquire new Awareness depends on how much accumulated Awareness we bring with us from previous worlds.

Awareness awaits discovery by those who are enthused and ready. If it were automatically available to all, even those without the enthusiasm to seek it, life would not be rich and interesting. There would be no complexity, no zest, no bewilderment, no amazement. It is God's plan for us to uncover, of our own volition, the secrets of our life's purpose. He understands that we have this capability. It is waiting for those who are deeply enthusiastic.

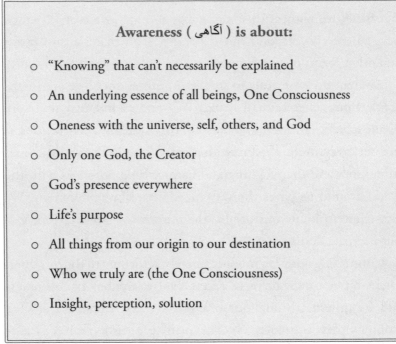

Awareness (آگاهی) is about:

o "Knowing" that can't necessarily be explained

o An underlying essence of all beings, One Consciousness

o Oneness with the universe, self, others, and God

o Only one God, the Creator

o God's presence everywhere

o Life's purpose

o All things from our origin to our destination

o Who we truly are (the One Consciousness)

o Insight, perception, solution

Enlightenment

FOR MILLENNIA, SINCE LONG before the days of Abraham, humans have tried to solve the puzzle of life's purpose. We have been stymied, however, because we have not established communication with our true self, the One Consciousness. It is this connection that yields Awareness about life's ultimate purpose, and that is Enlightenment. Our failure to solve the puzzle of our purpose may be, in part, because of the widespread influence of organized religions, which often disavow the belief that every individual can have direct access to God without their interpretations and interventions. Indeed, the teachings of many spiritual leaders, including Taheri, are valuable, but the discovery that, in our essence, we are one with other human beings comes from within.

Other complicating factors in solving the puzzle of life's purpose are the constraints of time and space, which make it difficult to perceive a world without these elements. However, when we become aware of our fullest potential—that is, when we reach the mountain peak of Awareness—our journey toward spiritual growth comes to an end, and we achieve spiritual perfection (كمال). The ultimate purpose of our creation is fulfilled, and we have full access to the treasure box of knowledge that God wants to give us (see "Perceiving Our Destination" in chapter 11).

According to Sufism, God is a hidden treasure who desires to be known; hence, God created human beings. This often-cited Sufi statement has many meanings, the most evident of which is that union with God is the purpose of creation. With great enthusiasm and through annihilation of the ego, we can become Enlightened and come to know Him—or, we can take the path of those who go astray, wander off the right path, and descend away from God. We have a choice. There is no guarantee once we reach a post-human state of being that we will continue to possess the free will we possess as human beings in this world. That is why Rumi, echoing the saying, "Die before you die," suggests that we discover who we really are while we can in this poem.

> *Go die, O man of honor, before you die,*
> *So that you will not suffer the pangs of death,*
> *Die in such a way as to enter the abode of light,*
> *Not the death that places you in the grave.*

> ~Rumi

It takes time to reach the divine state of Enlightenment, because with each new lifetime there are new lessons to be learned. With time itself as a Facilitator, it is possible to observe the sometimes-amusing thinking that the mind does without becoming involved in the dramas. While the collective consciousness remains constant, the progressive levels of Enlightenment go on and on, until we are finished learning. Setting the noble intention of reaching Enlightenment does not involve one-time experiences of being in the present moment. Rather, it requires sustained intention throughout our lives on Earth and beyond. This means our states of inner peace, love, and joy will likely continue to become more refined and intense as we climb the ladder to Enlightenment.

Additionally, seeking Enlightenment is not about setting goals (such as completing a degree, being promoted to a senior position, or getting a book published) that may emerge from a lack of satisfaction with who we are and what we have achieved in this earthly world. Improvement and happiness are what the ego strives for if unchecked. In Taheri's view, pursuing Enlightenment instead flows naturally from the core of our being, our One Consciousness. This "knowing" is not generated from the mind. It does not involve mental goal setting. It is devoid of the desire for personal gain or judgment about our progress toward Enlightenment.

What makes our journey to Enlightenment possible is our freedom to choose between divergent paths. We often get trapped in egoic thoughts and behaviors as we try to pump ourselves up or assert control over others, but these efforts ultimately lead to disappointment. Alternatively, we can gravitate to the kind of knowledge and Awareness that put us on the path to Enlightenment (see chapter 9, "My Path to Enlightenment"). We can detach from, while still enjoying, material things[39] and reach a higher vantage point from which to view our lives, the way an astronaut, from the vastness of space, views the beauty of planet Earth.

Nonattachment

Nonattachment merely means the ability to keep things in perspective, not letting our happiness or unhappiness depend on something other than our true self, the changeless One Consciousness or "nothingness."[40] Otherwise, we attribute an intrinsic value or meaning to things that are perishable. The first such thing is *form*, such as our physical body. Another way of understanding the body (besides organs, bones, and skin) is as the five senses that convey *sensory* information, such as the aroma, sight, or taste of chocolate. A second aggregate to which we attribute intrinsic meaning is *feelings*, such as an uplifting mood arising from our sense perceptions (for a full discussion, see "Psymentology" in appendix 2). A third cluster of things we hold on to is *perception*, through which the whole world of concepts comes into play and gets stored as memory for future reference. A fourth cluster we hang on to is *mental*, including emotions such as anger, greed, and compassion.

Attributing intrinsic meaning to passing forms, feelings, thoughts, or emotions leads us to grow attached to them. Attachment makes us become subject to what is happening in and around us, resulting in automatic reactivity, and consequently in suffering. We can see this tendency to cling to forms clearly in our own bodies. If we are holding on to staying slim and young, then when our bodies change by accident or just by getting older, we suffer. But what we're clinging to is really based on a surface-level understanding of what is there. As noted in chapter 5, if all the space created by "dancing electrons" were removed from the body, the matter that remained would be smaller than a grain of sand. There isn't much of an intrinsic value or meaning to be attributed to any form, feeling, thought, or emotion in our earthly world.

Without attachment, there is no possibility for suffering to take hold. Gain and loss, praise and blame, joy and pain happen to everyone. When we see life's impermanence, especially the deaths of people we love, we're less likely to hold on to things and, instead, see all experience as part of a passing movie. We may even develop a new philosophy about aging, pain, and loss.

Nonattachment doesn't mean withdrawal from the world, lack of enthusiasm, or fatalism. Actually, it is the opposite. Whereas the fatalist simply doesn't care and asks, "Why make any effort?" the doer of nonattached action, freed from fear and desire, offers everything he or she can. All work, for example, becomes vitally important. It is only the results of events or work (success or failure, praise or blame) that one remains indifferent toward. Desire for a certain result and fear that this result will not be obtained bind us to the world of appearances, and the results are miserable. Work done with anxiety about results is far inferior to work done for the work's sake, only in union with our indwelling One Consciousness.

> *Grow attached, and you become addicted.*
> *Thwart your addiction, it turns to anger.*
> *Be angry, and you confuse your mind.*
> *Confuse your mind, you forget the lesson of experience.*
> *Forget experience, you lose discrimination.*
> *Lose discrimination, and you miss life's only purpose.*
>
> –Bhagavad Gita

We strive for attachment to objects, feelings, concepts, or people when we identify with the ego. Attachments obscure connection with the real self, a state where real contentment lies. If, for example, this writing is done with an outcome in mind (such as becoming a "bestseller"), the creative energy will be dissipated in pondering about the ego-prompted results, rather than channeled toward the performance of the writing. When not fully engaged in the work itself, consciousness is clogged; therefore, the results may not give contentment to me or to my readers. The irony is that as soon as worldly success is of no concern, the way is open for them to flow in—as if the very act of wanting something pushes it away. Affirmation that success has already been produced and showing gratitude in advance for its deliverance may explain the changing of reality.

Nonattachment to our egoic tendencies—such as the need for praise, recognition, and control, or our obsessions with wealth, relationships, power, and fame—is a divine trait. There is a certain juncture in our spiritual development when nonattachment becomes a reference point for everything we do. When we are unattached to our external dimensions—that is, when we have gained the knowledge that our ego isn't us—we finally see who we truly are. We see that God has resided in us all along, though in times before we hadn't reached deep enough into our being to discover Him. That is, we hadn't connected with the One Consciousness, the portal to Enlightenment. And when we have reached Enlightenment, we will see the entire creation within our own soul and in God—i.e., pure Awareness.

Enlightenment (كمال) means:

o Peak of Awareness

o Spiritual perfection

o "Knowing" that emerges naturally, devoid of motive or the ego

o Full access to the treasure box of Awareness

o Demonstration of Godlike attributes such as love and forgiveness

o An end to learning the lessons of experience

o An end to being born on worldly planes of existence

o Entering a state of timeless peace and the all-good

o Oneness with God

o Nonattachment to impermanent entities, which, in this world, means:

    o Not holding on to the results of events or work

    o Not identifying with the ego

    o Recognizing pain, but choosing not to suffer

    o Not attaching to any purpose that is not a means for the journey to Enlightenment

7

Influencing Elements on the One Consciousness

The curls of alluring chain of the Beloved's hair,
Keeps away the troubles,
The one who is out of this chain (links),
Is disengaged from all these ventures.

~Saadi

IN THE ILLUSTRATION shown earlier, the triangle within the circle represents the relationships among three concepts: Presence, the state of being that is a prerequisite for connecting with the timeless One Consciousness; Facilitators, which we might think of as divine grace that helps us achieve the state of Presence; and Inhibitors, which are habits or ways that prevent us from reaching Presence. The Facilitators I will explain in this chapter come from Taheri's teachings and prominently include the divine Links of Grace. The Inhibitors, the effects of which can be minimized by use of the Links of Grace, are either thoughts stemming from the concerns of the ego or random thoughts, both of which we stumble on repeatedly on the pathway to Presence. I refer to these types of thoughts as "debris." They are to be distinguished from the focused thoughts that spring from enthusiasm and that we use to accomplish goals and solve problems to serve humanity.

Overcoming our Inhibitors by employing divine Facilitators

such as the Links of Grace opens us to Presence. This, in turn, deepens our realization that we are all of the One Consciousness. This understanding will ultimately lead to Enlightenment, the place where we discover the truth about ourselves. In Enlightenment, we are finished learning the lessons of experience bound by space, time, and duality.

Facilitators

AS NOTED ABOVE, FACILITATORS, as I refer to them, are divine grace that helps us reach the state of Presence. Among the many types of Facilitators is Taheri's spiritual Law of Relativity (not to be confused with Albert Einstein's Theory of Relativity). According to this spiritual law, everything in the universe is relative (dependent on something else) rather than absolute (independent of anything).

The dependency of relative things is illustrated by the motion of electrons in the molecules of all matter, without which there is no universe, as noted earlier. Because the universe is relative, everything in it is relative. For example, while my body is absolute in relation to its image on the Zoom screen, it is also relative to something higher that is independent of my body (متکی به خود), something that is absolute (مطلق) and real (حقیقی)—i.e., the One Consciousness. Taken to ultimate logic, we cannot experience our essence until we've encountered what we are not; it is only through evil that we know the good; and without pain we cannot experience joy. This is the goal of the Law of Relativity and all physical life: a thing cannot exist without its opposite. While all the experiences of our lives are contained in the "relative truth," the "absolute truth" is a world of "no things"—i.e., there is nothing ultimately there to be separate.

An application of the Law of Relativity I have personally

discovered is that no individual, no experience, and no action can be evaluated as good or bad until I look at it in comparison with something else. For example, I may think of myself as having had a bad childhood, but that's because I had friends and relatives who had happy childhoods. My experience was bad relative to theirs. Yet when I compare my childhood to that of a homeless child, I see my experience in a different light. By making this law part of my worldview, I am less critical of others, more willing to understand a person's flaws in relation to his or her virtues or situation, more able to value multiple perspectives on any issue, and more likely to feel gratitude for what is good. In the spiritual realm, I recognize that without anti-Enlightenment factors, mainly the ego, Enlightenment wouldn't be valuable.

Another Facilitator is Taheri's spiritual *Law of Uncertainty.* Taheri recognizes Werner Heisenberg's Uncertainty Principle, published in 1925, which states that there is a fundamental limit to the precision with which the exact position and speed of any photon[41] can be known, whether by experimental observation or by mathematical prediction. However, Taheri suggests that the origin of the Law of Uncertainty (which he says applies not only to atomic particles, but to every aspect of our daily life) is much deeper than the emergence of photons after the Big Bang. The spiritual Law of Uncertainty is a function of an absolute truth, consciousness, untied to dualities, time, and space—a truth that began *before* the creation of atomic and subatomic particles. These tiny building blocks of matter which make up our bodies and the universe, such as electrons, were initiated by what Taheri calls *fundamental vibrations* before the Big Bang. This inexplicable "emptiness" or "nothingness" (هیچ) which is outside the realms of matter and energy is the One Consciousness in which existence is in perfect unity.

So, whereas Heisenberg's Uncertainty Principle stops at the level of particles created by the Big Bang, Taheri's theory keeps going. The idea of fundamental vibrations emerging from the One Consciousness to create the universe makes Taheri's theory unequivocally distinct from all others.[42] What is invoked here is an interpretation that has *explanatory power* (makes sense), is *internally consistent* (doesn't contradict itself), and is *parsimonious* (uses no tools and few postulates—existence is simply an appearance of a singular truth, the One Consciousness).

The Divine Intelligence "does not play dice" with the laws of the universe prescribed by itself, Einstein famously said. Each factor in our bipolar universe is subject to dualities, such as birth and death, heart and mind, domestic and wild, work and play. Without dualities, motion and, consequently, the universe[43] itself wouldn't have existed. Dualities were incorporated into the design of the universe for a purpose, primarily to give life meaning and interest. It is duality that opens the windows of opportunity for humans to exercise choice, put effort into whatever they do, manifest with enthusiasm (see "The Spiritual Law of Enthusiasm" in the following text), and eventually die. If there were no limits to the existence of human life, we would have a completely different universe.

A personal facilitative application of the spiritual Law of Uncertainty for me is to accept life events, realizing that there is always uncertainty surrounding every event no matter how well I plan and how hard I try. This is an inevitable result of the way the universe works. The commonly used Persian phrase انشاالله (God willing), pronounced formally as *en shâ Allah*, is related to this spiritual Law of Uncertainty, according to Taheri. It implies that there are many factors in the universe that have to come together in order for something that one hopes will happen in the future to come to pass.

Facilitators provide access to our "positive axis of being" (محور وجودی مثبت), which, according to Taheri, is our birthright. Indeed, it is part of what he calls our *original personality blueprint*, which accompanied us when we entered this life (see chapter 11 for more discussion of our personality blueprint). The blueprint evolved from being self-centered to understanding that we are all one in our deepest essence, that our gratitude belongs only to God (الحمدالله), and that wherever we look, we see God's reflection (وجه الله).

The most prominent Facilitators discussed by Taheri are the Law of Enthusiasm and, especially, the Links of Grace, both of which are described in the text that follows.

The Spiritual Law of Enthusiasm

What is enthusiasm? It is the key characteristic that unlocks both our worldly (کمیت) and our spiritual (کیفیت) potential. When we are highly enthusiastic, we experience deep enjoyment, eagerness, and excitement in what we do. When we bring the energy of enthusiasm to whatever it is that we are doing—whether that's improving our physical stamina, writing a book, preparing a memorable dinner, engaging in charitable work, making jewelry, or becoming a ballerina—we bring our full selves. Obstacles are no longer amplified, insights pour in, and we enjoy each step toward the goal. We don't have to labor by ourselves anymore. Enthusiasm lifts us up and takes us, like a divine current. It makes tasks feel almost effortless, or inspires the energy to carry on when tasks feel daunting.

Enthusiasm is the quality that unifies our human dimension

and our divine dimension. In fact, the word "enthusiasm" comes from the Greek *en* (to be with) and *thios* (the divine). It offers us the opportunity to become fully present to our lives in whatever it is we are doing, unobstructed by the ego, which is solely concerned with outcome. When enthusiasm and vision for improving the human condition exist, coupled with the power of the Divine Intelligence, naysayers and critics become unimportant. Energy and vitality grow from within, as do optimism, determination, confidence, and enjoyment. When a person is empowered with these traits, compassion for and forgiveness of others naturally follow.

How do we cultivate enthusiasm? I don't know. Taheri acknowledges that by nature, every newborn arrives in this world with his or her own personality traits. Some will cultivate deep enthusiasm more easily than others. Taheri says that we each develop distinctive personality traits with the help of the Divine Guide (روح هادی), which was bestowed by the Divine Intelligence to show the path to Enlightenment. This compass guides us out of the labyrinth of our ego toward full self-knowledge leading to the perception of God, which is always combined with love and gratitude for His creations—from the air we breathe to the food we eat to the earth we walk upon. The grandeur of the human state lies not only in our ability to conceptualize complex theories but in being worthy of receiving divine guidance.

Borrowing from the *Bhagavad Gita*, at the end of its life cycle, the universe returns to the One Consciousness that sent it forth, remaining there in an unmanifested state until it is manifested. In this phase of potentiality, the original, "clean-slate" personality blueprint (*Gunas*) is in a state of perfect equilibrium. That is, personality traits are the same in everyone. Creation is the disturbance of this equilibrium. The personality blueprint, which includes ego, begins to enter into a vast variety of combinations from the force of *Praktiri* (consciousness) and partakes in multiplicity. (The one exception to this rule is our "soul," a divine presence at the heart of our being, detached from here and now, which enjoys a very special affinity with God; see detailed discussion in chapter 11.)

While all traits are present in everyone, one always predominates, representing the different stages in any particular individual's evolution. One can be calm, another restless, and yet another lazy. Depending on which trait is predominant, our character varies accordingly. While our personality traits are programmed prior to our arrival on Earth, we can cultivate any one of the traits by our actions and thoughts. For example, regardless of our personality blueprint, we can still create and sustain enthusiasm if we choose to. Nobody needs be the victim of his or her peculiar talents. Everyone is capable of making use of other talents than that to which they are naturally drawn.

I know from personal experience that, first and foremost, we need to start a *vision* for that which wants to be born. This vision isn't entirely our own invention. It is a calling, the radiance of something that wants to illuminate Awareness into the service of something that is real. When we speak of or write about something that is real, the words have power. Others can feel its reality too.

For example, in 2010, I received a vision to write a book on a new theory of literacy, and in 2021 another book on the reading skills of children, focusing on children from high-poverty schools—the wounds that the vision illuminated. I made each vision come alive via intense enthusiasm, followed by unwavering commitment and perseverance. I sustained the latter over a period of seven years in each case, despite difficulties and delays, with no expectations for monetary or any other kind of reward.

What created and sustained that enthusiasm is still somewhat of a mystery to me. No one had advised, convinced, directed, or encouraged me. My graduate training, knowledge, and professional experience likely stimulated the enthusiasm, yet enthusiasm coming purely from my mind would have been temporary on its own.

Enthusiasm comes from a deeper place beyond thoughts, a place Taheri calls the "realm of love" (پله عشق). This is the domain of absolute truth, which can only be experienced. Enthusiasm is in the nature of consciousness, which gives meaning and purpose to our lives (see chapter 5, "What is the One Consciousness," for details). It motivates our worldly activities via the "realm of the mind" (پله عقل). According to Taheri, we become a complete human being (رند) when we are able to acknowledge the interdependency of love and mind and embrace both.[44]

Our external and internal perceptions are inextricably intertwined. This way, the eternal self is not overwhelmed by externals, unable to reflect on and refine its ego. Human nature is bipartite, consisting of a mind and a soul. We live on the borderline between the temporal and the eternal, the physical and the divine. The key to living in a state of harmony (*juste milieu*) with these levels of our being is to respond to circumstances, not with craving for material outcomes, but with the enthusiasm and hard work that permit outcomes to spontaneously be what they like, rewarded with the workings of divine insights (see discussion of "Presence as a Bridge between Zero and Focused Thoughts" later in this chapter).

Enthusiasm is thus necessary, but not sufficient. It needs tools unique to the realm of the mind—such as knowledge, thinking, logic, determination, effort, focus, follow-up, perseverance, and patience—to fulfill a goal. Similarly, without enthusiasm, nothing we do with our mind is sustainable—at least not with enjoyment, quality, or meaning. By staying enthused, we can attend to every detail as well as the overall quality of whatever we do that is prag-matic—writing a book, learning about Enlightenment, making bread, or practicing for a Broadway play. At points, when we like what we have accomplished and sense that others are inspired by it, we find our enjoyment of the process intensified and can further sustain our enthusiasm, courage, and resolve for moving forward.

Enthusiasm is not the same as attachment to our physical enti-ties, achievements, possessions, and the rest. Passion for what we do can be practiced mindfully, provided we avoid giving it an in-trinsic value it doesn't possess. For example, at this very moment, I'm enthused about writing these words for you, my readers. I'm paying my focused attention to what I perceive is a need to be met, informed by a clear sense of my true self, the One Consciousness. However, I'm unattached to the product—and when I don't iden-tify with the outcome, my mind is filled instead with divine in-sights and joy. Winning and losing are like happiness and unhap-piness, good and evil, truth and falsehood, or light and darkness. None of these dualities has any intrinsic value or meaning. If I were to think otherwise, the writing would become the means to an end, likely to be driven by ego, such as making the *New York Times* bestseller list. It is the ego that gets upset about losing or boasts when winning.

Beyond enthusiasm in service to something that is real, beyond the mind, there is something more mysterious at work as well—a kind of magic described in the text that follows.

What is the Law of Enthusiasm? The Law of Enthusiasm is a spiritual law discussed by Taheri. It postulates that individuals receive divine rewards for their enthusiasm, passion, and com-mitment (مزد اشتیاق). As such, this law favors no one, including ego-driven individuals who pursue their agenda with intense enthusiasm. The reward, which comes to us through the Law of Enthusiasm, is called upon by specialized Links of Grace. We enter into alignment with this Law and receive our reward: an insight, a revelation, a solution, or a person who can help us at just the right time. When the insights come, they amplify enthusiasm, which, in turn, leads to further insights. In this realm, enthusiasm may be seen as currency. The most enthusiastic individuals are indeed the wealthiest, though not necessarily in earthly/material terms. We become a channel or a vehicle for the Divine Intelligence to give to the universe. It is no wonder the Greeks define enthusiasm as "the God within."

In chapters 1 and 2, I described how the Divine Intelligence guided me toward actualizing both my education and career, despite monumental challenges. I now see these achievements as rewards given through the Law of Enthusiasm for the sustained, enthusiastic effort that I put into pursuing a vision. Back then, I did not know about the Divine Intelligence or the Links of Grace and how to access them. I now know that the Links of Grace are inherent in all of us, and that the opportunity to use them is there for anyone who has the thirst. This idea is beautifully expressed by the following Persian poem:

> *The water of mercy falls on the face of such earth*
> *in whose soil are the thirsty inhabitants.*
>
> ~Maraghei

Enthusiasm (اشتیاق) is:

o A key characteristic that unlocks our worldly and spiritual potential

o A quality of Presence that unifies our human and divine dimensions

o Rewarded by the Divine Intelligence with sudden insights

o Required to facilitate a strong connection with the One Consciousness

o A calling from our innermost self, not the ego, if positive-enthusiasm

o Like a divine current, making tasks feel effortless

o Experienced as deep enjoyment and excitement in what we do

o A potential source of inspiration for others

o Something that can be cultivated

As indicated earlier, there is room for a range of spiritual opportunity to achieve a state of union with God. However, for the particular exploration we've undertaken together in these pages, I'll present one such spiritual practice—the only one I know. This spiritual practice requires the Links of Grace—divine mercy available to everyone as an inner facilitator.[45]

Links of Grace

Taheri's ideas about the Links of Grace are consistent with the mystical tradition of Sufism that emphasizes the inward search for God through direct experience, which is beyond the reach of ordinary comprehension or science. Thirteenth-century Persian Sufi poets, like Rumi and his spiritual guru Shams, referenced in their poems what Taheri has labeled حلقه های رحمانیت, and which I translate as the Links of Grace. It was after receiving personal revelations about the Links through his own intense enthusiasm that Taheri learned about the similar revelations by ancient Sufi masters. However, besides poetic references, there were no historical documents, books, or even vocabularies that would clearly explain these Links. Taheri is the first spiritual leader to reintroduce the Links of Grace, explain them meticulously, and demonstrate their effects on physical and mental health.

There is no direct translation from Farsi to English for the specific Links of Grace. Any approximate translation is likely to create nuances that were not intended by Taheri. Therefore, I've withheld the Farsi titles of the Links and described their admittedly imperfect equivalents in English in the hope that the descriptions will convey their general meaning. In truth, any key conceptual word used in this book, English or Farsi, is simply an approximation of something that is beyond words. Words themselves seldom reveal the depth of the concepts they represent. The One Consciousness, Awareness, Links of Grace, and other concepts can best be understood when they are accessed and experienced directly.

If the universe is designed with a purpose, which according to Taheri it is, then our life journey must be purposeful as well. The Links are God-given gifts to help us fulfill that purpose. By gaining Awareness on our journey to Enlightenment, we grow spiritually toward oneness. These divine gifts are not mandatory. We've been given the free will to either accept or decline them.

Taheri teaches that divine mercy through Links of Grace is available to all people as an inner resource for purification, regardless of their religion, spiritual experiences, nationality, personal attributes, level of enthusiasm, gender, wealth, education, effort, or even sins. This poem by the celebrated Persian poet Tabrizi artfully delivers that message:

> *Love treats rich and poor alike.*
> *This scale balances stones and jewels as equals.*
>
> ~Tabrizi

The Links of Grace are not rewards for our good deeds or spiritual beliefs. They are divine opportunities for all humans, including criminals, to receive the kind of Awareness that would help them climb toward the mountaintop, Enlightenment. The Links of Grace are unconcerned with one's morality, religion, or belief in God. No one is viewed as being a sinner. That's because once the individual awakens and acquires divine Awareness, his or her character will be different. There will be compassion, enthusiasm, and a sense of wonder. We change the within, and the whole edifice will be different. However, not everyone is enthused and ready to grab on to God's Links of Grace inherent within each of us. There are no requirements to access them, other than an inclination toward connecting with one's own true self, which is the One Consciousness.

The facilitative functioning of the Links of Grace is a universal process for all individuals across the globe. Throughout time, people have likely been tapping into the same essential spiritual fields of consciousness, referred to here as the Links of Grace. What the Links are called, the manner in which they are accessed, and how the "linking" experience is interpreted are likely influenced by context—such as Christianity, Buddhism, or Sufism—each with its own application.

A key objective of the Links of Grace, however, is to facilitate the experience of self as an integral part of the universe. This experience, which brings humans closer to their being, others, and their Creator, is accompanied by an opening for Awareness without the use of rational or mental processes. This instinctive "knowing" is more than a philosophical concept. It is a way of seeing, a way of being, and a way of perceiving who we are, why we are here, how the world came to be what it is, and what may come next. In this way, individuals expand their personal boundaries and overcome the limits of the discrete, separate self. This mode enables the Links of Grace to act effectively because it is based on the reality that we are part of the world, as the world is part of us.

In Taheri's theory, there are many Links of Grace that lead us toward Enlightenment. Some are especially useful in certain circumstances. For example, some Links help us abandon our attachments to material things. Others help us navigate obstacles and avoid setbacks or negative vibrations. Still others improve our physical, psychological, and emotional health and well-being, as discussed later in this chapter (see "The Complementary Medicine Link of Grace").

According to Taheri, access to specific Links for specific purposes is available only through his trained instructors. However, another Link, حلقه عام, or as I call it the *Shared Link of Grace*, (see discussion below) is available to everyone. The Shared Link of Grace includes a number of subordinate Links. It is our birthright; that is, like all other Links, it is already inside us when we enter this world. We need only use a "glance" to access the Shared Link and then be a nonjudgmental witness to our spiritual growth.

Taheri likens those who use the Links of Grace to seek Awareness and Presence to passengers on an ocean liner. On such a large ship, they will more easily survive a violent storm. Others who do not access the Links are like sailors in smaller vessels. They are more likely to be tossed into a turbulent sea. The key to accessing the Links is to quiet anything that distracts from achieving Presence and to witness ourselves as we pull ourselves up by God's rope of salvation. Distractions often come in the form of egoic thoughts, such as impatience, the desire for time to pass rapidly, or a wish for time to be stopped. In each case, the individual has disharmony with time.

The Links of Grace are especially advantageous at times of large-scale suffering and upheaval, such as a global pandemic or periods of deep and sustained political unrest, the kind observed and experienced worldwide in recent years. This turmoil creates enormous suffering, anger, and angst. However, the more people engage the Links to seek Presence and peace, the quicker and easier we will extract ourselves from the grip of this pain.

Taheri notes that we must access individual Links of Grace or combinations of them to connect with the One Consciousness. It is highly improbable, he says, that we can ascend to Enlightenment without them. Hafez's poem below expresses this:

Never can you reach the jewel of the desire by your own endeavor.
It's mere fancy to do this without the Divine intermediary.

-Hafez

I think of the Links of Grace as a ladder stretching from my current state of consciousness to the more mature consciousness I desire in my journey toward Enlightenment. I have come to approach access to the Links with great enthusiasm. Each time I establish connection with the One Consciousness through a Link, I know there is the likelihood I will receive insight and, greater divine Awareness, often in unanticipated ways. As I sit quietly and connect, I enjoy a rare opportunity to be without the constraints of time and space that characterize our earthly world. The whole room is filled with a powerful aura of divine love when I'm rapt in the state of connection with my essence, the breath of God.

It is important to clarify that the effects of the Links of Grace cannot be attributed to Taheri or his expertise, or to that of his instructors, all of whom serve as connectors to the Links and to the Divine Intelligence. Taheri emphasizes that the effects come from the divine power that flows through all of us. This is nicely expressed in the following poem by the revered Persian poet Hafez, who says the essential condition for receiving divine awareness (wine) is becoming an impartial witness (an observer).

> *Drink from this wine and let your heart become an observer,*
> *as His beauty is not dependent on embellishments.*
>
> ~Hafez

The "Complementary Medicine" Link of Grace

A Link of Grace that has been extensively studied by Taheri and his research team, and used by his students during the past four decades, is called Faradarmani (فرادرمانى), which roughly translates to "complementary medicine." It is beyond the scope of scientific medicine but may be used alongside it in the treatment of disease and ill health. Unlike conventional complementary medicine, such as acupuncture, meditation, and osteopathy, this Link uses the divine power of the Links of Grace.

As we know, the human body is a highly complex and interrelated system. Our physical, mental, and cognitive dimensions do not operate independently. A friend who had been treated for chronic clinical depression once told me that the more he learned about the deeper meaning of life, the less depressed he became. It was his lack of a sense of purpose that had induced depression. Because the human body relies on interconnected systems to function, any impaired functioning in one part of the body has the potential to negatively affect other parts of the body. Western medicine typically relies on focused examination of specific body parts to make a diagnosis and suggest remedies. This myopic approach opens the possibility of unwanted and unexpected effects on the rest of the body.

Taheri acknowledges the value and importance of medical diagnosis and treatment, yet he also recognizes that medical science doesn't have full knowledge of the nuances within our complex bodies. Therefore, it cannot accurately diagnose and treat every health condition, or do so without side effects. There is, therefore, a need to also look at the human body from a deeper and holistic perspective (فراکل نگری).

This Link of Grace is intended to complement the field of medicine to achieve optimal health and wellness. It does this by bringing together (a) historical records of ailments unique to the individual that are stored in body molecules and (b) the distressed molecules in our body. Once scanned and diagnosed by the Divine Intelligence, the distressed molecules become exposed to the relevant consciousness fields (میدانهای شعوری) and correct themselves to their original state without any physical or chemical interference.

Consciousness fields, as noted earlier (see "Divine Intelligence" in chapter 6) are dynamic yet invisible pathways within the substrate of overall cosmic consciousness. Each consciousness field has a potential influence moving in a particular local region. These fields have the Awareness of all that is. The physical universe, on the other hand, while a dynamic process nestled within an even bigger dynamic process, exists only as long as energy created by the orbiting electrons keeps it moving.

As discussed in chapter 5, consciousness emerges from the One Consciousness, functioning as the cosmic software (نرم افزاری). Once the Complementary Medicine Link is activated by the Divine Intelligence, our body molecules, analogous to computer hardware (سخت افزاری), become exposed to specific consciousness fields to produce desired health outcomes. The body is guided by the cosmic software, in the same way that computer software controls its hardware so that it can effectively manipulate data. Examples of hardware-driven remedies include the use of surgery, drugs, and massage therapy. A software-driven remedy, instead, consists simply of nonjudgmental witnessing. Thus, behind our bodies' hardware there is a cosmic software capable of healing our ailments after a precise scanning, without the use of any tools or techniques. This way, we humans have a second chance to improve our eternal self on our path toward Enlightenment.

Our body molecules possess local consciousness (شعور جزء).[46] Given the vastness of the information it holds, each molecule contains full knowledge relevant to the onset and various phases of our health conditions—yet this molecule alone is unaware of the overall strategy. As such, it relies on the coordinating function of the Divine Intelligence with the other fifty trillion cells in the body to begin correcting itself to its original state.[47] Once scanned, diagnosed, and exposed to consciousness fields that surround us, the damaged molecule uses its reservoir of information about the individual's health history to correct its own misfunctioning.

The above is a good illustration of how molecules, which consist of atoms of chemical elements (such as carbon, hydrogen, nitrogen, and oxygen atoms, which make up 99 percent of our bodies), have the *potential* (توان بالقوه) to carry out an *action* (توان بالفعل)

given proper conditions. That potential stems from the inherent intelligence or consciousness of the molecules. The consciousness that underlies the molecular potential within our bodies cannot act on its own. To actualize its potential, it needs to become part of a larger consciousness that pervades the cosmos through the mediating function of the Divine Intelligence. Another way to see it is that consciousness and matter become allies, each level reinforcing the other toward order, organization, and healing under the oversight of the Divine Intelligence.

Science (physics, chemistry, biology) aims to describe molecules and their subatomic particles from which everything is made, together with the laws that govern them. Arguably, it has to describe the world of materialism, since its resources—empirical observation, theory, and conceptual reasoning—are only suitable for describing structures, processes, and quantities, not intrinsic qualities such as love, pain, or the taste of pomegranate, which require quiet introspection and experience.

Yet science seems to have left out a very important ingredient from its picture of the world. The missing ingredient that affects all components of the universe, including our body tissues, is consciousness. The universe of consciousness, in comparison to the universe of materialism,[48] is fundamental. It can be argued that it is more parsimonious and empirically rigorous (that is, verifiable by accurately reported direct experiences, rather than third-person data, theory, or pure logic) than the mainstream doctrine that the real world consists simply of the physical. There is only One Consciousness, and we are surrounded by it. We, other living organisms, and the inanimate world around us are the extrinsic appearances of this cosmic consciousness.

The view that everything material (from electrons to rocks to trees to us) is an extrinsic expression of consciousness is increasingly being taken seriously as interest in the scientific study of consciousness grows. This isn't meant to imply that particles have a coherent view, merely that there's some inherent consciousness in even the tiniest particle. In proper conditions, these particles *combine* with millions of subatomic particles in the right way under the oversight of the Divine Intelligence. They are then exposed to specific consciousness fields incorporating the Complementary Medicine Link of Grace to meet needs. We can experience their effects as the disappearance of cancerous lung cells or the restoration of infinite components of the body to their original state of health.

Besides being purposeful, consciousness is limitless; therefore, no illness (hereditary or incidental) is beyond its repair capability. Similarly, because it is untied from time and space, it can rehabilitate from any distance[49] in zero time. Furthermore, because it looks at the human body as a whole, it doesn't have side effects on unaffected body cells. Finally, because it doesn't rely on human judgment for diagnosis and treatment, it doesn't make mistakes. That is why human effort, knowledge, and techniques become unnecessary while we seek help through the Links of Grace. Likewise, the Complementary Medicine Link can enable healing even if the exact source of the health problem remains unknown. All that is required, again, is nonjudgmental presence or witnessing. The working of the consciousness may be experienced as vibrations[50].

Taheri has introduced a companion complementary medicine called Psymentology, which, like *Faradarmani*, is a subset of universal mysticism, Erfan-e Halgheh (عرفان حلقه). Psymentology focuses on correcting the underlying causes of mental and emotional disorders, such as feelings of despair, apathy, and hopelessness, which tend to sap vital energy. (For full description, see appendix 2.)

The Shared Link of Grace

In addition to teaching for more than forty years about the revelations he received, Taheri has served as an intermediary, or "wired connector," to the Links of Grace for his students and trained instructors. Instructors, who train for approximately two years under Taheri or one of his masters, in turn pass on the means to establish the Links of Grace to their students, thus paving the way for a new generation to experience divine awakening.

The seeker–instructor–Divine Intelligence relationship that Taheri espouses is, in a way, like the Christian doctrine of the Trinity, which includes God the Father, God the Son, and God the Holy Spirit. The three have different personas, but, in essence, they are all one. In the case of the Links of Grace, there is the spiritual seeker; the instructor who provides access to the Links of Grace; and the Divine Intelligence, who makes the connection to the One Consciousness. All are manifestations of one God. It is when the three come together that the Link is formed. After the formation of the Link, God's grace is offered through the mediating function of the Divine Intelligence, and we get to glimpse the One Consciousness.

Instructors take an oath to honor the conceptual integrity of Taheri's teachings and facilitate connection with the Divine Intelligence only for higher causes (such as self-awareness and Enlightenment), not engaging in acts for personal gain, such as fame, prestige, money, entertainment, or other egoic concerns, like psychic powers.[51]

As noted earlier, full access to all the Links of Grace is available only through a certified instructor of Taheri's teachings. But the Shared Link, called حلقه عام, is open to anyone, anywhere in the world, twenty-four hours a day. This Link is actually a package of multiple Links selected by Taheri for the primary purpose of attaining health (فرادرمانی) and inner peace (طلب خیر). The connector for this Link is none other than Taheri himself. With a willing seeker, Taheri as connector, and the Divine Intelligence, the Link to the pathway to Enlightenment is formed. God is the fourth element, the creator of the trio.

With an awareness of the Shared Link of Grace, all the spiritual seeker needs to do is to initiate connection with the Divine Intelligence (see discussion of "How do the Links of Grace work?"), then impartially watch or witness (شاهد) any changes in the body without any judgment, prior assumptions, or interpretations of the changes that are observed during connection. This is the state of being Present in the moment with zero thoughts.

Closing the eyes helps to disengage from outside events and distractions, but it is not mandatory. The formation of the Shared Link is like that of all the other Links once witnessing has occurred and Presence is established. It then sets the stage for the connection to the One Consciousness to occur via the Divine Intelligence. Once connection has occurred, the Divine Intelligence starts scanning the body to assess what needs to be done and initiate the healing process. Gradually, with practice, connectedness with the One Consciousness through the Divine Intelligence begins to feel natural (احساس شناوری) and occur automatically, without an explicit attempt to establish connection.

It is important to keep in mind that hooking into the Links of Grace is not the ultimate goal. Here is an example: If you wish to achieve Presence, but frequent migraine headaches get in your way, you may call on a Link of Grace to alleviate the headaches. However, it is the attainment of Presence, not a cure for the headaches, that should be the goal. What impedes us from attaining Enlightenment is not bodily illness. It is the ego, looking to control our thoughts and physical comfort. We must let go of seeking to satisfy the ego and instead focus on inner transformation. As Hafez says in this poem, the veil that conceals our happiness is our ego. The Links of Grace facilitate that transformation for a much higher purpose.

> *Hafez! You, yourself, are the veil getting in the way!*
> *Arise from this midst and go away.*
> *Blessed is he who can go through the path with no veil.*
>
> ~Hafez

Some may read this book and decide to join Taheri's classes, or classes taught by his trained instructors, for the sole purpose of being granted the Links of Grace to address specific health issues or other concerns, without signing the pledge to be a force for unity among all humanity. These people will not benefit from either Taheri's teachings or possibly the Links of Grace. The following ancient Persian poems express beautifully the idea that those who want simply to protect their own interests must rely entirely on their own knowledge, wisdom, and ability with no divine aid (wine).

> *The wine of God's mercy is without boundaries.*
> *If it seems there are bounds,*
> *it is the shortcoming of the glass encompassing the wine.*
>
> ~Rumi

> *The sun of love shines on everyone.*
> *However, not all stones are the same. Not all transform into gems.*
>
> ~Saadi

Facilitators are:

○ God-given gifts to guide us toward Enlightenment

○ Universal, available to all people across the globe and through-out time

○ For a variety of purposes, including achieving Presence, controlling thoughts, attaining health, neutralizing nega-tive vibrations—all for a key ultimate goal of experiencing oneness with all beings, accompanied by Awareness toward Enlightenment

○ Implications of the Law of Relativity

○ The Law of Enthusiasm

How do the Links of Grace work?

As noted earlier, formation of any Link of Grace requires three parts: the spiritual seeker, a connector (a certified instructor), and the Divine Intelligence (God's deliverer). Once this spiritual connection (حلقه وحدت اتصال جمعی) is made, God's grace is be-stowed upon the spiritual seeker through His deliverer, and the seeker keeps the delivery—that is, the assistance given by that Link of Grace—indefinitely. The instructor is no longer needed, and the individual receiving any one of the Links of Grace assumes the role of connector for himself or herself.[52]

Some rare individuals with exceptional enthusiasm for under-standing life's philosophy,[53] such as Taheri, may bypass a connec-tor in seeking the full Links of Grace. These seekers serve as their own connectors, but such individuals are extremely rare, fewer than one in a million. That is why the Divine Intelligence created the opportunity for all to share the divine ration of those rare individuals who have created their own direct access.

Glance (a split-second union): Establishing connection (اتصال) with the One Consciousness requires only a split-second union, or "glance" (نظر), between the seeker and the Divine Intelligence for one or more Links of Grace to be activated. There is no way to describe the complex nature or source of the glance in precise terms. It establishes a connection between humans and relevant consciousness fields among the myriads of consciousness fields mediated and directed by the Divine Intelligence as chapter 5 discusses. More specifically, the glance serves the double function of (a) loading the Links of Grace, so to speak, and (b) keeping our secular self out of the way. The further we recede (حذف من), the more easily and smoothly the Divine Intelligence can activate the desired Link of Grace.

The glance exists on a non-physical, intangible plane, like the scent of a wild beach rose. It is not an eye-to-eye glimpse with another being, nor is it a mental visualization or making an intention, which springs from the mind. One might say that through the glance, we communicate with the Divine Intelligence our desire for connection with the ineffable One Consciousness. Then our communication with the Divine Intelligence activates the desired Links of Grace in zero time, because the Divine Intelligence is not constrained by the element of time. The shorter the glance, the more potent and efficient our alignment with the Divine Intelligence. This is because the glance is less obstructed by the mind and further removed from the constraints of time, space, and dualities.

How the Links of Grace generally work:

o A split-second union or "glance" for the Link to be activated

o Being an impartial observer of body changes during the connection

o Activation of the Link by the Divine Intelligence

o Connection with the One Consciousness

o Scanning of the body and healing, as needed, by the Divine Intelligence

o An opening through which Awareness and other benefits flow

Witnessing: The glance described above is followed by witnessing. Witnessing can be described as simply being an alert observer with no thoughts. When watching oneself from within, unexpected things start happening: thoughts and emotions disappear, and a silence surrounds us. When there are no thoughts and emotions, there are also no judgments, expectations, or assumptions—similar to how young children perceive the world with a sense of wonder without past experience to mediate their perception.

This is not to say that thoughts are our enemy. Thoughts are the most beautiful processes for which there are no parallels in science. They remain a masterpiece of tremendous complexity, power, and potentialities. We don't want to *change* or *shut down* our thoughts, and certainly not the mind which created those thoughts when witnessing. We want to go *beyond* thoughts in order to establish direct connection with our innermost essence, the One Consciousness.

Witnessing is always in the present, never the past. When we are witnessing, we are simply there in a state of "alert presence." We are nonverbally alert. Without any verbalization in the mind, we watch our thoughts, like clouds, come and go. Standing aloof and distant, *gaps* start arising between thoughts, and in those gaps, we will have glimpses of zero thoughts. Those glimpses are full of mystery because all barriers are dropped. The whole of existence becomes transparent. Everything we are surrounded by will come to life. The sky will be bluer than it looked before, the music more blissful, and our desire for peace stronger. The universe is won-der-filled. It creates a song, a dance, a poetry inside.

Thoughts step aside of their own accord when we simply wit-ness them. We cannot use our thoughts to fight our thoughts; oth-erwise, we go mad chasing them. Since no thinking or judgment is involved when witnessing, there is no ego, no sense of "I." Even for a few seconds, we position ourselves to have a glimpse of a different world, the real world. In the beginning, these may be rare moments, but over time the gaps or the intervals between thoughts will become wider, spontaneously, without being forced.

With practice, these glimpses become an integral part of who we are. Because we are not oblivious or in a state like a drunken stupor, but rather the complete opposite—a state of intensely heightened Awareness—the memories of those glimpses remain. More than that, they inform our mundane daily ego self even if only in a small and barely perceptible way. To give a concrete ex-ample, when I am an alert witness (هوشيار) in daily life, the dis-tinction between *feeling* the pain and *being* the pain becomes more salient. I am mostly an observer or a watcher of the pain, but not the pain itself.

At the center of that real world is the meeting point of our collective soul. We are one. And that's what God is—beyond time and space. Separation comes from the mind. Only the eternal self will remain after we die. Eventually, if we are patient, we become a master (رند), capable of attending to both the "realm of the mind" and the "realm of love." We think when thoughts are needed (which is most of the time) and allow them to rest when not needed.

In witnessing, instead of evaluating, attention is given to physical feeling that may result from being scanned by the Divine Intelligence, such as feeling warmth, seeing lights flashing, experiencing pain, or, in my case, feeling wavelike vibrations in the palms of my hands and tingling sensations in my feet.[54] This practice of self-observation by giving full, nonjudgmental attention to our immediate experiences is referred to as "mindfulness" by some spiritual teachers. From this position of self-observation or witnessing, we can see things that we are blind to when we identify ourselves with the roles we are playing—scientist, wife, friend, or spiritual seeker.

In seeking this connection, when you take away the human parameters, there is a sense that for a fleeting moment, there is nothingness. That feeling cannot be fully described, in the same way that being in love cannot be fully described to someone who has never fallen in love, or the taste of a persimmon cannot be described to someone who has never tasted persimmons. It can only be experienced. There is a sense of being of this world and, at the same time, not being of it.

Following activation of the desired Links of Grace by the Divine Intelligence, connection with the One Consciousness is established. The Divine Intelligence activates the Links for those new to seeking them, even in the absence of enthusiasm for, or faith in, their effectiveness. That's because it is understood that initially, the seeker may have feelings of uncertainty about the validity of the

Links. Similarly, it is understood that Presence and stillness (pure existence) may not be achievable, at least not at first.

There is one caveat, however. The Divine Intelligence will not act if the seeker ceases to be an impartial observer—i.e., a witness. This may happen, for example, if an individual mocks the healing power of the Links of Grace. If someone belittles, denies, or dismisses the influence of the Links, that means there is judgment. Judgment locks the mind and prevents it from witnessing effectively. As a result, desire for activation of specific Links of Grace cannot be effectively communicated to the Divine Intelligence.

As our Awareness grows and we begin to feel our oneness with the universe and our creator, our witnessing expands. It evolves from impartial observation to full surrender to God. When we have fully surrendered, our minds are free of concepts. We have no identification with the ego. We yield to the Divine Intelligence to help us with no resistance. We acquire full Presence and have peace with God, regardless of the hardships of our lives, because we don't let the mind use the situation, illness, or pain to create a victim identity. We do not feel sorry for ourselves. In this sense, witnessing and surrendering may be viewed as an uninterrupted continuum. Surrender transforms us to a higher level of witnessing, where we know who we truly are apart from our human condition.

Witnessing (Alert Presence):

o Is not a technique (using the body, objects, drugs, or thoughts)

o Requires impartial observation of thoughts, emotions, and senses

o Gets our mind out of the way so that our essence reveals itself

o Can't work if our mind is preoccupied with wellness

o Can only happen in the present moment

o Evolves into a higher form—surrendering to God

Scanning, healing, and awareness: Once connection with the One Consciousness has occurred through the Links, the Divine Intelligence begins scanning the body based on the information it already possesses within its imperceptible cosmic software and identifies the problem. Each of us, like merchandise in a department store, has a "barcode" of our physical, psychological, cognitive, and other dimensions that is readable by the Divine Intelligence when exposed to the Links of Grace (that is, to the fields of consciousness—that is, to intelligence). It then initiates the physical, psychological, or cognitive healing process without the need for medicine, X-ray, physical therapy, and the rest.[55] God's grace then flows through us, always mediated by the Divine Intelligence, His deliverer. I'm always grateful for God's grace after each connection. I see it as a blessing (بركت) that benefits not only me personally, but others as well.[56]

With health limitations behind us, we begin receiving Awareness and insights. We realize that there is an order and purpose to our lives. Suffering no longer appears to be random and haphazard, and we don't take issue with God. We accept events both small and large. It is as effortless as it sounds, assuming there is motivation, discipline, and practice.

Taheri and his team at the Taheri Academy in Toronto are in the process of documenting the effects of the Links on health and well-being through impartial witnessing alone (دنیای بی ابزاری) in the absence of any conventional interventions, such as drugs, surgery, psychotherapy, breathing methods, mantra, hypnosis, headstands, body postures, or massage therapy. To my knowledge, this is the first attempt by anyone to try to empirically describe the effects of the Links of Grace.

Over time, as we practice surrendering and feeling one with God, establishing connection with the One Consciousness becomes automatic. We no longer need to consciously solicit activation of the Links of Grace, although I find it helpful.[57] The switch to the healing power of the Links of Grace is activated automatically and instantly through the coordinating function of the Divine Intelligence, with whom we are now aligned. Among the outcomes of attaining health, as noted earlier, is Awareness about humanity's mission in the ecosystem: perception of the unity of the world of existence and the purpose of creation. This way, we will neither get entangled with our current struggles nor hold a grudge against the Creator.

Inhibitors

IN THE GRAPHIC REPRESENTATION shown earlier, in the lower left corner of the triangle are what I call the Inhibitors to Presence (شبکه منفی) and, consequently, to connection with the

One Consciousness. They prevent us from gaining Awareness that shows us the path to Enlightenment.

There are many Inhibitors to full Presence. Among them are painful events from the past, particularly childhood, that leave indelible impressions on us. These impressions can carry negative associations that compel us to resist the present moment. Despite the positive take on life I've developed, partly through triumphing over adversity, I harbor several of these impressions within me, including victim identity. The blocked energies arising from pain inflicted long ago by my family situation (described in chapters 1 and 2) occasionally serve as Inhibitors to my seeking full Presence.

Another inhibitor is our lack of Awareness about our collective consciousness. Our preoccupation with our earthly selves is reflected in our thoughts, words, and actions. It comes to us from our original personality blueprint (نفس), with which we were endowed when we entered this world. This original blueprint (see fuller description in chapter 11 under "Understanding Our Origin") is accompanied by other personality traits, such as self-obsession (خود شیفتگی), which is more likely to manifest in us in childhood, our key developmental stage.

Depending on how our original blueprint evolved (see discussion of our origin in chapter 11), we may become even more self-centered. This lack of Awareness creates a "negative axis of being" (محور وجودی منفی), which we pass on to others in the form of negative vibrations. The pathway to Enlightenment requires us to dissolve our obsession with ourselves and instead view the world from a spiritual perspective. In this daunting task, the Divine Guide (روح هادی) is always there, helping us to understand (a) our origin, (b) our destination, and (c) our life's purpose, if we don't resist. Our guide helps us perceive that in our essence, we are inseparable from other human beings, that our gratitude belongs

only to God (الحمدالله), and that everything comes from Him
(وجه الله). Using our free will, we can choose to either sustain the
negativity underlying our axis of being or reach for our connected
self, the One Consciousness, and practice what resonates with our
Divine Guide—discovery of the larger landscape of who we are.
Once we allow our true self to be revealed, our negative axis of
being starts to shift toward a positive axis of being. Then, positive
vibrations are more likely to flow naturally from our actions and
words.

Egoic Thoughts

THE MAIN INHIBITOR TO Presence and, consequently, to connection with the One Consciousness is egoic thoughts (تیک های شخصیتی)
generated by the egos (من های ضد کمال). Egos perform certain tasks
on our behalf. Chief among these is maintaining the boundary between self and the other by means of attachments to wealth, education, power, and approval. They assign motives where there are
none, and try to compete with others. They eventually become our
personal identity. As the Persian poet Lahiji says, by moving away
from our egocentricity, we find God's love:

> *While "you" are present, God disappears.*
> *"You" should disappear so that God appears.*
>
> ~Lahiji

When egoic thoughts become one's personal identity, they create a false self. Like a mother who protects, defends, and praises
her children in all situations so as not to distress them, even when
they are misbehaving, egoic thoughts create in us a fictitious sense
of who we are in order to lift us up, avoid any sense of inferiority,

and eliminate stress. To accomplish this, we sometimes find fault with, demean, complain about, or ridicule others—all without conscious thinking. When confronted, our ego vehemently denies accusations that, for example, it sees the glass as half empty or that it is acting like a victim, when, in fact, these are things that characterize the ego.

Signs that the ego is involved include stress, fear, anger, anxiety, depression, aggression, indifference, complaining, sadness, and overeating. These moods and emotions place us in a negative frame of mind (فاز منفی) instead of a positive frame of mind (فاز مثبت), which is characterized by enthusiasm, hope, liveliness, curiosity, joyfulness, and love. When we are in a positive frame of mind, we absorb positive vibrations that are directed at us resulting in improved mood. When we are in a negative frame of mind, we repel the positive vibrations that come our way and, instead, absorb negative vibrations, which suck out our bodies' cellular energy, leading to the disruption of the duties of the Divine Intelligence. When the Divine Intelligence is not allowed to do its job effectively, the result can be a breakdown of the immune system, which can then make us vulnerable to various illnesses— physical, psychological, and cognitive—and reduce our longevity.[58] Importantly, negative pulses created by the ego limit our connection with the real us, the One Consciousness, which we need as a prelude to Enlightenment, that is, to our true destiny—not a place or a time but a divine state of being.

It is difficult to successfully establish connection with the One Consciousness when we are feeling fearful, anxious, hateful, angry, or depressed. In these states, we let our ego react. We let the ego engage in negative activities such as seeking revenge, trying to impress others, overvaluing our self-image, worrying about how we are perceived by others, expecting recognition, or constantly having expectations of others. We may feel regretful, unhappy, irritated, nervous, impatient, overly sensitive, and on and on.

Initially, we try to defend our feelings and behaviors. We may engage in gossip, feel disdain and even hatred for others' political viewpoints, and ridicule others to give ourselves comfort and satisfaction. We make ourselves feel superior by making others feel inferior, but soon after, negative vibrations created by these actions return in the form of anxiety, stress, exhaustion, depression, sadness, and even physical illness. These can escalate into civil wars, genocides, and other exploitative behaviors on the collective level. Meanwhile, the cognitive energy that has gone into satisfying the ego and the amount of time that has consumed have taken us away from finding our path to Enlightenment—our real purpose for living.

Moreover, the negative vibrations created by our individual egoic delusion can affect not only our mental and physical health but also the quality of our work. Importantly, it can reach into the universe and affect God's creations. When we experience the One Consciousness, we can enjoy our achievements, possessions, and relationships without deriving our sense of identity from them. Rather, we are in touch with something much greater than any doing or pleasure of this world. It is comforting to know that from this vantage point, we can create a better world, offering true compassion and healing. That is because the Divine Intelligence is helping us by turning on the switches to the Links of Grace and thereby spreading the peace that we emanate into the universe.

Our egoic tendencies, like our preoccupation with self, come to us at birth, emerging from the original personality blueprint at entry into this world. Therefore, they can never be completely eliminated or denied. Misidentification with the ego creates a strong resistance because the ego identity is so familiar and because it exists from beginningless time. While we cannot let go of our ego, we can manage and control it. Indeed, we are given free will by our Creator to do just that—transcend the limitations of the lower us (our ego) and rise to the higher us (the One Consciousness). We are constantly challenged by these two inherent dimensions. In fact, it is this struggle that stimulates spiritual growth and puts us on the highest path. The ego can be reduced only by the earnest effort to live constantly in unity with the One Consciousness, using the facilitative functioning of the Links of Grace. The extent to which we can dissolve the ego is an indication of our success in meeting the challenges presented to us in this world.

We need to contain the ego, and we do this primarily by learning to recognize it and understand that it is unreliable. Learning about the nature of the ego and how it operates is important. If we don't recognize that it is our ego that wants to enhance our sense of worth with possessions, physical appearance, fame, social position, and achievements, it will trick us into identifying with it. When we identify with the ego, we strive for more external attachments to continue to feel special. That ultimately leads to our downfall. When we identify with our ego, it is difficult to connect with the One Consciousness, the ego's spiritual opposite, or the inner light that we listen to through Presence in the moment. The ego is oriented to the past or the future, not the present.

Once we recognize our egoic thoughts and understand that they are unreliable, we can merely witness them without judgment in our spiritual practices. In doing this, we create an opening to dismiss them. Without such an opening, the One Consciousness will remain elusive. Ironically, acknowledging the ego yet refusing to identify with it essentially leads to moral behavior such as forgiveness, compassion, and respect for mankind and nature. For some, letting go of the ego in spiritual practice is more influential in determining moral behavior than the teachings and advice of religious leaders, the scripture, the government, or other authorities. Unlike religious rituals, dogma, or doctrine, spiritual Awareness is profound yet indescribable. Once we feel our shared essence and connectedness to all of God's creations in our natural state of being, we automatically do not want to do harm. Like waves of uplifting energy, Awareness comes from the realm of love, not thoughts or the egoic mind.

Egoic thoughts (تیک های شخصیتی):

○ Are main inhibitors to Presence, and thereby to sensing our oneness

○ Are oriented to the past or the future, not the present

○ Seek power, approval, revenge, fame, being right, and so on

○ Create false stories about who we are

○ Stereotype and make judgments about people based on personal characteristics

○ Take on victim identity, which manifests as moral superiority

○ Eventually become our personal identity

○ Are associated with emotions such as fear, anxiety, guilt, and hate

○ Vehemently deny accusations when confronted

○ Create Negative Axis of Being, thereby spreading negativity into the world

○ Can be controlled by impartial witnessing, but not eliminated

---

Egoic Thoughts versus Random and Focused Thoughts

Random thoughts: Not all thoughts that distract us from connection to the One Consciousness are egoic. Some are random thoughts related to past experiences or future events that we have recycled a thousand times in our minds. Here are some personal examples: *I'm surprised how well Nelly did last night in the* Dancing with the Stars *semifinals! What shall I make for dinner tomorrow night?* Even thinking about good times in the past can be a dead end, for these kinds of thoughts are grounded in our human experience and offer no progress toward connection. Indeed, these rapid, never-ending, "machine-gun-type" thoughts consume our limited cognitive resources, which could otherwise be used to facilitate awakening, if we could just quiet them down.

Focused thoughts: In addition to egoic and random thinking, we also practice focused thinking. It is my personal belief that focused thinking to actualize outcomes that benefit humanity is not of secondary importance to zero thinking or stillness, which directly facilitates connection to the One Consciousness. Despite the fact that worldly achievements are often short lived, focused thinking enables us to understand and pursue the sacred, the One Consciousness, as I have done by writing this book and as you are doing by reading it.

When practiced with enthusiasm and the desire to lift humanity, focused thinking allows us to actualize outcomes for the human good. These thoughts are not ego generated. This feature of focused thinking is key. As noted earlier, the Law of Enthusiasm favors no one. It rewards the efforts of anyone with intense enthusiasm, including malevolent dictators like Adolf Hitler and Joseph Stalin, who pursued their agendas with relentless, focused thinking. Yet their thinking came from extreme ego separated from the collective consciousness, aimed at achieving power, control, and recognition at the expense of humanity.

Leaders such as Abraham Lincoln and Nelson Mandela were also engaged in directed focused thinking, yet they appear to have been inspired not by their egos but by the desire to seek equality for oppressed people. As Lincoln and Mandela strove for equality among the people of their nations, their focused thinking was aligned with the idea of oneness. Whether or not they were conscious of it, their thinking seems to have been aligned with the divine love, which is what changes the world for the better.

There will always be those who hate and persecute others, and there will always be those who choose the opposite—people who are moved to compassion and seek to help those who are less happy or healthy without self-righteous feelings of pride in their good-heartedness. The struggle between good and evil is an enduring theme of the human condition in our bipolar world. There never was and never will be a time when we all are equally happy or healthy so long as the opposites to those conditions exist.

The goal is not to rid the world of suffering or evil, but to choose how we respond when those things occur—to arrive at a place where we meet whatever happens with the same response the Japanese Zen Buddhist Hakuin gave when wrongly accused of fathering a child: "Is that so?" The choice here is between making an egoic response or seeing it for what it is: something that arises, lasts for a while, and then ceases, devoid of any intrinsic meaning. Saying something has no intrinsic value (such as a promotion, newly diagnosed cancer, recognition for an achievement, or a car accident) doesn't necessarily mean we should not engage with it, but rather that we should not identify with it or attach to it.

On the individual level, when we have enthusiasm for what we do and a calling that comes from our sacred, inner self, we do not cling to the ego. We find ease and joy in our work. We live more in the present. We give more attention to the journey and less to the outcome. Things fall into place in almost magical ways. Insights pour in, and people and resources appear to remove obstacles. Conversely, if we become excessively focused on outcomes, we do not honor the present—consequently, there is little intrinsic value or high-energy frequency in our work. The journey becomes a need to attain recognition, fame, or wealth, which the ego loves. We don't experience the fullness of life because the ego keeps us at the shallow surface of our being.

These days, I continue to devote time to focused thinking in my profession, even as I strive for a deeper spiritual practice in my personal life. I acknowledge that focused thinking, while helping me actualize my professional goals, is intimately related to the One Consciousness. The writing of this book, which required considerable focused thinking, was in response to a calling by the Divine Intelligence to pursue and then share the sacred. I "knew" I had to write this book. It is also a product of critical insights I received through the Divine Intelligence on various matters, including the logical relationships among the chosen key concepts and their collective relationship to the overarching theme, the One Consciousness. As someone with the lifelong purpose of lifting up my fellow humans, I rejoice in both modes of thinking: zero and focused. I particularly celebrate the thinker in me, which gives me the intense enthusiasm and full attention to devote to the process, not the outcome. And because I pay full attention to the journey, my creation enjoys a certain quality, a flow of joy. This allows positive vibrations to enter the world.

Presence

PRESENCE RELATES TO THE topic of time. Time, which is our label for a before-and-after sequence of events, is much like the frames of a film occurring inside the brain. The brain ties together events as we observe and choose them and then translates them into a coherent experience, a continuous flow in our daily life. In this sense, time is a relational concept, one snapshot relative to another.

Imagine a video feed of your entire life, a sequence of still images (frames) moving from birth to the present moment at a conventional speed of twenty-four frames per second. The quick succession of individual images gives the impression that you are changing, looking older now than you did as a newborn, a teenager, or even a year ago.

Similarly, in real life, our perception of time flowing from the past toward now is only storytelling created by the mind, according to Taheri and many others. Einstein once said, "People like us, who believe in physics, know that the distinction between past, present, and future is only a stubbornly persistent illusion." The brain creates the appearance of movement by thinking that the "you" reading these words now is the same "you" who ate breakfast this morning and the same "you" that went to the grocery store yesterday. The mind glues the past and the present together all the time to create a perfect unison. But in fact, all those selves are distinct, each one existing at a different point on the space-time continuum.[59] The mental stories eventually become our knowledge of the events; our stored memories.

Our flowing experiences (the "movie" version) are unique to our physical universe. At its deepest reality, however, the universe is timeless. If we were to step outside the universe—outside both space and time—we wouldn't see what we see today. We would see all these still frames, our individual images, from our birth all the way to the Big Bang (مهبانگ), which occurred nearly fourteen billion years ago—and even beyond, to the nothingness that is the source of everything in the universe, the One Consciousness. Every moment would seem to exist in perfect isolation, because the sequencing of events into past, present, and future requires intellectual connection which there is no brain to perform.

What is "Now"?

FROM THE SCIENTIFIC PERSPECTIVE, "now" or "present" is the smallest unit of time, called a Planck second. You may think of it as a single frame in the video described above. A Planck second is the smallest difference we can ever observe along the time dimension. It is conceivable that two distinct events in reality could occur less than a Planck second apart, but it is beyond the power of science to tell them apart if they do. Outside our deeper self, the One Consciousness, whatever we see is either an abstract representation of the past constrained by our dreams, or proclivities to act and react in certain ways in the future. They are both mental stories created by the mind.

> *But are not all Facts Dreams*
> *as soon as we put them behind us?*
>
> ~Emily Dickinson

From the spiritual perspective, the "now" is no longer here as usually understood, nor is it the eternal moment that comes after our earthly existence. Rather, "now" is the segue into and experience of connectedness with the One Consciousness, uncolored by the narratives we create. It is the pivotal point of power, which can only emerge out of our deeper dimension in the present moment. There is no before or after. "Now" is a key that can open the door to our inner existence and allow us to know who we truly are, where we came from, our life's purpose, and where we should be going. It also makes possible knowledge and love of God. That is why the Sufi poet, Rumi, reemphasizes the need to live in the now.

> *Past and future veil God from our sight*
> *Burn both of them with fire.*
> *How long will you be partitioned by these segments, like a reed*
> *So long as a reed is partitioned, it is not privy to secrets.*
>
> ~Rumi

Without an opening created by Presence, the inner light will remain elusive. We can have brief peeks into our inner being (that is, be in the timeless "now" with zero thoughts) for a fraction of a second, a second, or even more. The feeling cannot be fully described, in the same way that being in love cannot be fully described. It can only be experienced.

For most people, the present moment doesn't exist. They do not realize that it is the future they want to reach that doesn't exist. The future is only a thought, a thought that doesn't in any way diminish the sacred journey to Enlightenment, which is the eternal present moment. By resisting the present and waiting for the next vacation, for children to grow up, or for the book to be published, we create an inner conflict between where we are and where we want to be. And while the future is pure potentiality, the past is pure actuality. It has happened. Between these two, we stand in the present always thinking of the impossible. This resistance to the present moment merely serves to rob us of the now.

We walk from here toward God's "residence" only to realize that "there" is "now" in this very moment—that is, God is always near us. We have only to realize His nearness, which resides at the center of our being, the One Consciousness.

The present moment is not "now" as usually understood. Rather, "now" is the key that can open the door to our deepest level of existence, telling us who we are, where we came from, and where we should be going. This "now" is the only opening through which the soul can pass out of time into eternity, God's grace can pass out of eternity into the soul, and compassion can pass from one soul to another soul. It also makes possible knowledge and love of God (for more discussion of this, see chapters 6 and 11).

Being in the "now" to induce a state of connectedness with the One Consciousness requires no spiritual technique, meditation, correct breathing, hypnosis, or psychedelic drugs. There is nowhere to turn in search of Enlightenment but our innermost self. The indispensable prerequisite is simply nonjudgmental witnessing using the Links of Grace—a practice based entirely on the divine revelations of Taheri. Happy are those who can take advantage of the "now" while they are still in the human state.

In order to bring meaning back to the "now" of our lives (i.e., to be present), we must become a witness, or an impartial observer, to what is going on in our minds and bodies, after asking for assistance from the Links of Grace. Simply spectating our thoughts and bodies, without any judgment, analysis, or interpretation, leads to Presence, which, in turn, sets the stage for the activation of the desired Links of Grace. Gradually, as our Awareness grows, witnessing takes on the higher form of surrendering to God, as discussed earlier, which leads to full Presence. To quote Rumi, full Presence is an invitation to enter the sacred dimension within us.

Connecting with the One Consciousness

Silence is the language God speaks.
All else is a poor translation.

~Rumi

The state of being present cannot be understood intellectually or scientifically. It is a sense of being in God's presence, and when we are in God's presence, space and time lose their significance. We experience a touch of sweet timelessness. Loneliness and fear no longer have meaning because we have torn down the wall that separates us from God. And when we connect with the One Consciousness, our actions, thoughts, and words reflect that oneness. We come out of our individual selves and become aware of the beautiful surroundings that exist outside our solitary fort. However, Presence and the experience of divine joy aren't an end in and of themselves. They are merely a prelude to Awareness provided by the One Consciousness.

As long as you are engaged in your knowledge and superiority,
you are void of wisdom indeed.
I give you just one tip. Do not see self.
From then on, you are freed.

~Hafez

> ## Presence (حس حضور) from my own experience is:
>
> o Being an impartial witness, watcher, or observer
>
> o Making no judgment, assumption, or interpretation
>
> o Having zero thoughts or visualization
>
> o Accepting the now (not past or future)
>
> o Harmony with time (not willing it to pass rapidly or to stop)
>
> o Accepting, not resisting, situations as they are
>
> o Timeless and spaceless
>
> o The segue or doorway into sensing the power within, the One Consciousness

Presence as a Bridge between Zero and Focused Thoughts

While wisdom and intellect illuminate the way,
they can never take the place of the moonlight.

~Shah Nematollah Vali

OUR LIVES ON PLANET Earth are composed of two dimensions: the secular (the outer realm) and the sacred (the inner realm). When we turn off our thinking completely and become fully present to the inner realm, Taheri tells us that our activity becomes infused with the Divine Intelligence. To this I would add that, when we are fully present—our thinking focused toward actualizing a goal that lifts up humanity, discriminates between different choices, or makes consciousness available to others, all free from the entanglement of the ego—we are also awarded the gift of the Divine Intelligence. In both zero thinking and focused thinking for the good of humanity, we are guided by the helping hand of the Divine Intelligence, perhaps in the form of a person, a fleeting insight, or even a song. If ready for it, we can capture the Awareness that comes swiftly our way.

To me, focused thought is a medium for creative expression, unbounded to its fruit. Though not directly engaged in my creative work, the Divine Intelligence acts by mere presence, so my work is done as much by the Divine Intelligence as by my focused thoughts. As a result, the quality of my work does not lie in its mere performance but in the motive that prompts it and the frame of mind behind it; that is, detachment from the results, enthusiasm, humanity, and ceaseless effort.

The truth is, we spend most of our lives pursuing worldly goals through focused thinking, rather than spiritual goals through zero thinking.[60] Despite their relatively short lives, worldly achievements, like my writing and your reading of this book, can be portals to spiritual awakening. There is no real division between the two if we don't clump together all types of thought into a single category. Focused thought is different from both random and egoic thoughts. Focused thought can share most of the characteristics of zero thought plus another element—creation. Random and egoic thoughts, on the other hand, are distractors, or what I call "debris."

Indeed, in some cases, focused thinking is the basis for or portal to zero thinking. It enables us to describe, clarify, discuss, and work toward an understanding of the sacred. In some instances, it may be difficult to pursue the sacred without focused thinking. Similarly, when we evolve toward an awakened spiritual self, our secular life is positively impacted. Both focused thinking and zero thinking are essential, like two lenses in a pair of eyeglasses; neither alone is sufficient.

Viewed this way, zero thought and focused thought become interrelated, regardless of whether or not the primary goal is to connect with the One Consciousness or to fulfill an outer purpose of actualization. The link between both types of thought is Presence.

When we align with the present moment, having been driven by the sacred (inner) being, we gain Awareness that is transferable to the next world. We become aware that we are an integral part of the universe, that we are all one underneath the misperception of separateness, and that it is God that manifests through the Divine Intelligence. When we align with the present moment, having been driven by a secular (outer) purpose that is naturally rooted in the state of One Consciousness, our endeavor is one of joy and quality. Invariably, the result is a creation that contributes to humanity.

Being naturally rooted (شناور) in the state of One Consciousness while engaged in focused thinking is a key requirement for seeing the interrelatedness of zero and focused thoughts. Let me explain the concept of being in a natural state of connectivity from personal experience. Earlier in my life, as a competitive ballroom dancer and personal trainer, I learned to naturally engage the innermost part of my abdominal muscles, the *transversus abdominis*, throughout daily activities. I practiced this not only when I was competing in ballroom dancing but also when I was exercising or walking, in order to have better balance and stability on the dance floor and in life in general.

These days, in addition to my dancer's center, I've learned to engage the innermost part of my being, the One Consciousness, throughout my daily activities, so that I can be better aligned with the universe. Like my dancer's core, my spiritual core is always engaged. This impactful engagement not only gives me liveliness, joy, a creative spark, and appreciation for all the beauty in nature; it is also a reminder not to identify with and attach myself to the impermanent earthly world I'm passing through. Because focused thoughts arise from a natural state of oneness with the universe (anything else is ego driven), both zero and focused thoughts are assisted by the spiritual power of the Divine Intelligence, the initiation of which is an act of the Links of Grace. As a result, insights, helpful events, joy, and coincidences occur to guide our creation in a way that our mind cannot understand. As a research scientist who is always in explore mode, I especially cherish these insights.

A sign that we are not rooted in our spiritual core is *stress*, which is not to be confused with *intensity*. Stress blocks the flow of insights, whereas intensity that is aligned with our being, the One Consciousness, transforms obstacles into insights, as if riding a huge wave.

In short, neither zero nor focused thinking, as defined here, is identified with the ego. Moreover, both have the potential to lift up humanity with the gift of the Divine Intelligence. The Awareness of the One Consciousness lies at the heart of many spiritual traditions, including Sufism, Buddhism, and Abrahamic religions. Similarly, insights from current science, as I've noted in chapter 5, contribute to our perception of ourselves as being intimately interwoven with the universe. What a beautiful convergence of two areas previously thought to clash: science and spirituality!

The main difference between zero thinking and focused thinking is that in zero thinking, we connect directly with the all-inclusive collective consciousness, leading to divine Awareness without a thought, technique, effort, or even an outcome in mind. This is because Awareness is already complete and will reveal itself to us once we take a witness seat with no prior judgments. In focused thinking, however, we do put effort into studying, analyzing, and manifesting something to improve our lives or make knowledge available to others, all the while being anchored to our essence. That is, we are in a natural state of alignment with the One Consciousness while fulfilling a vision, regardless of how that vision changes over time.[61]

Yet both zero and focused thinking are necessary, and both have the potential to send out positive vibrations that can spread across space and time. In a sense, these are two sides of the same "universal coin," as Taheri would say. While there is within our bodies a reality that is already divine arising from the One Consciousness, there is a degree of our body in the soul. In other words, there is a fusion of body with soul. We thus have existence in all realms from the spiritual to the physical, from the sacred to the secular, from microcosm to macrocosm, from qualitative to quantitative, from local to global, from "mind" to body, from subjective revelation to objective knowing, from reality to its animated representations, and from the divine spark to intellect.

These realms are not additive, such that cognition is added to divine experience or insight; rather, each allows something yet to be determined. For example, within our secular realm, every act turns into perception, every act of perception into reflection, every act of reflection into the making of associations, and every act of making of associations into creation. Manifesting within a world of potentiality, in turn, helps us become aware of who indeed we are, resulting in the growth of our eternal self in the here and now (see discussion of "The Eternal Self" in chapter 11 for further details).

I thus recommend oscillating between zero thinking and focused thinking in order to access our true self and creative potential—both of which only arise in the now. This way, we also won't miss what comes our way. We can choose to be present either way, by stepping out of focused thinking only to enhance it with zero thinking. When we return to focused thinking, it will be even sharper. Life is a dance between the inner and outer. We need the outer experience so that we can learn, create, and evolve. But if we don't tend to the inner, we end up empty, hurt, and confused. Conversely, if we just retreat to the inner world—unless we have chosen the life of a monk—we'll likely experience isolation and loneliness. The key is not to confuse focused thinking with who we are in our deepest essence, although all true creations are anchored to a state of consciousness, whether we know it or not.

Both zero and focused thought are:

o Driven by enthusiasm

o Essential (neither is sufficient by itself)

o Inspired by a deeper connection with all beings

o Connected through the bridge of Presence

o About being in the now, not the past or future

o Unobstructed by the ego seeking praise, power, or wealth

o Concerned with the journey itself, not outcomes

o Guided by fleeing insights from the Divine Intelligence

o Able to send positive vibrations into our world

o Capable of lifting up humanity

o Joyful

8

Connecting with the One Consciousness

You won't gird your waist with such a tight, binding belt
if you see that the one in the midst (who becomes squashed)
is nobody but yourself.

~Hafez

S PIRITUALITY IS AN expansive concept with room for many perspectives. We each have our own way of understanding a given spiritual approach or theory, and none of us is in the position to judge the validity of another's chosen form of spirituality. While there is room for a range of spiritual possibility and opportunity, when we find a theory meaningful, we must then move from learning and intellectualizing to deeper perception, and then, most importantly, to practice to see if it actually works for us.

In the context of this book, it is the practice of "alert witnessing" or "alert presence" that ultimately leads to Awareness and helps us move toward Enlightenment. When we practice witnessing and, eventually, surrendering, the One Consciousness becomes a living reality. Our spiritual dimension emits high vibrational frequencies into the world, thereby bringing healing and compassion. One of the earliest Sufi masters, who lived in the eleventh century, had this to say about surrendering:

Know that when you learn to lose yourself,
You will reach the Beloved.
There is no other secret to be learned,
And more than this is not known to me.

~Ansari of Herat

Taheri teaches that connection with the One Consciousness through Presence requires (a) no effort, thought, self-discipline, or skill; (b) no techniques such as meditation, repetition of the divine name, imagination, intense concentration on an image or a sacred symbol, energy therapy, journaling, body movements, suffering, or self-deprivation; (c) no schools of thought such as psychology, philosophy, alternative medicine, chiropractic, homeopathy, shamanism, astrology, hypnotherapy, dream interpretation, or numerology; (d) no medicine or psychedelic drugs; and, (e) no education, belief system, imagination, concentration, or knowledge.

Taheri eschews dependence on effort, techniques, schools of thought, drugs, and the rest when connecting with our true essence because (a) the goals of many of these approaches are primarily to seek relaxation, peace, or general health, rather than Enlightenment as defined in this book; (b) positive outcomes could be attributed to personal efforts, techniques, or drugs rather than to divine grace, which could create egoic pride; and (c) these approaches may become distractors, blocking the flow of insight and Awareness about meaning of life and who we are, which are key outcomes of connecting with the One Consciousness.

Instead, given our *goal* of receiving divine Awareness[62] and given the accompanying *approach* of relying on God's Links of Grace to fulfill this spiritual goal so that we are on the right path toward Enlightenment, all that is required is a split-second union or "glance" for the Divine Intelligence to turn on the desired Link's switch and for us to then sit in the witness seat. We watch impartially, and the One Consciousness responds.

My Spiritual Practice: Visiting with My Sacred Self

MOST DAYS, I SET aside ten to twenty minutes for a visit with the sacred part of myself, which I call "visiting with my sacred self." Essentially, I try to connect with "who I really am," the One Consciousness, the one who knows the whole story from beginning to end. The length of time varies depending on the individual; some are sooner able than others to dismiss their thoughts, experience the Presence of this timeless/spaceless truth, and realize that they're not separate from it.

To friends and family for whom the concept of visiting with sacred self is new, I simply call it *spiritual practice*. By that, as you might guess, I mean a practice that takes me to the depths of who I am—my essential self, stripped of all the perceptions I have about myself and my history. This practice pays back through my recognition of the marvel of being alive, my gentle appreciation of the air I breathe, and how I am humbled to be in the presence of God, who created this aliveness in me. God's boundless love for me (and everyone else) will never go away, even though the edges of everything else in my physical life will begin to soften and eventually dissolve.

This invisible, sacred "me" that I visit daily is inseparable from the One Consciousness. My body, my secular self, is only a veil that covers my reality. What is more, even the apparent solidity of my veil is a mental abstraction, according to Taheri. It is a vibrational frequency of electrons. Yet it is through my body that the One Consciousness reveals itself—and when it does, that state of consciousness flows into whatever I do in my daily life, from ironing my tablecloths to opening the shades of my dining room windows in the morning to writing scientific journal articles to sharing my personal stories with you at this moment. Notice the connectedness of zero and focused thought that I explained earlier: Through zero thought, we perceive oneness. Being rooted in oneness, creativity flows into our focused thoughts, and we begin to actualize.

For my spiritual practice, I prefer a quiet room. Rather than lie down, I sit on a chair to help me stay alert—always with my "glance" (نظر) at one or more Links of Grace to be activated. With my palms facing upward and fingers slightly splayed, I choose to close my eyes so that my attention is inward (although others may prefer to keep their eyes open) and plant my feet flat on the floor. I let my shoulders drop down, thereby relaxing the body. Then, as I begin to connect, I simply watch and witness any changes occurring in my body, typically as wavelike vibrations in the palms of my hands or tingling sensations in my feet. Some of my friends have reported feeling warmth within their body, seeing bright lights flashing, or even experiencing pain.[63] These are just indicators of the Divine Intelligence at work. I witness these bodily sensations without any judgment, expectations, speculations, prior assumptions, doubt, or interpretations. In other words, I try to be present in the moment.

Witnessing, which can only happen in the present, sets the stage for the activation of the specific Links of Grace I seek. Then, the Divine Intelligence steps in and makes the connection with the One Consciousness. Once connection has occurred, the Divine Intelligence begins scanning the body and initiating the physical, psychological, or cognitive healing process. It is amazing how the Links, once activated, help ignite the healing process.

When I observe a thought in my mind or feel an emotion in

my body that hinders my connection, I know that I am not being present to the moment. I don't fight these distractions which arise in my mind during spiritual practices; in trying to forcibly abolish my daydreams, I would merely deepen their effect.

How do I find the "off switch" for this compulsive thinking mind? I gently dismiss the thought or feeling by witnessing it and then trying to perceive the Presence underneath it without fighting, controlling, or analyzing the thought or emotion itself. Notice the difference between being lost in some drama created by the mind, and then recognizing it as a thought. With that recognition, there is an immediate sense of waking up. I no longer identify with the thought or the emotion but am, instead, its observer or watcher. I just see it happening as if it is happening on a TV screen or as if I'm looking at somebody else. In this way, I create *gaps*[64] in the steady stream of my thoughts and emotions—moments of Presence—which, in turn, help provide glimpses of the One Consciousness.

I think of witnessing as the door to my soul, the One Consciousness. I know I'm witnessing when I'm not thinking. The moment I think, I've begun judging; if I tell my mind "Stop the judging," I've imposed something between the witnessing and me—a judgment on judging. I've allowed my past knowledge and experience to penetrate into the present. When I say "Stop the judging," it has already become the past. I've known and I've judged. Witnessing is only in the present.

Thinking is a mechanical habit with us. My spiritual practice doesn't mean never having any thoughts, but rather being aware of thoughts instead of unknowingly feeding them. In many cases, the effortless circumvention of distractions causes them to lose their obsessive presence and, for a time at least, to disappear. This I perceive as real joy and peace. The longer I am in this state of connectedness with my inner self, the higher the resulting vibrational frequency. With a higher frequency, there is greater power to discharge negative vibrations that might otherwise impede my progress toward Awareness.

When I first tried to attend to my inner self, I felt anxious and slightly agitated, and I even developed headaches. Those feelings of discomfort haven't completely gone away. A chief problem is clinging to my thoughts instead of the laudable goal of being in the now. At a certain point, I've even found myself saying things like "This is boring," or "This isn't working." These are judgments. When they come up in my mind, I try to recognize them as judgmental thinking and remind myself that spiritual practice involves suspending judgment, simply watching whatever comes up, including my own judging thoughts—without pursuing them. Interestingly, the moment I realize I'm judging, I am present. Whenever we are able to witness our mind, we are no longer trapped in it; another factor has come in—the witnessing presence, the awareness that we are aware.

Despite failing to be present from time to time, I'm still able to see the transformation. In my relationships, for example, I keenly recognize how defensive and ego driven everyone around me is (including, sadly, spiritual thinkers and leaders with delusions of grandeur), and how I too have been defensive and ego driven. Occasionally, I still see feelings like pride and selfishness in myself, but I've come to feel grateful when I see these patterns arise. It becomes another chance to perceive their nature and to let go of the burden they bring.

I now see unconsciousness more clearly around me, especially in social and mainstream media. Those who listen four or five times a day to newscasters and commentators on multiple forms of technology—each one of them the servant of their advertisers, of a pressure group, or of the government—are not taking an intelligent interest in world events, but rather magnifying world events by indulging in idle curiosity. News commentaries penetrate the mind, filling it with repeated doses of drama that merely create a craving for daily or even hourly emotional injections. Advertising is the organized effort to intensify and extend that craving. I view mental noise and noise of desire, when we identify with the ego, as the greatest obstacles between the eternal self and its God—a separate and hollow existence.

The journey to spiritual awareness takes time, even if one is enthused and ready. It takes discipline and practice, based on my personal experience, but there is no more worthy effort. There may come a time when you will experience the connection more often, in greater intensity, and beyond sensation—all without having to sit down for the spiritual practice. In a sense, you will have embodied (been immersed in) it. As such, you will be able to carry it wherever you go for the rest of your life. I carry God with me into everything I do and into all places, and He does most of my work. I become one with God in every thought, and He acts through me. Nothing can stand in His way, and in the same way nothing can scatter me.

Now, whenever I'm in a state of connectedness with my inner self and the universe, I feel a sense of aliveness and renewed vitality, which is there for everyone. What's more, as Taheri teaches, this sense of renewed vitality, unlike our physical bodies, does not change as we age. Rather, it slows the aging process by strengthening our immune system and improving our mental health. I don't look for scientific evidence; I *am* the evidence. The empirical knowledge derived from either scientific experiments or spiritual insights is the only type of knowledge accepted in these fields.

Initially, if I achieved connectedness and Presence for a fraction of a second, I was very pleased, considering where I was in my spiritual practice.[65] Now I know that if one practices regularly, with genuine desire rather than duty and without judgment, connectedness lasts for longer periods. With it comes the highest and most enduring level of spiritedness and joy, without any of the side effects (such as boredom) associated with the repeated pleasures of the physical world (like having a favorite meal four nights in a row).

In addition to my regular practice, I seek to reconnect with my inner self throughout the day, especially when I feel negativity rising within me. This may happen, for example, when I anticipate worrisome news from my doctor, when I have a disagreement with a family member, or when I experience other negative, external influences. In those instances, I may succumb to egoic thinking, hoping to make the fear, anger, or other distress go away, and thereby create a wall of resistance to connectedness. Yet, through my spiritual practice, I dissolve these walls with surrender. Rather than being defeated, I use a Link of Grace that helps me yield to and accept whatever the situation is. When I am fully confident that my inner self can see with my eyes, think with my mind, and walk with my legs, necessary positive actions are more likely to result.

Earlier in my life, I called this surrender "forgiveness," as chapter 2 describes. Intuitively, without any spiritual knowledge, I sensed that by forgiving, I could come to grips with my hurt and angry feelings and prevent them from controlling me. I could move on with my life despite the disturbing actions of others. This way, I became invulnerable to my life challenges.

Reading books and attending workshops on spirituality can only take us so far. We must practice connecting with our sacred self and accessing our inner strength. That inner strength, the One

Consciousness, remains unaffected by the circumstances around us. We access it through Presence and surrender.

Only when we access the One Consciousness collectively will we be able create a world that is less negative, though never completely free of negativity; the best we can hope for in this world is a balance between the positive and the negative. But change must start with us as individuals. If one individual becomes aware of the oneness of humanity, it will influence others. Soon, we will see no real boundaries between us. We'll become one in our essence, just like the beautiful blue planet Earth seen without national boundaries from space.

Once we are infused with the One Consciousness, a flow of divine vibrations provides help in miraculous ways, for the quality of both our work through focused thought and our spiritual awakening through zero thought. Once we are awakened and in touch with our own depth, true compassion for others becomes possible, because we can look beyond our individuality and feel the bond we share.

As Taheri explains, having compassion and empathy for those who are suffering, and helping to alleviate their suffering, are necessary and important human actions. Yet these activities are limited to the human realm. True compassion goes beyond empathy and charity toward others. It happens when we go a step further and feel our eternal bond of the One Consciousness with those less fortunate. It happens when we are aware of the source of all creation, God. It happens when we understand that everything that exists, including all of humanity, is a reflection of God's love. Importantly, it happens when we realize that our physical bodies, minds, and emotions are misrepresentations of our true selves. Our true selves are one with God's love. The path to Enlightenment is both our gift to the world and our main purpose for living.

Calling on the Links of Grace

ONCE I AM PHYSICALLY settled in my spiritual practice, I decide which Link of Grace or combination of Links I want to be activated. The Links that I appeal to on a regular basis include those that expand my capacity to perceive the vastness of the universe, to not want time to pass rapidly, to help heal sick people I know, and to create unity with the universe.

The readers of this book would seek activation of the Shared Link of Grace. The Link(s) of Grace are turned on by the law-abiding Divine Intelligence, assuming the condition of witnessing is met. The more confidence I have that the Divine Intelligence will deliver help, the more successful I am in exploiting the specialized Links of Grace. Silencing my mind, to the extent that this is possible, helps create Presence. While in this state, I experience timelessness, spaciousness, and nonduality.

On multiple occasions, connection with the One Consciousness, the universe, and God has brought tears of wonder and joy to my eyes. I am overwhelmed with gratitude. Acknowledging the good in our lives awakens the dormant sense of abundance within. Then this abundance naturally flows out. Knowing that God doesn't need my praise or appreciation, I feel motivated to give back to the universe through any means available to me: research, writing, charity, and unconditional love and respect for all of God's manifestations. I do not practice these things with all my being because I fear hell, because "God said so," or because I am trying to otherwise bribe the Divine Intelligence. I do not pray, "Dear Divine Intelligence, if you please get rid of my headaches, I promise to give money to a charity." I pray to perceive the nature of my being, the vastness of the world, and the existence of my egoic thoughts so that I am able to quiet them through spiritual practice and create an opening to the One Consciousness. The irony is that the Divine Intelligence helps me no matter what, precisely because I didn't expect leniency in exchange for doing good.

The Divine Intelligence is always there to extend a hand to anyone who longs for and believes in its power. I know this from personal experience. When we lack enthusiasm, it is often due to our doubts about, or lack of confidence in, the Divine Intelligence. This is a judgment that locks the mind and prevents it from creating the necessary conditions for receiving help.

If we practice seeking Presence and witnessing throughout the day with genuine desire, not duty or judgment, establishing connection will no longer be a peripheral activity but an automatic one. In other words, we will always be connected to our sacred part. Then, we will no longer need to consciously solicit activation of the Links of Grace. Their healing power will be activated automatically through the coordinating function of the Divine Intelligence. Awareness will pour in, different kinds for different circumstances.

All we need to do is simply "be," with a strong sense of who we truly are at all times. We do not feel sorry for ourselves, or proud of our achievements, or angry with others for their political views, because there is no ego to protect or defend. We are at one with ourselves. There is then a sense of inner peace, even if things do not go our way on the personal or societal level.

Here again, it is the enthusiasm for connection with our deep inner state that propels us forward and helps generate a positive vibrational frequency. It becomes a way of living that offers comfort and depth, especially in those moments when disaster strikes, such as in the form of a life-threatening illness or a near-fatal injury that leaves us incapacitated. In these situations, we use the threat or tragedy to intensify our connection with the One Consciousness.

This way, we ensure that the situation does not become who we are. When we realize that our One Consciousness can never be threatened, this assurance enables us to accept "what is" even in the most trying times.

Recently, a dear friend undergoing cancer surgery wrote this to me: "I am too busy living in each present moment to be anxious about the future." Her statement came from her strong spiritual foundation, a place where her ego is dissolved. Here, there is no place for blame, guilt, fear, or failure, which are all forms of negativity and resistance to illness and pain. There is no place to establish victim identity so that she feels sorry for herself. Rather, her Presence and acceptance of the challenging situation allow the peace and serenity of her essence to shine through. They allow the realization that in the depth of her being, there is the sacred, which we call God. Awareness of her sacred self made it easier (over a period of time) to move into acceptance, which, in turn, opened her to the reality of "what is." In this state of inner peace and clear-mindedness, she knew whether or not to take action, and if to take action, what the best course would be. Her acceptance didn't mean ignoring what had happened, but it did bring a healing power through an act of God's grace.

How Does Witnessing Lead to Awareness?

How do we explain the subjective experiences—such as a sense of unity, eternity, or ego dissolution—that we get from witnessing facilitated by the Links of Grace? The most straightforward explanation is the "eclipse analogy." We know that the stars are in the sky at noon because we can see them directly when the moon eclipses the sunlight out of our field of view. The noonday stars are always there, but they are "shouted down" by the intensity of the sun's light. Notice that the sun doesn't dissolve during an eclipse. It is obscured.

Likewise, we have two sources coupling information into our spiritual experience. We have a torrent of physical sensory data coming in from the material world. The brain translates the sensory data into the language of the body. Because this information is indispensable to the development of a coherent experience so that we can survive in this earthly world, the brain's activities shout down other information that is also present—divine Awareness residing in the One Consciousness. It, like the stars in the noonday sky, cannot be perceived unless the information coming from the brain is obscured. When this happens, we experience the sense of oneness directly— like opening a valve that admits trickles of Awareness to help us gain a sense of who we truly are, the One Consciousness.

Materialist scientists assume that spiritual experiences are the product of the brain (that is, purely biological) and therefore can be explained by the chemistry of the brain (serotonin) and by the region in the brain where the chemical is found (the posterior cingulate cortex). Another explanation given on behalf of those who practice Buddhism is that when we diminish the activities of the thinking mind, we are quieting the ego. When we quiet the ego, we don't get caught up in our attachments to the physical world. Achieving detachment from our thoughts, feelings, and desires, we reduce misery. So far, so good. But materialist scientists, again, want us to believe that these attachments have their mooring in some brain cortex, where they are nurtured and sustained.[66]

Based on such assumptions, they study and analyze the chemical properties and structure of the brain when presented with activating events, like psychedelics, to explain the subjective spiritual experience. This could be seen as "confirmation bias." That is, from the gratuitous hypothesis that our spirituality is manufactured by the brain, it is straightforward to construct experiments that seem to "activate" spiritual experiences—a solipsism problem where people can only speculate about what goes on within the prison of their own minds. If they succeeded in discovering a correlation between brain structures and spiritual experiences, it wouldn't imply causality. And even if it did, multiple highly correlated phenomena are often found to be coincident entailed effects of an as yet unidentified common cause.

Taheri offers a few intriguing clues to this unidentified common cause. The sense of oneness, eternity, and dissolution of the ego that is afforded to those who've had mystical experiences is due to the mediation of our Sacred Cognitive Dimension (كالبد ذهن), which reveals itself when the filters we impose on it through the brain are removed. As described in chapter 11, the Sacred Cognitive Dimension is separate from, but in charge of, the brain. It arose when our soul was first spun off as a "divine spark" from the One Consciousness. It preserves its integrity through all of our lives in various worlds, managing our cellular-level consciousness, archiving our takeaway lessons, and acquiring wisdom. When we turn off our thinking mind completely and become fully present to the inner realm, the Sacred Cognitive Dimension—through a process that originates from the One Consciousness and then becomes infused with the Divine Intelligence—uses the brain as a conduit or a channel to unload divine Awareness. Our brain cells do have inherent intelligence that is the same for all human beings, but to actualize their potentiality, the cells need to become part of a larger consciousness—in the same way that a computer hardware (brain) has potentiality to provide information, but cannot actualize that potentiality without a software (Sacred Cognitive Dimension).[67]

PART THREE

Enlightenment

9

My Path to Enlightenment

The one who seeds desire and dreams of the green path of Your residence,
Won't step out of this circle as long as he is alive.

~Hafez

THE PURPOSE OF our creation is to reach Enlightenment, God's residence, located at the end of what the poet Hafez calls "the green path." Hafez indicates that even though God resides in the realm of Enlightenment, He is not bound by space and time and therefore can also be with you while you're on the path (i.e., in the circle of becoming). Our duty is to remove the veils within us that prevent the divine spark from shining.

The spiritual perfection, or peak of Awareness, that awaits represents the accumulated knowledge and Awareness from our current life and our previous lives. To reach it, we must rely on the navigational guidance of the soul's compass. In what follows, I'll explain the concept of "Enlightenment" in terms of the following:

o   Experiencing oneness with the universe,
o   Seeing God's presence everywhere,
o   Perceiving life's purpose, and
o   Knowing who I am.

Whenever possible, I will illustrate these ideas with my personal stories.

Experiencing Oneness with the Universe

ONCE I UNDERSTOOD THAT the One Consciousness expresses itself through me, all people, and all life forms in the universe, I suddenly realized that I am you, and you, and you. In other words, we are all one being, disguised by our physical form—which includes gender, age, nationality, and skin color—located in a certain place, time, culture, and family that affect one's personal history and worldview. Once I sensed my oneness with the One Consciousness, all these external factors suddenly receded into the background.

When I worked in Hawaii as an educational researcher in the 1980s, I occasionally swam to Flat Island from Kailua Beach in Oahu. I have vivid recollection of finding myself in every colorful fish (including parrot fish, butterfly fish, and angel fish) that came and went alongside me as I swam toward the shore in the warm waters. I almost experienced the fish within myself, and the ocean perhaps experienced me. There, I was utterly one with the world, so much a part of it that at times I forgot who I was. We were all fishes swimming the ocean together. At the time I didn't have any conceptual or theoretical understanding of oneness, yet I recognized that identity experientially. There had to be some consciousness that inspired this sense of oneness. This reminds me now of Carl Jung's description of the One Consciousness (which he called "Collective Unconscious" in his autobiography)—"At times I feel as if I am spread over the landscape and inside things, and I am myself living in every tree, in the splashing of the waves, in the clouds and the animals that come and go, in the procession of the seasons."

This sense of oneness has, especially since my more formal spiritual awakening, invited me to treat everyone with greater love and respect, to seek the goodness in all people, and to listen to them with particular attention to the essence underneath their words. I hope that you, my readers, will sense the One Consciousness yourselves as you read this book. The key here is to not let our divine Awareness be filtered through our logical mind and be censured by thoughts such as, "No, there can't be such a thing as oneness. Look at our bodies, cognition, and emotions. We are all different." Thoughts like these come when we are unaware that our physical bodies are like separate applications (Word, Excel, and PowerPoint) within a single computer software, the One Consciousness. While our bodies are indeed separate, the One Consciousness is fundamentally connected. Once we drop the notion that our consciousness is confined to our biological body, it becomes possible to perceive our essence as united at the deepest levels.

Since perceiving the One Consciousness, I have developed a greater appreciation of not only my fellow humans but also all living things. In my winter home, I am surrounded by nature. I sense the sacredness of it, which is an expression of the One Consciousness. While my front yard has been neatly landscaped, the woods behind my house have grown organically and not been touched by human beings. Whereas I used to see disorder there, I now sense hidden order, harmony, and sacredness. All the sentient life forms I see in my backyard rely on the trees—their trunks, branches, berries, flowers, and fruits, and/or the shade and shelter they provide. The oxygen they produce in exchange for carbon dioxide provides animals (and me) with most of the oxygen we need to breathe. Even their dead branches and leaves provide vital nutrients to the soil when they fall and decompose.

Yet the trees continue to lead their quiet life, indifferent and unattached to the uses they are put to. This order ultimately relies on a cosmic order, whereby the earth spins on its axis, creating the right amount of dark and sunlight to nourish the trees through photosynthesis. These orderly patterns in nature leave the reflective mind with a wondering sense of the Divine Intelligence that has patterned the universe. It is impossible not to witness God everywhere.

As soon as I sense the sacredness of the woods—that is, their quiet yet concealed vitality—I feel a deeper connectedness with my own concealed vitality, my One Consciousness. When I am connected to the One Consciousness, I too am quiet—that is, fully present. If a thought comes to my mind, I'm more likely to witness it and realize that I am not that thought but rather the one who is aware of it.

Relaxed and attentive, I give my complete attention to the trees, to their every detail, and sense how still yet alive and surrendered to life they are. I feel the liveliness of songbirds, geese in the pond, squirrels reaching for red berries, and occasionally a rabbit or two nibbling grass. Nature is teaching me to be one with all forms of life. I find it amazing how life grows out of nowhere. I listen to any sounds that may be present without judgment: birds singing, rain pattering, and wind blowing, as well as human-made sounds like the whistle of a faraway train, an occasional ambulance siren, or even the roar of the neighbors' leaf blowers. I pay particular attention to the *ending* of each sound I hear, where I sense a moment of stillness. An analogy from my ballroom dancing days is the full extension of legs, arms, and fingertips to express the character of the dance. Observing these end points creates a moment of quietude in the same way that listening to the ending of a piece of music played on the saxophone or the conclusion of an outbreath creates a sense of peacefulness.

I've also developed more appreciation for the inanimate objects around me, such as my beautiful turquoise-blue vase and the small mahogany table it rests on. While these objects don't share in the One Consciousness with humans, they exist in consciousness, possessing their own spiritual essence. The power to make the table and the vase never originated in the creators of these objects; rather, it emanated from God. We have to conclude that there can be no table or vase *without* God. I'm also reminded that these inanimate objects, like me, contain molecules composed of atoms that are, in turn, composed of protons, neutrons, and electrons that are constantly on the move. In short, every inanimate object in the universe is a manifestation of God. As such, each has a spiritual essence to which I am related.

Having experienced connection with the One Consciousness, I now feel a stronger tie to the larger universe. I know that the cosmos is not chaotic. In fact, in the Greek language, the word *kosmos* means order, harmony, and the sum total of everything. The ancient Greeks thought that the world was perfectly harmonious and impeccably ordered. We cannot see or perceive that order with our minds, although we can sometimes glimpse it. An understanding of the cosmos as a qualitative phenomenon unfolding in consciousness is an insight into myself. It's easy to see that all matter arises in consciousness—the very essence of who I am—which I access through my inner experiences.

Our planet, Earth, to which I now feel intimately connected, is part of a solar system[68] that includes everything else bound to it by gravity—the sun and the other known planets, some with their own moons. Our solar system, in turn, is part of the Milky Way galaxy, containing millions of stars dancing across the sky that I love to gaze at on summer nights when I'm in Maine. Our Milky Way is one of billions of galaxies in the universe. Our universe may even be part of multiple universes. The vastness is so great that light from some stars[69] takes thousands of years to reach Earth, compared to the light from the sun, which takes only eight minutes to reach us.

So, you and I are an intrinsic part of this vast web called *universe*. In a sense, our inner space is the doorway to outer space, or, more appropriately, to God, from Whom all manifestations flow. The doctrine that God has created the world has a practical corollary—the sacredness of nature and the immorality of human efforts to oppress her in service to our needs, rather than working as her collaborator. If every human being were in a proper relationship with natural environments, the innocent wouldn't suffer.

This Awareness of oneness with the universe propels me to treat not only all living things but also our climate and our environment with tender respect. When I am a good "neighbor" to the world because I sense the oneness, my body takes on a positive vibrational field of good will; as a result, adversarial stances dissipate. Conversely, when I carelessly burn too much fossil fuel, such as oil and gas, they release carbon dioxide into the air, causing the planet to heat up. At that point, I am within the field of ill will. That's because global warming, among other things, causes rising sea levels. Rising sea levels threaten human and animal communities. They threaten people's livelihoods, which could push them into poverty, thereby increasing income inequality within and between countries.

I view climate change as an expression of a deeper condition, a manifestation of a spiritual crisis. I use the term *spiritual crisis* to encompass the feelings of those who believe that the more control we can exercise over the ambiguously organizing universe with our intelligence, the better the world will be; that we have been given only limited stewardship of the universe by God; that government solutions that protect the environment are not good; or that we have a political "group identity." These belief systems push to the margins anything that is not easily measurable or that doesn't fit into our quantitative models. They leave out the core theme of this book: that the universe is a whole living thing and that we should allow its mystery to touch us. They suggest that mankind is separate from both the universe and its Creator. They go against the central idea of loving every living thing on the planet, especially one another.

If we look at Earth as an inanimate object or an arbitrary, purposeless life rather than one whole living planet containing "organs" and "tissues," then maybe there isn't much to love about the climate. Those who see nature and the environment as something separate from themselves value our precious natural resources only to the extent that they can use them for their own purposes. Destroying habitats, polluting waterways and air, and extracting resources irresponsibly is but a reflection of feeling separate from the universe. Indeed, this is the basis for the ego's sense of identity. No amount of governmental regulation, scientific persuasion, or advice from environmentalists is likely to change this view, because it is driven by egoic greed.

Only by understanding our connection with all things can we break down the adversarial stances that we tend to take toward the environment. Ecological crisis is asking for a revolution of love to heal the soil, water, air, life, and beauty, one that sees species as sacred not only in theory but also in action. Any damage to the integrity of the planet inevitably damages human beings as well, whether or not that damage is visible. The people hardest hit by climate change, including those in the developing world, often are least responsible for causing it and have the fewest resources to handle its impacts. An Awareness of our oneness with the universe includes a genuine expression of "love the stranger," or expanding our circle of caring to include all people.

Society has evolved considerably in its understanding of scientific principles, but we remain infants as regards our perception of collective consciousness. We are vulnerable and even at risk of extinction on Earth. It seems to me that our best option is to practice connecting with our collective consciousness by quieting our egoic thoughts and making them subservient to our sacred selves, through whom we receive Awareness and the power of oneness.

I regularly solicit the facilitative powers of the Links of Grace to help me contribute to the cosmic consciousness, which is intended to curb the negative collective fields and create a sense of togetherness with the universe. This link is especially needed now to remind us of our connectivity and collective vulnerability. In the case of the COVID-19 pandemic, one cell within one body went awry; as a result, many in the world's population of nearly eight billion suffered greatly. Yet each positive pulse that emanates from a positive thought can influence the entire universe, because the Divine Intelligence is unconstrained by time and space. Recognizing that there is a Divine Intelligence governing the universe, everyone's cooperation is required to bring unity to the universe. We are one united body connected in a complex web. As such, our survival as a species depends on having each other's backs and collectively illuminating consciousness.

Connecting with the One Consciousness

Be a lamp.
Or a lifeboat.
Or a ladder.
Heal someone's soul.
Walk out of your house like a Shepherd.

~Rumi

Seeing God's Presence Everywhere

SINCE I HAVE BECOME aware of my oneness with the universe and practiced connecting with the One Consciousness, it is easier to fully attend to the beauty around me. I'm becoming more intensely conscious of all life forms and the majesty of nature, especially when I am in Maine in the summer months. I try to sense and appreciate the essence of the pine trees, birds, and flowers, rather than figure out what particular species I am seeing. Since I began my spiritual practice, my love for my fellow human beings, my inner peace, and my joy in living—things that truly matter but can't be achieved by focused thought alone—have increased.

I am more alert to, and appreciative of, everything in my life, including the simple act of breathing, the sound and smell of the ocean, and even the little black mink that appears on my deck in the morning while I'm having my breakfast in Maine. I am more attuned to the ten-foot tides that rise every six hours, the full moon that appears at daybreak sometimes, and the million-year-old rocks around my cottage. I notice the life force in my tiny herb garden, the delicate wildflower blooms, and the ocean sparkling in the sun.

I'm more aware of man-made objects too, whether beautiful or mundane: a painting of a single rock by the fireplace, a crystal vase that glitters in bright light, my electric toothbrush and iPhone. Like me, all these objects have matter, energy, and intelligence of a different sort. But more than that, they, like me, are manifestations of one God. I see these manifestations not only with my eyes but, more importantly, with the eyes of my inner being. I see God's presence in everything, and as a result, I view everything with greater respect.

I also see birth to this world as a divine grace that God gave to humanity. Unlike other living beings, we are given extraordinary perception, Awareness, judgment to ask questions (*Who am I? What are my origin, destination, and life purpose?*), and the free will to act accordingly. The more we perceive ourselves as being deeply connected with everyone and everything else, the closer we get to God and Enlightenment.

I call on the Links of Grace to help me perceive that this tree, this body of water, this bird, are all manifestations of one God. When I perceive the earth's holiness and our oneness, I don't want to harm any of God's manifestations—not a honeybee, a wild rose, a leaf on a tree, or even a little spider in the corner of my office—because I revere these things, and harming them would create negative pulses in the universe. I have an obligation to care for these things because they are precious gifts entrusted to me by God. The Links give me the capacity to perceive and begin to feel the grandeur, splendor, and wondrous world around me.

Moving toward inner being, we see our place in the universe, our relationship to nature, and our relationships to each other differently. The Divine Intelligence runs through all living and even nonliving things. We are all connected in a vast and complex web, as the diagram on the cover of this book illustrates. To put this vastness in perspective, far less than a single percent of the cosmos lies within the view of our most advanced telescopes.

The more I appreciate God's presence everywhere, in the sacred quality of nature and in all the other good things around me, the more opportunities I create for being in the present moment. Appreciation requires attentiveness in the absence of distracting thoughts—a state of being by which I measure my success in practicing Taheri's teachings. When I am more in the moment, I am also more attuned to the everyday activities I perform unconsciously—for example, using my muscles to keep my posture aligned, walk upstairs, and type these words on my computer. I use these opportunities to disengage myself from darting, random thoughts, including memories that trap me in my past history or egoic thoughts that give me a false sense of identity.

Perceiving Life's Purpose

OUR WORLD IS IN turmoil, and we are each paying the price for the other's actions. Often those actions are unexamined, driven by cultural and religious beliefs, and based on faulty assumptions rather than eternal truths or an understanding of our purpose on Earth and the interconnectedness of each person's actions. For example, some may think it's "smart" or "strong" or "right" to take advantage of everything and everyone, accumulate wealth and power, and thereby live a "happy" or "successful" life. All this is in the realm of the ego. To truly take care of ourselves and one another, we need to raise Awareness about our higher purpose for being on this planet.

The dominant tenet of Taheri's philosophy is this: We are here to walk the path toward Enlightenment. We are given the free will to either give in to the temptations of egoic thought or gain Awareness that is transferable to the next life. Giving in to our egoic thoughts, which invariably results in fear and anger, does not prepare us for stormy times in this life or in other lives to come. As Taheri says, being in this small boat only ensures that we will succumb to violent seas and get tossed overboard, yet gaining Awareness is like being on the big, stable ocean liner, where the dreadful ocean waves are navigable. The purpose of life, then, is to gain wisdom from the fact that each life is a sequence of events in which we have to make choices, then experience the consequences of those choices.

Knowing Who I Am

In other living creatures, ignorance of self is nature;
in man it is vice.
~Boethius

"VICE" IN THE ABOVE quotation may be defined as behavior sanctioned by the will that has bad results. It is bad because it is harmful to others. Without self-knowledge, there can be no diminishment of the ego, therefore no divine Awareness, therefore no sense of oneness—therefore, no compassion for others. Spiritual progress comes through growing knowledge of the self. I don't mean it in the purely theoretical sense—to be effective, such knowledge must be realized as an immediate experience. Ego (which creates fear, worry, anxiety, and more) cannot be easily gotten rid of by personal effort, but through connection with the divine, the One Consciousness, it can be done.

Connection with the One Consciousness has led to a flow of Awareness in my daily living, including a more mature Awareness of who I am. I am not the identity created by my ego. Rather, I've come to experience my real self as part of one endless thread woven into the tapestry of the universe. In this unbounded web, compassion, gratitude, and creativity are natural. They flow within me and from me without effort. I've become more alive and real, emerging through superficial coverings and radiating positive vibrations into the world. I am in a constant state of gratefulness, appreciating everything, accepting everything in my life as a divine blessing. I am at peace with the universe through my connection with the One Consciousness, made possible by God's Links of Grace. The way I've experienced various changes, insights, and transformations within myself is beautifully expressed by the Persian poet Sepehri:

> *I turn into the direction of a red rose when I pray,*
> *I stand in a spring while I perform my prayers,*
> *I bow and put down my forehead on the light,*
> *My prayer carpet is the grassland.*

> ~Sepehri

With a deeper sense of "who I am," I've become more grounded in my secular self as well. With pure joy and excitement, I bring my full attention and Presence to my intellectual pursuits without an agenda for praise, fame, or monetary reward. In this sense, my secular part and sacred part are not separate but intertwined. Both are driven by enthusiasm, unobstructed by the ego, guided by the Divine Intelligence, and thus capable of lifting up humanity.

Because I feel anchored to my true self and am beginning to know who I really am, it is easier to approach everything I do from this state of being. The more I enter this life within, the less likely I am to be drawn into commentary from "experts" in mainstream and social media who are fueling separation and polarity rather than seeking solutions. There is less risk of my engaging in toxic conversations about politics, existing in noisy settings, acquiring possessions, or surrounding myself with people who gossip or self-aggrandize to get attention and feel important.

Instead, I experience exceeding delight in walking in nature;

relating to friends from a deeper place; being a custodian of the planet; contributing financially to people in need through various organizations; and sitting in stillness before dinner and calling on specific Links of Grace to extend a prayer[70] of good will, including the following, to which I am particularly drawn. I refer to this prayer as my personal "Ten Commandments." It begins with gratitude, moves through the requirements for connecting with the One Consciousness, then finishes with my being healed so that I can "give back" to others by being a conduit for healing and unity.

My self-discovery hasn't ended. I continue to find it in myself to fully forgive wrongdoings by my family and those who are blinded by their ego. I am able to send a bouquet of flowers, make a phone call, or send a text message, regardless of whether or not I want to restore a relationship—simply to promote well-being. These days, stickers and emojis attached to text messages that have "sorry" written all over them make it easier than words to express desire for forgiveness. Nonforgiveness is a form of revenge by the ego to foster separation, and, like all other forms of ego, it sends negative vibrations. From Taheri's spiritual perspective, while nonforgiveness isn't a crime, sending negative vibrations into the world does constitute a crime because it derails us from walking the path to Enlightenment.

There was never a time in which humans were flawless. Enlightenment proceeds by gradually making the flawed into the flawless. That's when we finally see through the veil of "illusion" of separation from God and recognize that, in our essence, we are all one. And since we are all one, there is no "other" to blame. As Rumi said, when we see things as coming to us from outside ourselves, we perceive ourselves as victims, which incites us to blame someone else or something else for our experiences.

Prayer of Good Will

~

May I . . .

Be grateful for this food and the cells that sustain my life.

Neutralize any negativity I encounter.

Detach from egoic thoughts that separate me from others.

Quiet my mind to experience oneness and to manifest.

Awaken to my true self and the shared essence of all living things.

Perceive the vastness of the universe so that I may glimpse God.

Receive Awareness about my life's purpose, Enlightenment.

Be healed, and sleep well tonight.

Be a facilitator for others' physical and mental healing.

Be a force for unity among all of humanity.

Yesterday I was clever, so I wanted to change the world.
Today I am wise, so I am changing myself.

~Rumi

Goodwill and service are never imposed upon us when we "know who we are." They come from a natural capacity to love ourselves and to extend love to all living beings. The more we know about who we are, the One Consciousness, the more effortless and automatic our ethical and value decisions become, rather than responding to "oughtness." As we extend love to others and all life forms, we have a heightened sense of well-being. More than that, it opens the way for our love to flow into the universe.

10

Controlling Thoughts and Exploiting the Links of Grace

Those whom you see gloomy and sad are in love with "self" affairs.
Let's not remark affairs of "self" but see affairs of "ours."

~Rumi

I N OUR JOURNEY toward Enlightenment, perceiving oneness, God's presence everywhere, and who we truly are (discussed in chapter 9) necessitates that our egoic tendencies gradually dissolve. This is a key requirement that makes our journey to Enlightenment (راه وحدت) possible. Egoic tendencies trap us in thoughts and behaviors that separate us from each other (راه کثرت), such as the needs to be recognized, control others, and accumulate wealth. Ultimately, this path leads to a dead end, causing us to wander and creating confusion and unrest.

We can only control the ego; we will never eliminate it. With the bond to our One Consciousness comes the joy of connectedness with all of God's creations. This state of being, I believe, is needed now more than ever—not for just a few moments here and there, but as a core practice and perspective.

Controlling Thoughts

IN WHAT FOLLOWS, I'LL describe four forms of thought that get in my way as I seek Enlightenment, and the Links of Grace that I call upon to quell these thoughts and neutralize their associated negative charges around me. I hang on to these steady Links like the trunk of a tree in a windstorm. In my experience, some of their benefits occur instantaneously, some over a few days' time, and some, especially those that support unity with the universe, over a longer period of time.

During my spiritual practice, I use the Links of Grace that Maryam, my instructor and connector, has granted me. Each of the Links is accompanied by a protective layer (لايه محافظ), which is experienced uniquely by each individual.[71] The protective layer, which, like its associated Link of Grace, is embedded in universal fields of consciousness, shields both me (the spiritual seeker) and Maryam (the connector) against the potential interference of negative vibrations and other inhibitors coming from individuals, groups, or the society at large.[72]

For this reason, readers of this book are advised not to attempt to use the Links of Grace unless they have received them from Taheri or one of his certified instructors. However, they can safely use the Shared Link of Grace, the connector of which is Taheri himself. It incorporates many of the Links I like to use.

Controlling Random Thoughts

Like most people, I cannot fully prevent random thoughts. Mine, which are often entangled in thoughts about what I was working on yesterday or might do tomorrow, cycle in my head, especially when I'm trying to sleep. With no immediate professional or personal activities to occupy the mind, it is free to wander: "I need to fall asleep, but I'm fully awake." "Tomorrow is a big day and I need to be rested." "Oh, I forgot to add thus-and-so to the introduction of the book." "I wonder what happened to my red blouse?" The idle voice in my head never quiets down, one thought leading to another. No wonder I can't sleep. Even if I don't give my mind something to occupy itself, it goes off and finds entertainment.

To a lesser degree, I also get immersed in these chaotic and futile thoughts during the day. This makes me absent to the present moment. As long as I am in this state, my attention and even my short-term memory sink, and Presence is lost. When Presence is lost, I can neither connect with my inner essence nor actualize effectively. This is because, just like zero thinking, focused thinking on a task requires being present, and being present means being alert and poised to receive divine insights, either those related to the state of oneness or those related to solving scientific and other types of problems.

Taking energy away from random thoughts means that my now-alert energy can be sensed by the people around me on an unconscious level. I can now relate to them on a deeper level. It also means that I'm more observant of my surroundings, which can help prevent bad things from happening. Once, lost in random thoughts on my way to my office in Washington, DC, I drove through a stop sign. Not only did I not see the sign, I did not see the police car that was next to me. After the officer stopped me, he said, "Didn't you see me in plain view?"

I said, "No." Then I added, "I don't even recall not stopping at the stop sign." Somehow, the policeman seemed to understand that I had been trapped in thoughts and oblivious to the sign. My random thoughts had taken me completely out of the present. The officer lectured me about paying more attention when driving and then let me go. I was lucky I did not get a ticket!

The extent to which we become absentminded is a function of the degree to which the mind has become immersed in random thoughts about the past or the future. These conversations that we're having in our head while driving cannot be forbidden by legislation in the way that phone conversations or text messaging while driving are, yet the consequences are similar when attention is elsewhere.

The mind has its momentum, like a raging river, which is hard to stop once started. Exerting willpower is futile, as is making a decision to not think. Raging thoughts create a feeling of distance between us and the One Consciousness. It is difficult to step into the zone of zero thought and achieve presence without divine help.

By asking for help from Links of Grace that serve to quiet the mind, I am more able to manage this silent chatter. I often pause during the day and ask myself: "Right now, where is your mind?" This practice serves as an internal alarm. I consciously witness my random thoughts without judgment and allow them to be, because I know I can't stop them by suppressing them. The practice is not to concoct stories or to stop the thoughts, because they will arise. The practice is to observe them (that is, to use the mind to observe the mind) and to surrender control of them.

Witnessing and accepting random thoughts, in turn, creates gaps in thoughts, allowing the Links of Grace to do their job. I'm hopeful that this meta-awareness will help the gaps in thought grow in frequency, as I become more and more a watcher of my random thoughts in various circumstances. Anytime I hear a random voice in my head, it is usually a waste of energy, and I know it is not the real me talking. That me is always silent. That is the one who watches the voice and waits at the doorway to connect with the depth of my being, the one who knows the One Consciousness.

If I am witnessing my random thoughts but still trapped in them because of some discouraging or exciting event in my life, I sometimes "cheat." I begin to approach Presence by first focusing on my breathing, or the tingling in my fingertips as I bring my palms closer together in slow motion, or on other sense perceptions—looking at the formation of the clouds in the sky, listening to the foghorn or a bell buoy, smelling a beach rose, or simply enjoying the sound of silence. When we are not lost in wandering thought, we hear sounds with amazing clarity and ease.

This nonjudgmental self-observation takes my attention away from my thinking about the past, the future, or the problems the world is facing. But it still requires directing my attention to something, which is not full witnessing. The moment my attention is directed to my breathing, I experience it meta-consciously; that is, I'm aware that I am breathing, rather than being unaware of this autonomous biological function. That is why I call it cheating. Taheri cautions that relying on this in the long term could confine us, rather than free us from ourselves to seek oneness with help from the Links of Grace. That's because in its primordial configuration, the One Consciousness is clearly not meta-conscious. It unfolds the way it does as a result of what we do. To connect with it, we must set aside all self-reflections, because they eclipse our immediate, direct experience with the One Consciousness.

Soon after self-observation, I try to become aware of the single fact that I'm here as the One Consciousness, my *essence identity*. When I realize that there is more to me than my *form identity* (name, email address, gender, profession, relationships, possessions, accomplishments, mental concepts, and history), suddenly a glimpse of Awareness that is inseparable from who I truly am opens up. That relaxed Awareness is beyond the conceptual or sense perceptions, although I can almost feel a rise in its vibrational frequency. It is deeper than me, a person with some personal history, which is rarely enough. As I become more aware of myself as the collective consciousness, the need to understand my life history, which is filled with conceptual and egoic thoughts, diminishes.

Once I have a glimpse of myself as the One Consciousness, I try to reconnect with that Awareness while I'm engaged in my daily activities and interactions with people. This *spiritual awakening* has become the foundation for everything I do. It helps to free me from the ego, which is just about everything I tend to identify with, including my worldview. There is an enormous liberation that comes with the sense that I can operate in this physical world I inhabit in a way that is more beneficial to humanity and to myself, especially when faced with life challenges. The key is the perception that I'm not simply a human being with thoughts, regardless of how creative or contributive they may be. Against this background of Awareness happening in the field of consciousness, I may get a little closer to the enlightened state, which is the destiny of each human being, albeit not in this lifetime.

Controlling Egoic Thoughts

Egoic thoughts, as I've described earlier, are key Inhibitors that keep us from experiencing Presence and thereby from experiencing oneness and receiving Awareness. Awareness and ego do not coexist easily. The purpose of our life is to be challenged by our egoic tendencies, which were a part of humanity long before you and I arrived. They will likely be with us until we are, at some point, awakened through Presence on our journey to Enlightenment.

Connecting with the One Consciousness

THE EGO MANIFESTS IN many different forms. Among them are stereotyping, arrogance, feelings of superiority, judgment, assumption, self-centeredness, and jealousy. Other behaviors that suggest the ego is in charge are name-dropping; withholding due credit; feeling pleased when we exaggerate or attract attention to our achievements and possessions; saying how fortunate or unfortunate our lives have been; living through the accomplishments of our children or spouses; feeling impatient with time because we are often ahead of it; feeling guilty or like a failure; and creating stories and interpreting them as good or bad—all of which are egoic thoughts, limited personal narratives about ourselves that we create and then falsely identify with. As Shakespeare's Hamlet said, "There is nothing either good or bad, but thinking makes it so."

Let's talk about one of these forms manifested by the ego—judgment. I don't mean the type we make when selecting between two courses of action. I mean the judgments we make about others. We judge others and every daily situation we encounter, including our spiritual practice, without seeing the whole person or the situation; that is, we judge without a basis. Nothing seems to escape our judgment. We judge or make assumptions (a disguised form of judgment) because we can't live with uncertainty. There is no room for judgment in connecting with the One Consciousness during spiritual practice, because judgment necessarily comes from the belief that we are separate beings. That belief runs counter to what we're trying to do, which is to sense our oneness and to tap into the treasure box of Awareness to access the wisdom of God and His attributes.

Although we cannot fully counter our ego and associated emotions, we can help clear the way for consciousness to prevail. My husband once took me to a fine French restaurant. After dinner, we ordered a dessert, Grand Marnier Soufflé, to be shared. While

I was relaying a story, he started eating. When I finished my story, I found he had eaten all the dessert and left me with none. I called him selfish and uncaring. I now realize that what I said was a judgment. What I'd probably say today is something like, "You've eaten all the dessert and left me with nothing," which is a bit freer of judgment, labeling, and negative emotions. I would then accept what had just occurred and ask him to give me a "rain check" for another Grand Marnier Soufflé in the near future.

Negative emotions such as fear, anger, guilt, anxiety, depression, aggression, and sadness—all Inhibitors to connecting with the One Consciousness—are signs that the ego is involved. The ego needs to win at all costs. In this regard, it may seem like an ally, yet it creates loss for the individual, in both body and mind. How common is it that we eat with presence, just enough to satisfy our hunger? It is the ego that demands indulgence beyond what is sufficient for energy. We can allow ourselves to enjoy the pleasure of something we love (dark chocolate, in my case), so long as we know when to stop and don't feed a craving. This we may do by witnessing the urge to indulge (i.e., the ego). The freeing insight here is to just sit and observe the desire. Soon we'll see that it goes all by itself. Like everything else, it passes. There is nothing more we have to do to make the desire go away.

The ego is never the spiritual winner, and acting with it can even make us physically sick. Worse, the ego, when amplified through mainstream and social media, creates group identity without Awareness of the One Consciousness. This kind of identity, especially political ideology, can take possession of the minds of a large group and result in destructive collective thought, like a mental virus. Group identity can be marked by anti-intellectualism, or the willingness to ignore facts that challenge the group's narrative. This further propels the "us versus them" belief, or worse, "us versus the enemy" rhetoric. Inflammatory rhetoric and quickly drawn conclusions played to an impatient crowd, many of which are not based in truth or motivated by a desire for the common good, are used repeatedly by social and mainstream media as well as many political leaders. Such rhetoric incites further division in a country already "on edge."

Imagine the negative vibrations emanating from the egoic thoughts of millions of people who regard as "enemy" or "evil" millions of others who don't share their ideologies. Conversely, imagine the positive influence in what humanity could experience if only 1 percent of the nearly eight billion people in our world—meaning eighty million worldwide—realized their sacred oneness underneath their surface ideologies. If we can feel our own essence, we can also feel it naturally in others. This connection can motivate us to choose positive actions to benefit others. I'm reminded of Mother Teresa's response when someone asked her why she didn't participate in anti-war demonstrations: "I will never do that, but as soon as you have a pro-peace rally, I'll be there."

As noted earlier, egoic tendencies can never be completely eliminated. Humans constantly judge and label others without thinking, based on personal characteristics such as their dialect, gender, sexual orientation, socioeconomic status, geographic location (rural versus urban), nationality, ethnicity, political affiliation, age, education, religion, profession, disability, clothing, weight, and skin color. Because egoic tendencies are in our original personality blueprint, we often unthinkingly practice stereotyping by classifying and comparing people. As soon as we meet a person, our assessment of who they are, based on external indicators, begins. Once those first impressions are made, it takes considerable work to change them. The one thing that cannot be assigned a category, however, is the One Consciousness, which removes these layers of judgment as we grow in connectedness and Awareness. When we recognize another person's essence as our own without judgments, we manifest a flow of positivity that is recognized without even having to say a word—a beautiful process!

How do I control the problematic egoic thoughts? I have discovered that when I recognize that my irritation toward an undesirable event is caused by an egoic thought separate from my essence, and also recognize that it is the nature of the ego to create emotion with the false hope that it will dissolve the undesirable event, I can bring a new dimension into my interaction with others. I am learning to *watch* the part of me that is trying to defend, protect, or entertain itself and decide to let go of it. The ego cannot survive for long when we are witnessing it, because when we witness, we are bringing our essence in the present moment, not the past or the future, where the ego resides. Once I've made the commitment to free myself of that thought without fighting my mind, I stop feeling the tightening in my chest and start to feel my energy change. Once I'm free from the hold the negative vibration has on me, I can experience the collective consciousness that exists within me. If we all sense our connectedness by watching thoughts and events come and go without getting drawn into them, a new mindset will be created. This vibrational field will be capable of resolving the irritation, sadness, or anger within us and replacing them with inner peace. It is comforting to know that we can let go of difficult experiences by treating them as another element of the universe, like the moon, the ocean, and the sand.

For example, if a friend says or does something hurtful or demeaning, instead of attacking or withdrawing, I allow the negative vibrations of the hurt to pass by without wounding my inner self. I do this by inviting a relevant Link of Grace to connect me to the Divine Intelligence, which will help me dismiss my emotional egoic response, such as disappointment, rejection, anger, or sadness. If I do not seek help with my egoic response and instead confront, complain, or even back off, I become a victim, carrying a negative charge that has no place to go but through me.

At the same time, I also try to practice forgiveness and not to dwell on people's faults. I do this by recognizing

o   their true essence through my own;

o   their virtues;

o   the fact that the faults of others are easier to see than my own;

o   the fact that everyone will manifest occasional unconsciousness in their interactions with others;

o   the fact that I don't know the situational or cultural context that may have contributed to the behavior;

o   the fact that the person may have misperceived my meaning or motivation, and vice versa;

o   the fact that I have the opportunity to use a Link of Grace; and

o   that if I amplify their behavior, I would be making it part of their identity, precisely what the ego wants.

Only after I begin to feel compassion for that person can I begin true communication with him or her. I do this by telling the person what I felt as I witnessed or experienced their behavior, without labeling them as rude, cruel, or inconsiderate. If I do this, the behavior does not weigh on my mind and bad feelings do not accumulate. In short, by reconnecting with my deeper self, I can become centered and therefore less vulnerable. Negative emotions cannot survive when there is a deep bond between people. This bond is not about liking or disliking people, but rather about letting go of the like or dislike when they do arise so that the One Consciousness flows unimpeded.

The One Consciousness never gets angry, afraid, or bored. It is our egoic thoughts that become identified with these feelings and make us believe that we're feeling these emotions. The truth is that these are just passing emotional states, which separate us from all others who are not angry, afraid, or bored. The sense of separation is the ego. None of these emotions have intrinsic meaning other than that which we attribute to them. During the COVID-19 pandemic, those on the front lines, such as health care providers and other essential workers, experienced a wide range of emotions. Some who didn't work during the pandemic described their daily life as boring, while others (myself included) were engrossed in their focused thoughts and writings. As Marcus Aurelius, a Roman emperor-philosopher, once said, "Men are continually seeking retreats for themselves. Where can a man find a calmer, more restful haven than in his own soul?" There is a sense of expansion and freedom from our endless preoccupation with ourselves when we experience our true self as universal.

History tells us that highly knowledgeable spiritual individuals are particularly prone to falling into the same trap of the ego, seeing themselves as separate from others. Their downfall, according to Taheri, is much steeper than the downfall of a person who is naïve because they haven't been exposed to the concept of Enlightenment. This is why there is no room for admiration and praise, the fuel on which the ego feeds, in Taheri's teachings.

There are times when I am inclined to be firm with my egoic mind. I want to tell it in no uncertain way, "Don't pretend to be me." This happens especially when egoic thoughts creep into my mind like unruly weeds in a garden: *What do you need Enlightenment for? Do you really think the Links of Grace will do you any good? It is too hard to still your mind. You don't have time for that.* At these times, I remind myself of the nature of the egoic thoughts and stay vigilant as to the angle from which the thoughts are attacking: *You'll get hurt. You'll become bored. You deserve better.* The higher I go on the ladder toward Enlightenment, the cleverer the egoic mind becomes in its sabotage. It is like a guerrilla fighter, working from within.

Knowing the nature of the enemy—my egoic thoughts—I am more able to accept people as they are, instead of becoming irritated with them and reminding them of their undesirable personality traits or viewpoints. I know that their own egos would immediately deny them. By recognizing and accepting my own egoic tendencies, I try to create gaps between my real self (the One Consciousness) and my fictitious self (my egoic thoughts). I observe and witness the latter nonjudgmentally using a Link that serves to bring to the surface egoic tendencies. That Awareness gives me a choice and an opportunity to lower the ego's attractive, shimmering light, much the way the stars' lights are dimmed when the sun rises. Because our ego is very powerful, we must be vigilant in our efforts to bring meta-awareness to egoic thoughts. New ones come into our minds constantly. They resist dismissal with all their might, because if we let go of them, our false self dissolves and we transcend into the realm of consciousness, where our true selves reside.

I tell myself that if I am the one who is observing the egoic thought, then the thought cannot be me (حقیقت). Rather, it is something that happens to me (واقعیت). When I am in the zone of witnessing and zero thought, I get an instant snapshot of who I really am, the One Consciousness. This is the me that is purely aware of where I've always been. I watch my egoic thoughts and emotions come in through my senses, and with that meta-awareness, a great mystery begins. When I am aware that I am aware, I no longer become completely immersed in negative events that previously drew me in with worry and fear. I can even sit quietly, looking at negative media and the false information that it spreads, without leaving my center. If I need to re-center, which I do sometimes when I lose my witness seat, I solicit the facilitative function of the Links of Grace to reconnect with my inner self and the simple awareness of who I am and always was.

At first, dismantling my egoic thoughts felt like standing shakily in the world without anything to hold on to: no personal name, roles, titles, academic degrees, or career successes, not even my physical body, mind, or emotions. There was only my true self. Falling into what felt like nothingness was quite unsettling. I feared the emptiness and wondered who I was and what I was doing. My ego made me doubt myself until, in my own time, I dropped into a deeper realm, where guidance arose from a higher source. I noticed my boundaries dissolving into a vast web of interconnectedness. The feeling of emptiness gradually became peaceful. Now I dance with an aliveness unbound by earthly identity. I've become one with the rhythm, melody, and harmony of the universe.

The true value of a human being is determined primarily by the measure and the sense in which he has attained liberation from the self.

~Albert Einstein

Controlling Stereotypic Thoughts

As noted earlier, because it is composed of egoic thought, the tendency to stereotype people (based on their race, political affiliation, ethnicity, gender, socioeconomic status, education, nationality, or other personal characteristics) can never be completely eliminated.

However, it can be managed. Indeed, it is imperative that we control these thoughts—stereotyping is an overgeneralization that doesn't take individual differences into account ("Those people are the problem"), and it doesn't feel good to the stereotyped individual. Oversimplifying and disparaging large groups of people is itself a form of prejudice. In some individuals it may even lead to discrimination, feelings of superiority, and antagonism. Stereotyping also engages the egos of those we discriminate against; it is an underlying factor in today's political unrest and violence, in America and elsewhere.

Taheri tells us that by inviting Presence through the Link of Grace related to egoic thoughts, and by witnessing and observing our own thoughts and emotions without judging them, we can create *gaps* between ourselves and our stereotypic thoughts. We can thereby help to dissipate the anger that follows these thoughts. All we need to do is be aware of our thoughts as they occur, separating us from other people who are not like us. Separateness is the very quality of the ego. Some of the Links of Grace are intended to free us from seeing ourselves as separate from others. The term "others" here includes individuals who are both similar to and different from ourselves. We can keep our company with like-minded people without seeing ourselves as separate from those with different ways of thinking, thereby acknowledging the unity of the undivided One Consciousness.

How do I challenge feeling stereotyped? For example, say I am stereotyped by someone for my political views, and my principal response is irritation. Instead of making the perpetrator wrong by claiming my superiority, I accept and acknowledge my irritation and silently watch what happens inside me. Sustained attention to my thoughts helps bring about the process of transmutation, which lessens the irritation so it can no longer replenish itself. In addition to observing my annoyance, I tell myself that the rhetoric I've heard isn't necessarily representative of the other side, which is more varied than the stereotype. I also recognize that the life experiences, cultural forces, and environment that inform the political views of the other person are different from my own. Nearly all major newspapers, websites, radio stations, and television (from which I've taken a long break) are driven by ratings, which often lead to content that disproportionately amplifies negative news to keep the audience emotionally charged and, thereby, "addicted."

My anger having subsided, I can begin to sense the divine essence of the other person beneath their viewpoints. His or her essence is also my essence. We are of one essence, the One Consciousness.

If we cultivate some of these practices regularly, we may shorten the time in which our anger stemming from stereotyping dissipates, as well as lessen its frequency. As Taheri reminds us, if we try to fight our stereotypic thoughts, it creates inner conflict. The more we function from the deeper core of our being, the more we become empowered. This is because we are then in alignment with the purpose of the universe.

Controlling Victim Identity Thoughts

As a young child, I learned not to let my thinking be controlled by my family, my society, my religion, my poverty, or my gender (as I've described in chapters 2 and 3). Intuitively, I rejected seeing myself as a victim. Period. Had I not done that, I could not have taken responsibility for myself and worked hard for what I wanted. Even worse, I might have suffered from moral superiority—just what the destructive ego would use to distract me. Instead of acquiring a victim identity by blaming my family and my circumstances, I transmuted the pain and the suffering into education, then to contributions to my profession—all along feeling the power of God coming through me.

There is a difference between recognizing and accepting past wrongdoings by family, friends, and groups and taking on a victim identify. The former propels us forward to acknowledge abuse or dysfunction and make positive changes. This dynamic also holds true on the governmental and societal levels. We can recognize and accept the mistakes of leaders without feeling victimized. This allows us to work, for example, to address corporate greed, environmental degradation, economic inequality, and educational opportunities for children in high-poverty schools.

When we take on victim identity, on the other hand, we look for enemies. We may label them as homophobic, racist, sexist, Nazi, un-American, or socialist and therefore inferior. This creates moral superiority in the collective mind. Fueling this way of thinking are some mainstream and social media outlets, which engender hate and fierce anger for those with different viewpoints or perspectives. This hatred sometimes gets transmuted into physical action and violence. The insincere ego believes that by creating negative vibrations, it can strengthen its moral superiority. Thus, like a nonorganic virus, it spreads through, occupies, and possesses our minds. Fooled by our ego, we think it is the real us fighting for a good cause.

Once we have identified with the ego, we don't want to let it go. We may even prefer to stay angry, emotionally charged, and depressed, which, sadly, sabotages the positive vibrations in us— the One Consciousness. Yet, when we let go of victim identity, which manifests as moral superiority, compassion arises. In the context of this book, concepts of moral and racial superiority serve as Inhibitors to oneness, which results in separation from the One Consciousness.

When we think of ourselves as victims, we never heal, because we see things as happening to us. It is impossible to blame and feel empowered at the same time. When we blame others for past wrongdoings, we often use them as scapegoats so we can feel justified in not taking responsibility for our lives the way they are. We can correct that perception by reminding ourselves that our true self, the One Consciousness, cannot be a victim of anyone or any circumstance.

Identifying with the past keeps us imprisoned in egoic thoughts and the negative emotions that go with them. Beyond the consequences of toxic emotions (i.e., anger, fear, and grief) on the universe and our physical bodies, egoic thoughts work against connecting with our inner self. Failing to sense our oneness with those who think or look differently, or even behave in ways we would not, creates division, not empathy. This leads to degradation of society.

Correcting injustices is most effective when it arises from our sense of oneness. We are much better off as a society if we derive our sense of identity from the One Consciousness, rather than from the ego. Once we can each see ourselves as a single cell within one body, and once we recognize that our political or moral views are just that—viewpoints—we naturally want to be forgiving. We can recognize the other's flaws without personally judging them—no matter where they are on the consciousness continuum. We feel love and respect toward those we disagree with or even dislike, because they are part of us. With forgiveness in particular, we have the opportunity to dissolve victim identity and open the path for the power of the One Consciousness to emerge. Finding common goals ("freedom," for example) and working together to make positive changes toward those common goals is a good place to start.

We live in a world of gray, not black and white, as described in chapter 7 and its discussion of the Law of Relativity.

The mysterious thing is that when we bring oneness into the equation—without the polarities of good and bad and without antagonistic stances toward each other—the positive vibrational energies that the One Consciousness creates through the mediating function of the Divine Intelligence, though they are invisible, cause circumstances to improve on our behalf. It is suddenly no longer the same turbulent situation. Our primary responsibility in this life is personal growth and development, but that has the potential to affect others, because deep in our inner selves, we are all one. Any change in one person's consciousness is a change in another's consciousness. This ultimately results in bringing consciousness into the world.

Yet bringing oneness into the equation requires controlling egoic thoughts, as noted earlier. When we're aware that certain thoughts, such as perceiving ourselves as victims, are being created by our ego, we increase our capacity to converse with individuals with whom we disagree without getting resentful, angry, or physically violent, and without using demeaning labels such as "racist." We can accept viewpoints, compromise on them, or reject them. We can choose to take positive actions, such as participating in peaceful demonstrations, writing letters to our representatives in Congress, or writing a spiritual book to encourage others to seek guidance from their inner selves, as I am now doing. But we must do these things without letting "the story" become our identity. When we extract ourselves from the anger, demonization, labeling, and victimization, we regain our natural connectedness to the collective consciousness. Now, because what we do flows from our deep connection with all beings, we can more effectively bring about change without losing the better angels of our humanity.

Exploiting the Links of Grace

DIVINE GRACE, WHICH I call Links of Grace, originates from the One Consciousness. It is given to help us ascend and achieve our final end, which is out of time, space, and duality. In any given instance, divine grace may help us toward the achievement of Enlightenment if we are ready.

Our built-in Links of Grace facilitate our journey to Enlightenment. To the extent that I'm successful in making use of these Links, I can perceive God's grace and grandness in everything through my connection with the One Consciousness. That perception is then reflected in everything I do and results in high-frequency vibrations flowing into the universe. What's more, the Links help me to avoid egoic distortions, such as catastrophizing, discounting positives, or blaming. Instead, I can mentally detach myself from material things, even while enjoying them. Using the Links, I can reach a higher vantage point from which to view my life, much the way an astronaut, from the vastness of space, views the beauty of planet Earth.

In what follows, I'll describe three categories of the Links of Grace that not only facilitate my steps on the path toward Enlightenment but also enrich my life as I create on this earthly plane. When my creations enrich lives, are unobstructed by the ego, and send positive vibrations into our world, they too put me on the path toward Enlightenment.

Creating

The artist's, the poet's, the writer's, the scientist's, or any creator's inspiration is a mixture of intellectual and divine grace, a dance between the secular and sacred. High achievement is impossible without at least some divine grace appropriate to what is being created. These gratuitous graces, which have inspired some splendid works of art, science, and literature, belong to sudden and profound perception of ultimate reality, the One Consciousness, expressed as the formidable God. We know by immediate experience that divine reality manifests itself as a power that is loving, compassionate, and wise. The following quotation from Meister Eckhart (and similar statements from writers within other mystical traditions) about the role of divine grace bears a striking resemblance to Taheri's statements (see discussion of "Links of Grace" in chapter 7).

> *God is bound to act, to pour Himself into thee,*
> *As soon as He shall find thee ready.*
>
> ~Eckhart

Now that I perceive my true essence as the universal One Consciousness, my work as an educational researcher has taken on a new reality. I view creativity, such as writing peer-reviewed professional books and journal articles, as being empowered by both my human dimension (the creative mind) and my transcendent dimension (the One Consciousness). An analogy related to my current research may shed some light on the relationship between the One Consciousness and creativity.

Through effective and systematic teaching in early school years, children develop an understanding of how sounds are represented alphabetically. Later, with sufficient practice in reading, they achieve fluency with different kinds of text, such as fiction, nonfiction, and poetry. When we reach our highest level of education, we apply our accumulated knowledge of reading to critique and evaluate arguments and counterarguments within and among scientific and nonscientific texts. That application of reading skills is creating.

When the creation is carried out through focused thought inspired by the inner being, and especially when it is in harmony with the universe, there is an essence it possesses that touches everyone. A sculpture, a painting, a song, a poem, a piece of writing, a waltz—all present a message beyond what the eyes can see. They connect the artist or the writer with other humans, transcending cultural and linguistic backgrounds. That connection is empowered by the One Consciousness. To be engaged in both dimensions of our humanity, the sacred and the secular, is deeply enjoyable. There is no self-seeking in it, not for fame, power, or money. I try not to take too much credit for what I've accomplished; otherwise, the ego will arise.

We all have a wellspring of unlimited energy inside us that we can draw on when there is an opening—that is, when we feel enthusiasm. As I write these words, I can feel energy spontaneously flowing through me in waves. If I experience a setback and my energy wanes, a Link of Grace recharges me. It is our choice how much enthusiasm we want to have for the things we do. If we can always feel excited about the experience of creating in the moment, then the stumbling blocks matter less. Suddenly we get recharged. What is more, the enthusiasm and the vibrations flowing from us affect other people. This way, we become a source of inspiration for all those around us, another reward for enthusiasm.

Neutralizing Negative Vibrations and Toxic People

As negative events take place in our immediate or collective world, they emit invisible, negative vibrations that impact our inner state, causing fear, anxiety, and disturbance. The realization that, underneath my physical appearance, I am the One Consciousness has affected how I create inner peace, especially when adversaries come, which they inevitably do. In the world of dualities, for every Facilitator there is an Inhibitor. Therefore, I don't put undue expectations on myself. There will be losses, illnesses, and collective chaos, but, hopefully, I won't be flabbergasted when they come. Rather, I will calmly view them as invitations to go deeper, find inner refuge, and through them grow spiritually.

Adversaries can sometimes become fuel for metamorphosis—that is, a blessing in disguise. The process is a bit like weight lifting. From my earlier life as an American Council on Exercise (ACE)–certified personal trainer, I know that lifting weights can result in microscopic tears in muscle tissue. Over time, as those tears heal, the muscles grow stronger. Because of the tears, the muscles can eventually carry more weight. Similarly, adversaries, or "life tears," prompt us to tap deeply into our transcendent dimension, which is healing and, over time, makes us stronger.

My own experience has shown that when, with an understanding of the deep dimension of life and oneness, I experience gratitude, accepting and surrendering to whatever I'm feeling in the moment, an influx of positive vibrations is created from the Divine Intelligence through various Links of Grace. We can't fight adversaries, real or imagined, or else we create negative vibrations, which, among other things, helps accelerate the body's aging process. When we are rooted in our collective consciousness, which is who we truly are, adversaries don't translate into suffering because we accept them and then send away the emotions associated with them.

The realization that we are all one underneath our physical, emotional, and cognitive dimensions has also affected how I set priorities. For example, I now see negative politics and mainstream media, which tend to distort or amplify the worst aspects of humanity, as temporary. They are thus not seriously important to me or even worth my television subscription, which is now cancelled. Spending precious time trying to awaken to the sacred oneness, which is eternal, means far more to me now.

By helping me to become an impartial observer of my mind and not identify with it, the Links of Grace provide an additional benefit: I am not at the mercy of what happens around me. Because I don't get emotional as easily, I don't overreact or try to interpret others' actions and thereby annoy them. Because I offend others less often, meaning I amplify their emotions less often, I may even become a Facilitator in changing their attitudes.

When I am highly annoyed, it is sometimes difficult to become an impartial observer. My ego instead chooses reactivity. In these situations, I quickly use the relevant Links of Grace. Then, if I do react, I replay the event in my mind, reflect on possible egoic interpretations, and try to sense the One Consciousness, retrospectively, beyond personality or ideology. Sometimes I even go further and consider difficult people a blessing because they help me get in touch with my own consciousness.

Attaining Health

Our dualistic world is full of reactivity that is amplified with every challenge. When challenges appear in our daily lives, from the personal to the large scale—such as global pandemics or political unrest—many of us start complaining, even about the slightest inconvenience. Those things we perceive as adversaries lead to unhappiness and suffering, and they ultimately affect our immune systems. When the immune system is weakened, it can lead to chronic inflammation, which, over time, may cause damage to healthy tissues and trigger diseases like diabetes, cancer, dementia, heart disease, arthritis, and depression.

I regularly use the healing Links as divine aids, recognizing that the world of medicine, despite all its advances, cannot answer every question or resolve every health issue. These inherent Facilitators have the potential to heal the body, mind, and emotions; help with sleep patterns; and align our energy centers (*chakras*) so that life force energy (نیروی کیهانی), referred to as *prana* in Ayurvedic medicine and *qi* in traditional Chinese medicine, can flow easily.

This life force energy is all around us like a running river that nourishes the existence of all living forms, yet it is void of any physical characteristics. It can only be experienced. While the goal of energy flow for improved vitality and renewed energy is shared with practices such as Taiji, Qigong, and Yoga, these approaches differ vastly from Taheri's. Activation of the Link of Grace allows the life force energy to flow instantly without the use of any technique, because it is the work of the Divine Intelligence. These other practices rely on a variety of techniques to bring the energy flow into the body so that practicing individuals feel less tired and more energetic.

Taheri makes it clear that activation of the Links of Grace to attain health is not intended to replace medication or consultation with a medical expert, but rather to complement them with behind-the-scenes divine remedies (see "The Complementary Medicine Link of Grace" in chapter 7). He also makes it clear, as I mentioned earlier, that self-correction of bodily cells using the cells' own local intelligence, in response to communication with the Divine Intelligence, is not the ultimate goal. Rather, it is part of a much broader philosophy of knowing ourselves anew and of connectedness to the larger universe and the One Consciousness.

Based on the Link of Grace that has been activated, information is conveyed from کالبد ذهن (most closely translates as "Sacred Cognitive Dimension" or the "mind"), which is in charge of cellular management, to distressed cells in our body that have been scanned by the Divine Intelligence. Upon receipt of directives from the Sacred Cognitive Dimension, the affected cells begin correcting themselves to their original state with the intelligence they already possess, regardless of the nature of the illness (e.g., physical, psychological, or emotional; chronic or acute). Cases of spontaneous remission from cancer and other serious illnesses have even been reported by Taheri and his team.

The longer the connection to the One Consciousness, both in duration and frequency, the more healing may occur. Still, there is no guarantee. In using these Links of Grace, I remain an impartial observer throughout the connection, without imposing my ideas on the Divine Intelligence so it pays attention to my headaches, low bone density, or high blood pressure. I leave it to the discretion of the Divine Intelligence to heal what needs to be healed, because for all I know my illness might be psychological or attitudinal. This connection leads me to show gratitude to the owner of this intelligence, God, for the health and ability that I enjoy, including being able to type and see these words. In this way, I also get to connect with God in my spiritual practice.

All in all, making full use of the Links of Grace is helping me evolve toward becoming the kind of person I want to be. I know for certain that today, I'm a happier and more compassionate person than I was before I began my spiritual practice. When I see another human being who's in pain or struggling, I know that a part of me is in pain or struggling as well, because in our essence, we are one. I begin to reach out. It is not about being morally superior to anyone else. It is about being happier and more compassionate human beings than we used to be.

11

Our Origin and Destination

Tomorrow, when the presence of the truth becomes apparent,
embarrassed and regretful will be the travelers who focused
on the virtual world.

~Hafez

Understanding Our Origin

IN CHAPTER 10, I explained the term Enlightenment, the ultimate end-goal of our journey in this life, partly as our ability to not give in to the temptations of our egoic thoughts. Instead, we must seek Awareness, through the built-in Links of Grace, that we can bring with us to the next world. Avoiding the temptation of egoic thoughts requires an understanding of how these temptations originated, and that is the purpose of this chapter.

The mainstream thinking that evolution occurred by chance precludes our conception of ourselves as One Consciousness, guided by the Divine Intelligence. Instead, it suggests that we are no more than individuals with an evolutionary history. Those who believe this will often argue, if a God with unlimited power existed, why would there be so much human suffering (the Holocaust, worldwide poverty, civil wars)? Why wouldn't He put an end to it?

Yet this is a very limited view of God, one that casts Him as a controlling father. Without free will, humans might avoid pain and suffering, but they would also have no choice, freedom of action, or moral responsibility. We would neither have nor need enthusiasm to actualize desires or connect with our inner self, even under the most challenging and difficult circumstances; nor would we have any need to curb the mind's natural tendency to wonder in favor of seeking Presence by quieting the mind.

We can also explain the reality of evil in a world created by a God Who is good. From the point of view of the divine reality, there is no evil because there is no opposite that can be separated from the source of the good, the One Consciousness. Creation is good since it comes from God. This is demonstrated by the overwhelming beauty of the natural order. But for human beings living in the realm of relativity, evil is real. The problem of evil becomes difficult when we absolutize the relative. To speak of a world without evil is to confuse the absolute and the relative and fail to understand that everything in the universe is relative (dependent on something else). Without the evil that causes us to forget our true identity, Enlightenment wouldn't be meaningful.

There is a purpose for these challenges in the larger design of the universe, and that is to help us stop identifying with our outer self. Our dualistic world, by definition, is capable of making us happy one day and miserable the next. But we only become miserable if we totally lose ourselves in our outer self (واقعیت), the self that is concerned with our appearance, our thoughts, our physical pain, and our social position. In this mindset, we're stuck completely in our human side. We don't even know about our divine side, the place where we truly reside. Because we don't know who we really are, we don't know how to deal with tragedy, like the death of a loved one. Miserable and suffering, we then turn away from God. The suffering persists, however, and, over time, we become weary of carrying the burden that we've created for ourselves. We could avoid this by perceiving the "art of living": that is, transcending the evil and beholding only the good.

Even amid what sometimes appears in life as the predominance of the evil, we need to cling to the good, which ultimately triumphs. But we can't accomplish that without help. We are in need of divine guidance combined with faith to remember who we are, where we came from, and where we should be going. This realization helps us, as travelers on the journey to spiritual perfection, to overcome the fear of an imminent event.

When we stop thinking that life in a world tied to dualism should contain no terrible things—no genocides, wars, broken relationships, pandemics, earthquakes, illnesses, crime, poverty, or floods;

When we recognize that the grand vision of human destiny is to help us gain Awareness, which sometimes comes as a result of suffering;

When we go beyond the surface and perceive the preciousness of our true essence;

And when we dissolve stirred-up emotions from the past that haven't gone away (i.e., our egoic thoughts), accepting the way things are today as a part of the natural human limitations in this world;

We then bring inner alignment into our relationship with God. When we do this, enormous freedom suddenly comes into our lives. We begin to recognize that our outer self is simply a short-lived shell, one that, if we let it, allows our true essence, the eternal One Consciousness, to shine through and lead us to Enlightenment.

As if by magic, our enthusiasm and creativity arise from the mind. We can play with our focused thoughts and creative insights to accomplish and manifest, always against the backdrop of our natural connectedness with our true essence. Here, where there is a flow of our essence into our actions, we no longer pollute the universe with our negative vibrations, which weigh heavily not only on other human beings but potentially on all life forms. And because we are not totally identified with our impermanent, external dimension, death is no longer the most dreaded event. We feel for the suffering that comes with the loss of the outer self[73] and, at the same time, feel the indestructible inner self that is beyond suffering. In this way, we honor compassion by both weeping for the loss of the impermanent outer dimension and celebrating the permanent inner dimension. Recognizing that we are more than simply persons, each with some history that occurred by chance, we are then likely to make peace with God.

Nearly fourteen billion years ago, a tiny (less than one-millionth the size of the period that ends this sentence) but extremely hot and dense state exploded with unimaginable force. Within far less than a millionth of a second (our time),[74] the ineffable explosion created all matter and energy in the universe, expanding it outward to eventually create the Milky Way, the galaxy that contains our solar system, which, in turn, consists of the planet Earth, the other planets, dozens of moons, and many luminous stars, one of which is our sun. This phenomenon, known as the "Big Bang," resulted from the continuous and meticulous planning of the Divine Intelligence, which also created the Laws of the Universe and the proper conditions for our journey.[75]

The purpose of the Big Bang, according to Taheri, was to lay the groundwork for the eventual creation of humanity on Earth, a planet at the center[76] of the observable universe that has been moving in space for the past 4.5 billion years and will continue to do so.

Our biological systems evolved later than earlier processes.

Those earlier processes corresponded to everything that happened in the universe before humans formed. We are the result of a long chain of extraordinarily well-tuned events. Since the entire universe is in consciousness, we might say that our bodies evolved in consciousness.

Humans are likely unique among all living beings in their ability to engage in abstract reasoning, perceive the vastness of the universe, and ask questions, such as "Who am I?" "Where did I come from?" and "Where am I going?" Our creation was for a purpose, and that purpose, from Taheri's perspective, is to pursue Enlightenment. To walk on the unsteady and arduous track of Enlightenment, we were given resources as well as divine gifts, such as the Links of Grace.

Everything in the universe is tailored to support life on Earth. If the Big Bang had been just slightly more or slightly less forceful, we wouldn't be here. If our moon didn't exist, the degree of tilt of our planet would have been off, creating chaotic changes, such as aiming straight at the sun to produce hot temperatures that would make life unlivable. Had our sun been more massive, it would have exploded, thereby ending the potential for life on the planet. The idea that we just happened to live in one lucky universe where all parameters are just right to support life isn't a tenable hypothesis.

According to scientists with access to powerful new technologies, an unknown form of energy intrinsic to space called "dark energy" is now continuing the expansion initiated by the Big Bang at an accelerated rate. Every galaxy is receding from every other galaxy. This finding is contrary to what scientists believed up until 1998—that the expansion of the universe would gradually decelerate because in an explosion, the rapid outburst of material generally slows down. Apparently, that is not the case in the cosmos. One hypothesis, finding varying degrees of acceptance among physicists, is that the influence driving the continued expansion of the universe is a phenomenon called "dark energy."[77] According to Taheri, dark energy may be a form of intelligence that occupies most of the universe to ensure each of its infinitude of components, like the solar system, works in perfect harmony with other components and in accordance with the Laws of the Universe—as they have for nearly fourteen billion years.[78]

Scientists who have studied the early universe have provided plausible, evidence-based theories for how it began, but their explanations unravel when it comes to explaining its origin beyond what is observable. There is no real understanding of how life began or why the universe appears to be exquisitely designed for life's emergence and its sustenance. Everyone can see how unsatisfying the narrative that "the universe created itself" is. It suggests that life is an accident and inconsequential to the cosmos, like icing on a cake.

Taheri doesn't reject science—quite the opposite. He challenges us, however, to go beyond matter and energy and place them into a deeper understanding of the universe—one that adds consciousness to the equation. According to Taheri, the Big Bang was the end of a process that began with the One Consciousness, not the beginning. All of science is based on Awareness emerging from consciousness, but science hasn't the foggiest idea what consciousness is.

The dogma of scientific materialism indicates that there is nothing but matter and energy, just as in the past we thought the earth was flat with only two dimensions (width and length), not recognizing its third dimension (height) because it was unseen and therefore counterintuitive.[79] Being trapped in a two-dimensional view of the universe (matter and energy), science doesn't seek to know its third dimension (consciousness). And when it doesn't understand beyond matter and energy, it thinks something must be wrong with the concept of consciousness itself. It is a common mantra among materialists to dismiss a claim by asserting that it is unfalsifiable. What it often means is that a falsification strategy is too difficult for them to uncover. Consequently, science finds no point in evolution at which life can be said to enter, and no point at which personality can suddenly enter the fetus. I call this "confirmation bias" (a tendency to give greater weight to evidence that confirms prior beliefs than to evidence that conflicts with them).

In fairness, science has limited techniques for investigating the concept of consciousness. Therefore, there are some domains that science cannot penetrate. Science is concerned with the physical world. It can bring us to the Big Bang, but it can't take us beyond it. A different approach is needed to see a totality that is not fragmentary. It is a deeper challenge. One has to experience it in a manner that is familiar to the soul (a "dance" in a web of connections) instead of discrete data and perfect objectivity, which too have given us so much. Science addresses the material world, and spirituality addresses the world of mysticism, which cannot be completely understood by studying physics, psychology, philosophy, and other intellectual disciplines. We gain insight into consciousness primarily by direct experience.

Taheri takes us into uncharted territory by providing an authentic means (without tools, techniques, or preaching) with which to see our connection with the One Consciousness. That's when science can see that a Big Bang can neither occur by itself (in the same way that our image in the mirror cannot occur by itself) nor create the intricate set of properties that are perfect for life's existence. I don't feel there's a contradiction between science and spirituality. I see the two ways of knowing not as mutually exclusive, but as capable of informing each other to answer the big questions we face.

Affirming the understanding that the universe is intelligent, purposeful, and whole need not oppose what science tells us about the nature of reality. Using a related example, the theory of evolution, formulated by British naturalist Charles Darwin in 1859, beautifully explains the improvements in species and adaptive strategies. While there is compelling evidence from the fossil record and comparative anatomy for natural selection (the process by which organisms better adapted to their environment tend to survive and reproduce), there is no compelling evidence, according to Taheri, for the hypothesis that *genetic variation,* on which natural selection acts, is random (that is, each species has an equal probability of being chosen). This opens the possibility that evolution is an iterative process to reach certain goals. The astonishing richness of human life, our complex biological systems, and our ability to perceive and be aware suggests that an intentionality is at play at the root of the evolutionary process.

In short, no scientific cause could be ascribed to this primary phenomenon I call the One Consciousness. It is the true breadth and depth of our existence, with which we can develop a direct connection. We can validate that with *direct experience* instead of merely engaging in conceptual exercises in abstraction. Modern science seems to have discovered a soul mate in the phenomenon of consciousness. Still, despite great strides in understanding consciousness, these studies seldom cover the phenomenon of *direct experience*, central to the study of human existence.

About 240,000 years ago, when the conditions were finally appropriate, *Homo sapiens* emerged on Earth. For the conditions to be appropriate, formation of a single cell through photosynthesis had to occur. This cell eventually evolved into complex life, including flowers, dinosaurs, and mammals, one of which was a small ape in Africa. Humans were then distinguished from chimpanzees, both of which had the small ape as an ancestor. This beautiful stream of humans eventually included Abraham, my ancestor, about four thousand years ago, then my parents, and then me.

Taheri teaches that once *Homo sapiens* emerged, with physical bodies that contained both cognitive and emotional dimensions, it was time to imbue them with (a) God's Soul (روح الله), which originated from the One Consciousness, and (b) the personality blueprint (نفس), both of which are eternal. Almost like workers on a vehicle assembly line, the Divine Intelligence created the human body and then added the Divine Guide (روح هادی), which, as noted before, aids us in our quest for Enlightenment—our life's purpose.

The car's driver, according to Taheri, is our original personality blueprint, endowed with a set of egoic and other personality traits, inclinations for good and bad, and a Sacred Cognitive Dimension (کالبد ذهن) that doesn't contain any brain cells but has its own "brain system." This dimension is capable of perception, decision-making, archiving information eternally, and cellular management (when we are in physical bodies). We are perpetually aware with no intrusive gaps in which oblivion makes an appearance. Our Sacred Cognitive Dimension can learn new lessons and draw appropriate conclusions to overcome challenges in the different worlds we will inhabit on our way to our desired destination—Enlightenment.

Once in a new world, the Sacred Cognitive Dimension (کالبد ذهن) can either lead its assembled car toward the destination (Enlightenment) or "flip it into the valley," so to speak. That is, motivated by the need for egoic satisfaction in the form of wealth, power, title, accomplishments, relationships, or fame, we may attempt to fulfill unmet needs and desires through others in the physical world. For example, an individual with an addictive personality blueprint will likely be attracted to vibrations coming from a person with a similar personality in the material world, and may try to "drive" that person's car (mind and physical body) rather than stay on the road to Enlightenment. Note that infusing or occupying someone else's mind or body is different from being reborn with a new body (human or animal), as is the case with reincarnation.

These egoic pursuits may serve the personality blueprint well in the earthly world, but they will also enslave it into separation from other beings and thereby delay its progress toward Enlightenment. Eventually, however, it will enter other lives and continue to accumulate knowledge toward Enlightenment. With each subsequent life, it will live with more Awareness, having carried at least some lessons with it from each previous life.

Through our many lives in the bipolar worlds prior to the current one, our original personality blueprints were gradually programmed such that each of us developed distinctive personality traits, depending on our ability to control or enhance egoic tendencies using our free will. This is why we now have nearly eight billion different personalities on Earth, all of which stem from the same basic personality blueprint. This also explains why no identical twins have the same personality. One twin may be highly sensitive, the other more thick-skinned, despite having the same genetic makeup and being raised in the same home. [80]

The above description has, for the most part, reconciled for me the tension between Darwinian and religious viewpoints, recognizing that Darwinism is not inherently contrary to religion, nor are all religious viewpoints opposed to it. From the religious viewpoint, the creation of Adam, a symbolic figure who might be called our original personality blueprint (نفس واحد) was the establishment of a vessel for the One Consciousness to be carried over to the bipolar world from the unipolar world. The bipolar world, according to Taheri, is not a single world, as noted earlier. It is an "umbrella" world that includes many worlds that existed prior to the world that began with the Big Bang. We don't "know" much about these other consecutive (متوالی) worlds in the bipolar universe, other than that the last one had an extra dimension in addition to space, time, and duality. Accordingly, Adam was given a different form in each of these worlds in order to survive. In our current world, which began with the Big Bang nearly fourteen billion years ago, Adam ascended to the form of a "human being" (انسان), with physical, psychological, and mental abilities, in order to continue in a world that is characterized by space, time, and duality.

From the Darwinian viewpoint, we became *Homo sapiens* through years of evolution. This evolution was guided by the meticulous planning of the Divine Intelligence. How else can an "illusionary" universe (see chapter 5) be its own creator? Like an image in the mirror, it must have a reality somewhere else. How else can a primitive single cell come about in the first place much less be capable of giving rise to an organized cell—a phenomenon that is still not understood by science? God can work in magnificent ways!

Another way of saying the above is that human experience includes both the secular and the sacred. The secular, or human, side of us evolved during life in this universe over billions of years. It is confined within space and time. The sacred, or divine, side of us is the original One Consciousness, which is reflected in God's Soul (روح الله) in the unipolar world. It is timeless and energizes the secular self toward Enlightenment. God's Soul cannot be manifested to our human senses, or thought about by the mind.

Feelings of pleasure and pain are caused by the senses' contact with objects. They come and they go, never lasting long. God's Soul, the dweller in our body, passes through childhood, youth, and old age, and at death it merely passes into another kind of body or state.

In the next world, my eternal personality blueprint (نفس) will likely drive a simpler "vehicle" suitable for the new context, all of which will be assembled by the Divine Intelligence. With each subsequent death, I will be born into a simpler form of "me" because I will be in a world with fewer dimensions, that is, a world that is without space, time, and eventually duality, in that order. As part of the larger design of the Creator, I will no longer need *space* and *time* because some of my dimensions will have been eroded.

Perceiving Our Destination

BY NOW WE KNOW that our end goal for this life is to reach Enlightenment, which is the peak of Awareness or spiritual perfection. In order to arrive at this pinnacle, which shows us the path to our destiny, we need a level of understanding of our destination.

According to Taheri, Earth, within its galaxy and solar system, which began with the Big Bang, is simply one point in the much larger world that began with Adam in the unipolar world, noted earlier. Since God is limitless, His manifestations are limitless. Therefore, there are likely other worlds that we cannot even imagine because, as humans, we are constrained by space and time. It is hard for us to imagine something without a beginning and an end.

The metaphor of Adam's fall from paradise can be read as the beginning of duality in our world: What rises will also fall. Whatever is right also contains falsehood. Whatever gives us pleasure can also give us pain. There are Facilitators to Enlightenment, such as the Links of Grace, but also Inhibitors that distract us from Awareness, such as egoic thoughts. Whatever is born will also die.

When we die, our bodies return to the earth and our emotions vanish, but God's Soul[81], which has emerged from the One Consciousness and with which we are imbued, remains, along with our Sacred Cognitive Dimension (كالبد ذهن), which is separate from our physical brain. Our Sacred Cognitive Dimension accompanies our original personality blueprint (نفس) and has the primary function of perceiving, thinking, and archiving our takeaway lessons and wisdom related to Enlightenment. These takeaway lessons (which include knowledge of the true self and the One Consciousness with which it is identical), are not to be confused with knowledge of superfluous facts such as the distance between stars. Our eternal self (see discussion below) makes use of this organized spiritual knowledge and experience to become a unique personality.

These takeaways stay with us as we travel to our next lives, where, gradually, space, time, and opposites fade toward greater simplicity. When we leave life in this world, our next world may be one that has both time and opposites but no place. In it I can be everywhere and nowhere, with a 360-degree view but without the constraints of human limitations and life decisions or physical properties—everything from gravity to gender identity. With time constraints removed in the subsequent world, I can be everywhere in zero time. These freedoms could be immensely enjoyable.

With every new life we assume, we have an opportunity to practice oneness with God's manifestations, which vary from world to world. In doing so, we expand upon the Awareness, wisdom, and memories[82] we brought from previous lives through our Sacred Cognitive Dimension. In this sense, I would regard our personality blueprint as a "work in progress." We spend an eternity improving that blueprint with the increasing wisdom that we obtain through various lives, including material bodies in this physical world. That identity remains with us until we eventually merge back into the One Consciousness after having acquired the prerequisite Awareness. At that point, our individual identity dissolves and our memories become irrelevant and fade away.

Said differently, there is some individuality left after we die, up to the point of merging back into the One Consciousness we came from. Neither the Awareness nor the memories associated with our inner self stored in our Sacred Cognitive Dimension cease to exist upon death, for the same reason that the water in waves doesn't cease to exist when the waves dissolve. The water is simply released into the larger flow of the ocean, implying that our ongoing experiences in memory are also released into a larger context of consciousness.

In a sense, death is God's grace to improve upon our Awareness as we journey toward the summit of Enlightenment. Even the image of hell as a fiery dimension is viewed positively in Taheri's school of thought—an opportunity to burn our impurities, which are primarily egoic in nature. If death didn't exist, we would become more and more distant from God, and this retreat would cause increasing suffering. It is not true that there is no proof of the hereafter. How can a proof of immortality be found in mortal existence? Connecting with the One Consciousness allows us to find the seal. By opening it, we experience an Awareness of the continuity of life.

The more regret, guilt, unfulfilled desire, and attachment to wealth, fame, loved ones, and our bodies we cling to in this earthly world, the more difficult it will be to enter the next life and continue our path toward Enlightenment. So, if we are seeking Enlightenment, we must, while enjoying our relationships, wealth, and achievements, acknowledge them as attachments and then transcend the mind that created them.

Though subsequent worlds may have neither time nor place, opposites will likely be present until our final test, the filter before Enlightenment. The test will be whether we, with our newly acquired power that has become in some measure Godlike, proclaim to be our own God, or recognize that we, like everything else, are a manifestation of God and choose to be "one"[83] with Him instead. Our ego, which will still be with us and has free will, may seek power over Enlightenment. In this case, there will be no union with God. We will be sent to the beginning of the bipolar world. If, on the other hand, we transcend our egoic tendencies and choose to become united with God, the curtain will be removed, and there will be no more "you" and "I."

The divine spark in our inner being unites with the divinity. In that state of union, God becomes the light with which we see all things. To quote Meister Eckhart, a thirteenth-century philosopher and mystic born in Germany, we are in a state of fusion with the ocean of divinity. We are what we were, the immovable which moves all things. That is, we become embellished with the qualities of God, which are also our true self residing at the center of our being.

Divine reality is at once transcendent (beyond us) and immanent (within us in the here and now). The spiritual person realizes that to be really "here" is also to be "there," and vice versa. Whenever we are in the present moment, we are connected to the One Consciousness by an unbreakable bond.

The here and now is the gateway to God. In the now, we will realize that God has been with us all along, but what kept us apart was attachments resulting from identification with the ego. When we finally let go of attachments, we fulfill the work in progress and enter the zone of Enlightenment, where we are no longer needy. Climbing the ladder is a slow process in a bipolar world in which there is an opposite for everything. Even the enthused rarely reach the top until they are well advanced in their spiritual growth.

Once Enlightened, our personality blueprint, having transcended the ego and acquired omniscient Awareness, exits the bipolar world and enters the unipolar world, where there is an intimate union with God, the One Consciousness. The personality blueprint that is attached to anything, however slight, will not arrive at the Divine union. It is only when we have renounced our preoccupation with me and mine that we can become united with God. Rumi thought that to seek union with God while holding on to (or taking advantage of) power was an undertaking no less senseless than looking for camels among the chimney pots.

In the state of union with God, our individual identity is extinguished—we cannot speak of the personality blueprint anymore, for it is reconnected with its Source, the One Consciousness, and remains where it has always been. In heaven (جنتی), all is one—a state of fusion with the "ocean" of the One Consciousness, which is also our true self.

Note that the order of events from our existence on the dry land of the planet Earth to the peace in our native "ocean" is not a sequential process—over many lifetimes, we'll gradually lose the dimensions of space, time, and duality in that order. Furthermore, an individual can move indefinitely up or down, toward union with God or toward separateness and selfhood. The more the personality blueprint separates itself from its ego and the multiplicity of dimensions, the closer it becomes to God—until such time that the ego and dimensions of time, space, and duality disappear altogether and we unite with God. The more there is of self, the less there is of God.

We unite with God and no longer need the Divine Intelligence to guide us because we already have accessed the treasure box of Awareness. Said differently, with access to the treasure box of Awareness, the personality blueprint and its indwelling God's Soul unify (وحدت)[84], at which time the concepts of space and time have disappeared. When we opt to be "one" with God, instead of proclaiming we are our own God (because we now have access to the treasure box of Awareness), we finally reach Enlightenment and duality disappears.

In short, according to Taheri, if we have done our work to ascend to Enlightenment in this world, then we zoom past crossroads between any two worlds (برزخ, pronounced "barzakh"[85]) toward perpetual joy and oneness with God, mirroring the One Consciousness. That is where we fully understand God's concept of creation and oneness and become Enlightened.

Full Awareness is, indeed, attainable in our time on Earth. That is, we are capable now of perceiving what it means not to have needs, but we cannot *experience* being without needs until we go on to other lives with different dimensions in the bipolar world. We must live in "time" in order to be able to advance to "timeless," no longer on the human but on the spiritual level. We must continually battle with our lower self, the ego, in order to transcend it and become identified with that indwelling higher self, which is akin to the divine essence. We must make use of our focused thoughts to be able to pass beyond them and perceive the immediate divine Awareness. It goes without saying that focused thoughts and knowledge are indispensable, but alone cannot be a proximate means of union with God.

Neither can we skip a life on our journey, much the way we cannot skip a grade in school. If we perform poorly in a grade, we can make up the deficiency in the next grade, but it is more difficult to do. From my experience as a research scientist in the field of literacy, I know that successful performance of virtually any reading task requires at least some foundational skills, the ability to decode unfamiliar words based on knowledge of spelling-sound correspondences. If these skills are underdeveloped in grades 1 and 2, reading will become more and more effortful in later grades, when children are faced with more demanding texts. So, it is with us in our continual challenge to accomplish our spiritual tasks on Earth.

To carry the analogy a bit further, development of reading skills is like learning how to dissolve, yet enjoy, our attachments to the worlds we live in. Being able to read any text in any subject area is like tapping into the vast cosmic library of knowledge or accessing the treasure box of Awareness. The better readers we are and the wider our vocabulary, the more texts in different disciplines we can understand, and thereby the greater use we can make of the cosmic library.

Research studies in the field of reading have shown that first-grade reading ability is a strong predictor of exposure to print even when controlled for IQ—meaning that early acquisition of reading skills might help develop the lifetime habit of reading. What these studies tell me is that in an environment where (a) organized religions often deny the belief that we can access our sacred essence without their interventions and rituals; (b) the public education system is rife with regional discrepancies and does not encourage young people to ponder the higher questions of existence; and (c) social media has a tenacious grip on the minds of our youth—that in such an environment, the ability to read independently may well be a major pathway to spiritual development. There are many genuinely spiritual insights to be gleaned from reading spiritual texts, literature, poetry, and essays to name a few.

As we lessen our attachments to previous worlds and augment our Awareness, we get to more fully access the treasure box of Awareness, which resides in our indwelling God's Soul (روح الله). That treasure is stable due to its nature, the One Consciousness. The inborn spark of God within us is always still and intact. Our personality blueprint to which the ego is affixed, however, is prone to destructive elements. Thus, our attention needs to be fixed on the delinquent ego. Once the lower elements of our personality blueprint, the variable we (من متحرک), and the higher elements of our personality blueprint, the constant we (من ثابت), are united, we begin to advance on the "green path" to Enlightenment.

We are all steadily climbing to the next life and, eventually, to the "peak." No one is left behind; sooner or later, every soul will attain the "high perfection."[86] Unlike orthodox Christian doctrine, which does not admit the possibility of any further growth toward the ultimate perfection, in Taheri's teachings, God's grace is matched by His patience. Both are infinite. There is no eternal damnation, only a series of second chances to go forward toward reunion with God.

All are called, but few distinguish the desire-prompted attachments (such as lust for power) from God's Soul. The series of existences is indefinitely long; therefore, there is opportunity for everyone to learn the necessary lessons. There will always be divine "helpers" until every eternal self has been delivered into union with God and eternity.

Whereas calling on certain Link of Grace provides insights into this cycle of births and deaths, another Link gives us the sweet experience of our actual death from this life. This "dying before dying" experience was one of the most powerful connection experiences I've ever had.

On October 27, 2020, I had just walked, as usual, into my

office in the quiet early hours of the morning, when I saw a text message from Maryam, my spiritual instructor, who at the time was overseas. The message indicated that she would be serving as the connector or intermediary (see chapter 7) for this Link at nine o'clock that morning. There was no telephone or Zoom call per se; this meant that our small spiritual group would sit quietly for a few minutes, each in our own home, and simply witness the connection process within our own bodies, as explained in chapter 8, in order to receive this new Link of Grace. No guided imagery or other technique was needed to help us access and experience the flow of vibrations via the Link, only our witnessing and unbiased openness to receiving the Link.

The moment I sat down for the connection, the vibrations emanating from what I assume was activation of this Link set off an explosive wave throughout my entire body. My heart started racing forcefully, and I broke down and began sobbing like a child. It wasn't that I was experiencing fear, anxiety, or stress. On the contrary, I was glowing with love and excitement. After about ten to fifteen minutes, this sensation was followed by a sense of intense calm and sweet peacefulness. I was transported in a sudden state of spiritual ecstasy or intoxication of love. There was no clear way of measuring this subjective experience.

I interpreted the joyful experience as the death of my egoic thoughts and attachments to this earthly world, and the illumination of my dominant real self. I had ceased knowing myself as "me" and instead relaxed into pure Awareness, which I understood to be the One Consciousness. I had found that there is no "death" through activation of this Link by the Divine Intelligence—the one that governs the entire universe, including the cellular structure of my body. What gets stripped away is all that isn't us. We will come to life. I will never forget this experience and my husband's curious look as he rushed into my office, having heard me crying.

I don't regard the experience of "dying before dying" as having goodness or sanctifying power in and of itself. It is merely an indispensable reminder of something else: breaking down the ego—which stands between God and us—through His Links of Grace. Otherwise, I would think it to be a real part of spirituality, and so look no further, but grow full of self-admiration for my own progress. Pride might then abandon my will to see the ego's separative nature and look down on those who are not like myself. Moreover, I'd be able to do harm on a large scale, while, at the same time, wondering why the world was such a mess. To the extent that there is attachment to *me* and *mine*, there is no Awareness of connectedness.

Many, if not most, people fear death and the end of this life, and so they postpone reflection on what is a natural event. We spend most of our lives pursuing everyday activities: exercising our bodies, accomplishing tasks, smoothing relationships. However, as we age, we begin to consider issues that don't concern the younger generation, such as the nature and meaning of death.

The fear of death—our own or that of a loved one—is one of our greatest fears. No one wants to talk about death. It is hidden because we identify so strongly with our surface dimensions. To the ego, death is always just around the corner. The anticipatory grief regarding someone we love dearly stems from the ego, which cannot accept losing joyful moments like holiday gatherings, intimate conversations, promotions, or awards. The ego begins to feel sorry for itself and takes on a victim identity. Consequently, the death of a spouse, a friend, or a child becomes excruciatingly painful. Moreover, by encouraging us to feel deep distress in the loss, the ego sends us the message that God's laws about death are worthy of criticism.

Fear of death, by its very nature, leads to the feeling that we are separate from God. Still, when a loved one dies, it leaves empti-ness behind. We miss their human dimension—their voice, their touch, and their companionship—because love wants to be con-nected in all ways to the beloved. Sometimes I cannot shake the anticipatory fear of losing my beloved husband, but then I ask myself, what would he be feeling if I die first? Wouldn't I want to see myself as suffering in his stead? The death of our body may be viewed as an opening into the One Consciousness—a sacred mo-ment—not to be distracted by statements from assembled family and friends, such as "Hang in there" or "Please don't leave me." The soul understands that there is no tragedy involved in leaving the body. It is reunion with God for which the eternal soul yearns.

Suffering is inherent in our dualistic world, but we have mech-anisms for "amnesty," such as recognizing the ego and quieting it (that is, deepening our soul) with help from the Links of Grace. We acknowledge pain but learn how not to let pain induce suffering by recognizing that while experiencing pain, our true self remains unchanged. Said differently, while pain is inevitable, suffering can be optional. Rumi reminds us through the following poems that if we surrender to suffering (that is, neither fight nor flee from it), we can live through it and survive it.

Every storm the Beloved [God] unfolds,
Permits the sea to scatter pearls.

~Rumi

Connecting with the One Consciousness

Today's misery sweeps your home clean,
Making way for tomorrow's felicity.

~Rumi

To the extent that we hold on to worldly attachments, we experience suffering as a consequence of pain. To the extent that we release our hold on worldly attachments, we reduce suffering while still admitting the reality of our pain. When the whole concept of ownership becomes meaningless, we have broken our worldly attachments, and death reveals itself to be a gift of liberation from attachments, unmet desires, needs, sufferings, and the egoic mind.

Even without the dissolution of the ego, which strives for attachments to things, people, or concepts, death may be viewed as a natural ascent to eternal life over many lifetimes. Fears and sorrows become insignificant. Never did we not exist, nor will we ever cease to exist. We are all eternally present. Our impartial witness neither affects nor is affected by events outside itself. Those who know the real nature of our "self" (what I call God's soul, روح الله) do not grieve.

Since our real self as the One Consciousness is known to be always constant (من ثابت), there is no place for grief over death. We will simply discard worn-out clothes and put on new ones. Birth and death never occur to the real self, since it is the primeval being—meaning it is not subject to transformations such as birth, growth, and death, all of which are defined in terms of time and changing states. A timeless self-existence in pure consciousness, unaffected by outside events, is intended to end suffering. The goal of creation is the return of all sentient beings out of separateness, which results in suffering—illness, injury, hunger, poverty, anxiety, boredom, and the like.

In "Song of Myself," a poem from *Leaves of Grass*, a landmark in the history of American literature, Walt Whitman sensed very powerfully that rather than the end of our existence, death is actually a kind of liberation, a transition to a fuller and more blissful state. Finally, there is no more duality, no boundaries, no separated "You" and "I." At this level, Rumi glorifies the death of the material human being and the unity with the Creator. It is then that the Sufi finds the true meaning of his spiritual journey.

> *Glory! Glory! I triumphed—no more do*
> *I Know myself as me. I burn with love.*
> *Glory! Joy! No mortal mind can fathom me.*

> ~Rumi

The Eternal Self

> *I maintain that I already possess all that is granted to me in eternity.*
> *For God in the fullness of His Godhead dwells eternally in His image—the soul.*

> ~Meister Eckhart

I USE THE TERM "eternal self" (آدم) to mean a set of enduring attributes, which began in the unipolar world where we were imbued with God's Soul (the part of us connected with the One Consciousness). This set of stable attributes has characteristics that are shared across the multiple worlds that our eternal self has thus far entered within the bipolar world—acquiring a different physical form in each world so that it could survive that world's unique conditions. As described earlier, in our current world, which began with the Big Bang nearly fourteen billion years ago, the "eternal self" took the form of a "human being" (انسان), with physical, psychological, and mental abilities, in order to continue in a world that is characterized by space, time, and duality.

The attributes of our eternal self can be reasoned from divine revelations[87] of ancient Persian mystics like Rumi, and Taheri himself, even if we cannot map them onto numbers. Every human is endowed with two sets of key perennial characteristics: (a) God's Soul (روح الله), which holds the treasure box of Awareness originated from the One Consciousness, and (b) a personality blueprint (نفس) to which many dimensions have been appended to escort it on its journey.

Among the accompaniments of our personality blueprint (which I view as "work in progress," because it has potentiality to improve upon its Awareness once it is embodied) is a set of personality traits, some of which give us inclination toward Enlightenment (such as enthusiasm) and some against Enlightenment (such as egoic tendencies). These traits can never be dissolved because they are programmed (برنامه ریزی شده) in our software or nature (فطرت).[88]

Another companion to our personality blueprint is the Divine Guide (روح هادی), our inborn moral sense or compass, which helps us make good choices along the way.[89] Our personality blueprint is also ushered by the Sacred Cognitive Dimension or the "mind" (کالبد ذهن), which is separate from, but in charge of, our physical brain. It has the functions of managing cellular-level consciousness, perceiving, reflecting, and archiving our takeaway lessons, wisdom, and memories related to our true self, the One Consciousness.

In short, God's Soul and the personality blueprint are the two key aspects of our eternal self which existed before we were born and will exist after we die. The personality blueprint is about self-preservation and is driven by the desire to connect with its

Source, the One Consciousness. Our lives at any given day are the story of the interactions of these two aspects—divine soul and human limitations—and the emotions they bring with them. The divine soul has the power to lead us to new heights; the egoic tendencies can keep us pinned down to our past if we are not aware of their workings, creating an outer shell that blinds us from seeing the treasure box of Awareness hidden within. Our personality blueprint needs a gentle reminder that its function is to gather the experience and wisdom it needs to fulfill our divine soul's calling.

The Journey of Our Eternal Self

While our experience on Earth is limited and will terminate with death, our eternal self will continue beyond space and time toward Enlightenment. Life on Earth is a specific step in a much larger journey of the eternal self that started and will continue on another world and in a nonhuman body. The process will go on until such time that we acquire the requisite amount of Awareness that we can "bring home," recognizing that we have full freedom of choice in which fork to follow when we come to a crossroad.

While we are incarnate, our body and the eternal self interact with and complement each other. The body facilitates distinctions between pleasure and pain, and the eternal self provides spiritual guidance. When we are discarnate, the eternal self leaves the body and the body returns to dust. Seeing my mother's Sacred Cognitive Dimension (her "mind") leaving the physical body at the moment of her death was a meaningful experience. Eons later, having gleaned all the Awareness that she can through the process of living in different worlds, each with its own context and dimensions, her personality blueprint will unite with the prime Source—God.

How the process feels from within is a mystery. We have three dimensions in this world (space, time, and duality). In the next world, it could be that we only have a two-dimensional representation of the world. My only clues come from Taheri's revelations, yet it is difficult to perceive, much less explain, that afterworld isn't in space and time (dimensions that are so intrinsic to this world). Suffice it to say that our eternal self will not cease to exist upon our physical death, not any more than the death of a loved one in a nightly dream can imply his or her physical death. Moreover, there is a possibility of transformation and continued development of our personality blueprint in the next worlds if we wish to walk this path with Awareness. These are a hopeful conclusion for me and hopefully for some readers.

Positive Influences on the Eternal Soul

From a Sufi perspective, there are three factors that affect our eternal self in a positive way on the road leading to Enlightenment: the *knowledge of God, love of God,* and *virtuous actions.* The first includes discovery of the ultimate nature of who we are, our life's purpose, where we came from, and where we are going, which has been discussed throughout this book. This Awareness, which we carry in our Sacred Cognitive Dimension in the greater cosmic journey, emerged from the One Consciousness.[90] Love of God includes compassion for all His creations, not only humanity. This includes animals and plants as well as air, streams, and oceans. To ponder the meaning of compassion, the famous Persian poet of the thirteenth century, Saadi, says this:

> *The children of Adam are member of a single body,*
> *For from the moment of creation they were made of one substance.*
> *When fate causes pain in any member,*
> *The other members cannot remain still.*

O thou who hath no sorrow in seeing the sorrow of others,
Thou are not worthy of being called a human being.

~Saadi

The third positive factor influencing the eternal self, virtuous actions, turns our free will away from the evil—mostly our egoic tendencies, which have a negative effect upon the eternal self because of their deceiving nature. On the plain of relativity in which we live, evil is real. For the eternal self to deny it would be a catastrophe. It is this opposition between good and evil that is the basis of morality in most religious doctrines. While Sufis attach great importance to this claim of morality, they seek to go beyond the realm of external action and, through oneness, transcend the relativity of evil to the absolutely good. Transcending evil through oneness is where spirituality differs from ordinary religious morality.

Spiritualism, as viewed in this book, seeks to transcend the duality of good and evil through connection with the inner self, the One Consciousness, without negating the significance of morality. It is through the knowledge and experience of the interconnection of all beings that we can transcend the false love of the ego, such as hypocrisy and ostentatious charity, and engage instead in ethical behavior, such as sincerity and truthfulness. God is aware of this challenge. That's why we've been offered His Links of Grace to unravel the ego and turn the eternal self toward Him.

Those caught in the merely earthly existence can hardly discern the evil (ego) for what it is. The only hope for such people is to perform virtuous actions, which are primarily through the body, the conceptual mind. But God wants not only our actions but our core, which determines the actions through its moral compass. We begin thus with connecting to the One Consciousness; through our twin faculties of intelligence and free will, distinction between good and evil will naturally and automatically follow. That, in turn, can affect the state of our eternal self. Every egoic act creates a blemish upon it, and every virtuous act helps to purify it. As the great Persian poet, Saadi, says in the following poem, the spiritual person who seeks Enlightenment performs an act of goodness not for the sake of compensation but because of goodness itself; otherwise, if the act is attached to the fruits of the action, the moral bearing of our actions will be meaningless.

> *Do a goodly act and cast it into the Tigris River,*
> *For God will recompense thee in the desert.*
>
> ~Saadi

Interplay among the Positive Influences on the Eternal Self

There is an intimate interplay among the elements that correct the imperfections of the eternal self and make it worthy of Enlightenment. As noted above, the first element is the One Consciousness, which comes before everything else. Then there is the knowing and loving of God, illustrated by the chapter 6 graphic titled "Connectivity of the One Consciousness." The interplay goes like this: Our connection with the One Consciousness determines the level of our Awareness and knowledge of God, which leads to loving Him. That love leads to actions, most notably surrendering to "what is," which can mean many things, including getting to grips with God's laws of the universe, being willing to not have life go the way we think it should go, and accepting people with different or undesirable personality traits.

Recall from earlier chapters that it is abstention from that which separates us from the universe and others—our egoic tendencies tainted by power—that makes these virtuous actions possible. What makes the abstention from the ego and hence virtuous actions possible is mainly our connection with the One Consciousness,[91] that is, the Awareness that deep down the other is also our self.

Relationship of the Eternal Self to the Body

The eternal self and the body, while distinct from each other, intermingle in the same way that fresh and salt water intermingle, but the river remains distinct from an ocean. The seemingly opposed functions of each are complementary in what they reveal to us. Our intellect shapes what we think and how we form concepts. Our thoughts, in turn, have the potential of reducing the influence of the ego, effectively making the eternal self to become wiser than it was before. In response, wiser eternal self raises the power of our thinking, thereby motivating actions that are more virtuous in nature. This view stands in contrast to the view of reductionists who claim that the concepts we employ are the functions of our brains alone, thus undercutting the validity of the eternal self. If life appears meaningless because we have invalidated that which cannot be explained by mathematical equations or by probability graphs, the locus of the problem is squarely in our court for allowing that uninspiring conclusion. There is no fault in our brains, but in our recognition and respect for the complementary roles that our body and our eternal self can play in our lives.

To give a personal example, as you may recall from the early chapters of this book, I had to make choices at age fifteen when considering whether I should take my mother's advice and marry the dentist. Had I married the dentist, I may have had a comfortable material existence—a relatively high standing in Tehran society—and the blessing and approval of my family, but at the cost of stifling my true identity. Choosing not to consent to the marriage gained me instant disapproval from my parents and left me very uncertain about how I would make my way in the world. However, the decision preserved my humanity and profoundly affected the direction of the rest of my life. As I look back on it now, it is clear that, as much as the choice cost me in a life of struggle, what I gained was worth the struggle. Thus, my brain, a component of my physical body, had a role to play in my sense of eternal self. It may lack that context and the emotional intensity that my choice had in that context, but not the kernel of my wisdom as it relates to "who I am." Over a lifetime of hard choices (of which I've faced many), I gained a modicum of wisdom, which I hope will elevate my eternal self by lessening its ego. Over the course of many "lifetimes," those increments of wisdom accumulate. I am evolving, I am becoming, I am creating "who I truly am" every day until such day that I predictably make the highest choice for me (rather than my ego), which then becomes the highest good for my relationship to all things.

A Metaphor for the Eternal Self-Body Relationship

To draw upon a metaphor that has often been used to show the relationship between body and eternal self, the latter may be viewed as the driver of our car (physical body). Without the driver, the car is a useless husk of matter; without a car, the driver is left in a state of immobility. The driver can inhabit many different cars over a lifetime, each unique in its quality, reliability, and other features. The driver has no Awareness within its own makeup but is imbued with God's Soul and a personality blueprint endowed with several dimensions, including a Divine Guide (see earlier discussion). This means that the driver can now move freely in the world by being carried by the car.

The origin of each trip is at the point that the "God's Soul + personality blueprint" duo enters the fetus of an unborn baby. It is said by the Torah that every fetus born in this world has had experience with God when the fetus needed Him the most—during the "valley of the shadow of death." This is a symbolic description of the blank spaces between lives—for example, between life in the womb and life outside the womb, or, conversely, between life on Earth and a new life outside this physical world. The valleys are believed to be traumatic spaces. The "eternal self" hovers and doesn't want to say goodbye. It eventually separates from the body in stages.

During the travel, this duo ("God's Soul + personality blueprint") develops itself within the sea of consciousness. A wise driver with hard-earned experience can find ways to improve the performance of their car through careful maintenance, the right fuel, and good driving habits. Such a driver would also be more likely to learn from each unique driving experience and bring those skills to each new driving condition. A less experienced or attentive driver would have to traverse many miles down lots of roads in various cars before he or she acquired the natural comfort of feeling at home behind the wheel.

The critical factor is the driver's desire to follow the Divine Guide to Enlightenment using his or her free will. Thus, at the end of the trip, the duo is not quite identical to what it was at the start of the trip. That difference is the divine Awareness that has been acquired during the trip. At some point the trip ends with the physical death of the body (the car); the carrier eventually dissolves back into consciousness but leaves it no wiser than before.

At that point, the carrier separates from the driver. That's how we strive as eternal selves.

Connectivity of the Eternal Self, the One Consciousness, and the Body

As noted above, we have a degree of holiness (cellular-level consciousness) in our bodies by virtue of the fact that we were imbued with God's Soul. For the sake of this discussion, let's call that degree of holiness "local consciousness." The local consciousness experiences divine qualities arising from the One Consciousness such as Awareness and insights, as well as direct experiences of joy, love, excitement, wonder, and beauty. The more such qualities we experience, the more they can get translated in the brain to safeguard our physical and mental well-being. The greater our physical and mental well-being, the more Presence we can achieve, because it isn't easy to be present with a headache pain. The more Presence we achieve, the more easily we can access the One Consciousness and further develop our eternal self. Repeating the cycle, the more we access the One Consciousness, the more Awareness, insights, and feelings of joy and the rest will flow to us effortlessly and easily.

The Full Story of the Eternal Self in a Nutshell

We are both human and divine, temporary and permanent, all at the same time. At the moment of death, our eternal self resumes its journey toward union with God, but it takes with it the effects that our knowledge, love, and actions have made upon it. These spiritual effects are caused by the Awareness that deep down we are all One. Those who remain solely bound to the realm of action in this world will also follow the path to Enlightenment in the next life, but it may be more difficult to do so. Surely, we are not judged negatively for what we don't know if there is no means to overcome our ignorance, but that doesn't alter the reality that in order to be spiritually Enlightened, the eternal self must eventually possess the spiritual effects of knowledge, love, and actions gained in the earlier stages of its journey.

> *We see the world piece by piece,*
> *As the sun, the moon, the animal, and the tree,*
> *But the whole, of which these are shining parts is the soul.*
>
> ~Ralph Waldo Emerson

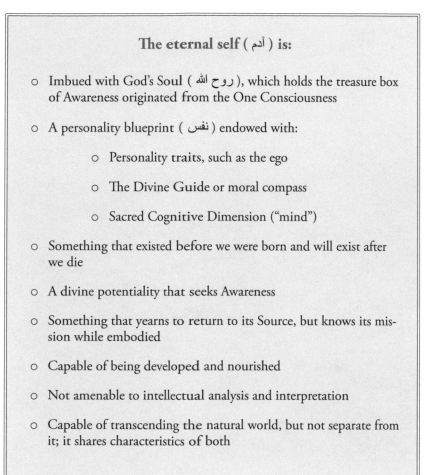

The eternal self (آدم) is:

o Imbued with God's Soul (روح الله), which holds the treasure box of Awareness originated from the One Consciousness

o A personality blueprint (نفس) endowed with:

    o Personality traits, such as the ego

    o The Divine Guide or moral compass

    o Sacred Cognitive Dimension ("mind")

o Something that existed before we were born and will exist after we die

o A divine potentiality that seeks Awareness

o Something that yearns to return to its Source, but knows its mission while embodied

o Capable of being developed and nourished

o Not amenable to intellectual analysis and interpretation

o Capable of transcending the natural world, but not separate from it; it shares characteristics of both

In Closing:
Remember Who You Are

You are the mirror reflecting His magnificence,
and your reflection is indeed all the universe.

~Attar

THIS BOOK IS neither a translation nor a condensation of Taheri's teachings. Rather, it is a melding of some of his most powerful ideas and some of my personal insights and experiences. I hope this book will be the beginning of a new spiritual practice for you and will, ultimately, motivate you toward a new spiritual life. I encourage you to visit Taheri's websites (www.mataheriacademy.com, http://mataheri.com, and https://cosmointel.com) for his original and more comprehensive coverage of topics presented or not presented in this book.

In the poem above, the Persian poet Attar tells us that the wholeness of humanity is a reflection of the image of the beloved God. It reminds me anew of my purpose in writing this book. With the challenges of our times, especially the extreme political and racial divisiveness in America, my goal was to deliver the single, overarching message that we are all part of the consciousness of humanity as a whole. Neither theoretical concepts nor scientific formulae alone can explain this infinite dimension of us encapsulated in the vastness of a unified whole.

If we feel oneness with humanity from within, we naturally

see others as companions on the spiritual journey whose differing views can strengthen and complement our own. There are no longer enemies whose decency is questionable and whose actions must be demonized. Feeling connectedness with humanity is a major challenge when mainstream and social media amplify negativity that we absorb like sponges without even knowing it. We thus isolate ourselves even further from who we are in our essence, the One Consciousness.

We can continue to have political viewpoints yet avoid getting caught up in negative vibrations associated with those views. How? By simply recognizing our viewpoints without identifying with them. It isn't easy, but we are capable. We can, without fighting it, simply watch our egoic mind conjure up stories and decide not to participate. For example, if someone cuts you off in traffic, the egoic story might be "That driver cut me off on purpose because she didn't like the political slogan on my bumper sticker. She's judgmental and reckless!" Stories like this in turn create the emotions we feel, such as fear and anger. The emotions seem real, even if the story is not true, and they can trap us in a negative state. This does not mean, however, that we do not follow through with actions we feel are for the good of humanity. For example, if the driver continues to drive erratically on the freeway, you might decide to notify the authorities to prevent a potential accident.

As I noted before, the mind can also be used for great focused thinking to solve scientific and societal problems and serve humanity. But here, I'm talking about egoic thoughts, through which we worry about what will happen in the future or create melodramas intended to appeal to the emotions. If we are increasingly aware that our ego is creating such thoughts and emotions, we do not castigate opponents as persons. Rather, without getting angry, we increase our own capacity to converse with individuals who question or contradict our position. We can still stick to our views, reject others' views, and say so with vigor, but without getting angry or losing the better angels of our humanity.

More than that, we allow an opening to our real identity, which lies in the One Consciousness, not in our egoic self, with whom we have an unavoidable relationship. When we allow this opening, we regain perspective. Instead of trying to control the world, we remember that we are seamlessly interwoven into it. True healing is a process that involves recognizing that we can be shattered by life yet still be whole with the universe. It is about coming to terms with "what is," rather than forcing others to be as we would like them to be. And so, the most important thing is to remember the beauty of who we are, our unbreakable wholeness, our origin, and our destination, before we act on egoic impulses. All else will follow. That's when we'll see the beauty all around us and the potential to live fully, in awe of the infinite universe we inhabit.

This awe and connection to the timeless One Consciousness come not through arduous discipline but rather through Presence and witnessing the egoic mind in action. The egoic mind tells us how hurt we are. It asks, "How could anybody do that to us?" It cries, "You can't just ignore that!" All these reactions put us in our comfort zone, like the soothing words of a second mother. But the confines of our comfort zone limit our ability to go beyond ourselves and access our sacred dimension, where there is direct connection to the Divine.

This timeless dimension of ourselves is connected to the source of all life—God. We can get a glimpse of God by perceiving the vastness and beauty of the universe and by feeling the underlying essence and holiness of all creations. Everything else is a "memoir," a story of past experiences, a surface phenomenon we live with for a while on Earth. We don't have to cling to these experiences, thoughts, beliefs, emotions, disappointments, self-concepts, achievements, titles, wealth, physical bodies, or even loved ones in the name of identifying ourselves. If we do, we will struggle perpetually to defend ourselves. We can expand ourselves instead into the brilliance of "what is," and what always was and will be. We give that new experience a name—Awareness of who we are, the One Consciousness.

At some point in our spiritual practices and growth, our thoughts naturally start to become quieter. The more we sit in the witness seat, the more independent we are of the thoughts, fears, grief, and even physical pain we watch. Mysteriously, when we form a relationship with our beautiful inner force and realize who we are, somehow the situation gets improved at God's hand through the facilitative functions of the Links of Grace. When that happens, we drift away from feelings of tension, anxiety, and resentment and move toward people. Now we can experience the high vibrational frequency of love for every human and for all the beauties of nature. This is the deep state of merging into God that the great Persian Sufi poets like Rumi have written about from their own experiences.

If we choose to live connected to the One Consciousness, we'll see that life can be lived in a state of peace, joy, and harmony, even in these turbulent times when the boundaries of civility are being tested in communities and families across the country. Living this way defines who we are, regardless of gender, age, race, nationality, family status, political affiliation, or disability. Having already experienced the spiritual realization of who we are in our lifetime on Earth, without too much clinging to our wants and needs, we won't face the next life in fear after our bodies have died. Our radiant inner self, which is what truly matters, never dies. Only the ego eventually dies. This will be painful only if we cling to our possessions, appearance, achievements, belief systems, and other externally derived proof of who we are.

I hope you have experienced some degree of inner transformation reading this book—that there is an awakening, however fleeting, that the universe is an indivisible whole in a way we cannot fully comprehend, that even the smallest event can generate positive or negative vibrations throughout the universe, and that you, in your own essence, are infinitely vast—then you are on the path to Enlightenment. Your outer self is now prepared to see its true essence and, in the process, contribute to the healing of this ailing world.

What I had hoped to offer in this book

o Raising of the individual and collective consciousness

o An integrated conceptual framework for the One Consciousness

o Fresh ways to reflect on what being human is all about

o First-person stories and poetic attempts

o Clear and complete explanations

o Perception of the other as ourselves in the deepest sense

o Answers to questions of who we are, where we came from, where we are going, and life's purpose

o Reduced loneliness through the experience of being alone with God and happy in this solitude

o The means for ascending to Enlightenment

o Knowledge that we are not our thoughts and that we can break the walls of the ego and experience presence

o Lessons in learning to face change, pain, and misery

o The ability to accept the reality of death

o Hope

Appendix 1

Key Concepts of Sufism
Shared with This Book

The result of my life is contained in but three words:
I was unripe, I ripened, and I was consumed.

~Rumi

What is Sufism?

PRESENT-DAY SUFISM HAS inherited valuable lessons from its long past, lessons it can offer to those on a quest for spiritual life and a path to Enlightenment. That past goes all the way to Abraham, who introduced monotheism to the Hebrews some four thousand years ago, according to Nasr. He was also the first to bring the tradition of mysticism to the world. Abrahamic mysticism called for approaching God directly, introduced the idea of migration of souls after bodily death, helped us realize that the ego is the source of all negative emotions, and told us that our manners and places of worship have nothing to do with talking to God. When we talk to God, we all speak one language, which transcends all religious separation.

Persian mysticism, which reached the height of its influence in the thirteenth century, may have also been influenced by primitive Buddhism, a philosophy founded by the Buddha, a Hindu, more than two thousand five hundred years ago. The Buddha's teachings extended over much of Asia, including deep into Afghanistan; at the time, it was a neighboring country to Iran, where many Persian poets, including Rumi, had lived. Huge statues of Buddha were built in Afghanistan nearly two thousand years ago to mark his life. They were destroyed when the Taliban seized power in 2001, in keeping with their fundamentalist strategy to obliterate all evidence of the time before Islam was brought to Iran via a bitter Arab invasion in the seventh century.

While reconciliation of early Buddhism's influence on Rumi and the ontological essence of the Self and consciousness, expressed through Rumi's own first-person experience and revelations, is a worthy objective, it is beyond the scope of this book. The practices of Buddhism adhere to the teachings of the Buddha to varying degrees. That is perhaps the effect of Buddha's teaching being statements of principle rather than guidelines for connection with the essence of Self and universal consciousness, as well as the effect of millennia of cultural evolution acting on the original teaching.

The themes of Sufism have been shared again and again, from the standpoint of every mystical tradition, East and West.[92] These themes include the following: (a) Human beings are not merely capable of knowing about God; they can also experience God by a direct insight, superior to reasoning. (b) Humans possess a double nature, ego and eternal soul (akin to the spark of God). (c) Humans' life on Earth has only one purpose: to identify themselves with their eternal soul and so to come to know God. The degree to which this is achieved (i.e., they can become what they potentially already are) here on Earth determines the degree to which their eternal self will be enjoyed after death.

With the emergence of New Age spirituality in the Western

world during the 1970s, Sufi mysticism experienced a popular renaissance that continues to this day. They both seek intimacy with God and a refinement of the eternal self, and they both adopt a belief in a holistic form of divinity that imbues all the cosmos. Both maintain a strong focus on healing using forms of complementary medicine, and an emphasis on the notion that spirituality and science can be brought together. Neither believes that adherence to religious law alone secures the perfection of the soul; instead, they teach that the believer must commit to God in the heart.

The Sufi path does not negate other paths, such as Buddhism, Christianity, Judaism, or Islam. A Sufi enters any house of worship and behaves as that denomination behaves, because at the heart of all worship is one message, one Truth, our deepest essence—or what I call the One Consciousness. Sufism would be the first to attest to its own universality. Rumi, in his famous verse above, is saying that there is such a thing as the Truth. On the basis of this certainty, one can advance to higher levels of the Truth until one enters the realm of Enlightenment, the Truth itself.

For Sufism, tolerance of others' beliefs, whatever they may be, is a key spiritual message, because its main idea is to remove distinctions which divide mankind. This idea is attained by the realization that we are all one in our innermost essence, regardless of whether we believe in Buddha, Christ, Mohammad, Moses, or Zarathustra. All these names are ideal human beings that have reached Enlightenment. As such, they are reflections of God on Earth. While every inspired person reflects, in his or her own way, some divine spark hidden in their soul, the central ray of light that these ideal human beings reflect falls upon every aspect of life, clearing away confusion and helping those who wish to advance spiritually toward the answers that lie in their own souls.

Message of Love

HISTORICALLY, THE ORIGIN OF Sufism is none other than Abraham's God, Who is never associated with fear nor reduced to religion but rather elevated as *love*. The earlier chapters in this book may have made this truth clear. Sufism recognizes love as a core attribute of God that is reflected within every human being. The Sufi message of love is the message of the day. Despite having existed for a millennium of history, this message isn't old or nostalgic. It has become a part of the contemporary American spiritual and literary landscape.

When a person begins to see himself or herself in others as a result of practicing connection with the Divine, great virtues, such as tolerance, humility, and forgiveness, spring naturally from his or her heart. What we call tolerance, humility, and forgiveness are forms of *love*. It is thus in love that we all unite, from East to West. A key idea that permeates all Sufi teachings is that the love that unites us all is the Divine spark, which is reflected in every human soul. The great Persian poet Rumi had the following poem engraved on his mausoleum, promising that no expiration date exists for accepting love's invitation.

Come back, come back,
Even if you have broken your repentance a thousand times.

~Rumi

When love emerging from the sense of oneness has awakened in our soul, it doesn't matter if we are in the church, in the marketplace, in nature, or in our own house. It is not the place that is holy; it is our own soul. Furthermore, truth cannot be spoken in words. It is something that is discovered through *experience*.

The Appeal of Sufism in the West

ALL THE POSSIBILITIES OUTLINED below are bound to be realized even more in the future, especially in the West, as the world evolves to oneness. The modern Sufi way:

o   Is easily accessible and understood by everyone, even if they have no previous knowledge of the subject.

o   Serves as an antidote to fundamentalism, which claims to return to the pure religion of the ancestors while giving a most sacred character to killings, oppression, and hatred; also acts against those who are infatuated with materialism and everything external to their inner self.

o   Has a vast literary treasure, including Rumi's mystical verses, with their startling freshness, playfulness, lyrical beauty, and most of all insight and spiritual profundity, which speak directly to contemporary audiences in the rare second person.

o   Exists in a language, Farsi, free from gender—with no "he" or "she" and no "his" or "her."

o   Is pertinent to our deepest needs, such as having hope, finding a purpose in life, learning to face sorrow, and being able to confront death.

o   Has intellectual unity, including the application of metaphysical principles to cosmology, such as consciousness, dualism, and causality—all of which are above the physical world in which knowledge has become so compartmentalized.

o   Defines mystic experience as being *ineffable* (difficult to convey in ordinary language), *noetic* (reveals absolute truth), *transient* (doesn't last long unless practiced regularly), *blissful*, and in *union* with all things.

Aside from the universality of consciousness, a message of love, tolerance of all religious ideals, and other familiar voices described above, there are some other key concepts of Sufism that are shared through this book's ideas. In the following paragraphs, I provide a brief overview of what I consider to be the most salient ideas that lie at the heart of both Sufism and this book.

What is the purpose of human life?

THE COSMIC JOURNEY THAT takes us to the abode of Enlightenment is the primary reason for our existence. Sufism is one of the major paths to this journey. It is the straight path of ascension over the cosmic mountain to reach beyond the cosmos, God's residence. The spiritual journey of the Sufi is therefore union with God through Awareness. Awareness is accessible by convening with the One Consciousness with the aid of the Divine Grace.

Seeking union with God helps us live on Earth in harmony with friends, the changing weather, what we eat, the place we live, surrounding wildlife, and the adversary. Things are unpleasant to us when we don't see the deeper meaning of life. Individuals, their health, or things of the earth are transitory, and we must someday lose them. There remains only one object of dependence—God, Who is not transitory and Who always is and will be. For the souls who are tuned to and reflect God, nothing frightens, for they possess nothing—all fright is connected to possessions.

How do we fulfill our life's purpose?

TO WALK UPON THE path to Enlightenment requires certain spiritual practices beyond simply reading and thinking about the spiritual world, although these are indispensable prerequisites for the cosmic journey. When a person wishes to ascend the cosmic mountain, they must first try to free themselves from the prison of the ego, which entertains superiority, pride, hypocrisy, disingenuousness, haste, anxiety, fear, envy, bitterness, and all the other roots of spiritual afflictions that create distance from ourselves, from one another, from nature, and from God.

This loss of the sense of spiritual connectedness in today's world has created a culture that emphasizes activity over contemplation through the creation of distractions, an atmosphere filled with information, advertising, and divisive social and mainstream media commentary. Fallen humans, cut off from the higher dimensions of their own beings, measure success based only on how the world reacts to them. Here, Rumi warns of not confining ourselves to the prison of the ego, which measures success by worldly pursuits.

> *Ego is the soul's worst affliction,*
> *No one lives outside its jurisdiction.*
>
> ~Rumi

It is worth noting that while the command of Sufism requires nonattachment to the material world, it does not advocate withdrawal from the world. The Sufi way brings the sacred and the earthly together in recognition of the inextricable interdependency of love and mind. This integration of the sacred life and the secular life is a hallmark of Sufi spirituality and a deep focus of this book.

One way to promote the quieting of the ego, a chronic condition inherent to the human experience, is to engage in virtuous acts such as humility, sincerity, forgiveness, and charity—recognizing that virtuous behaviors like charity are performed not simply to feel good, but for the awareness that the other is in the deepest sense ourselves. That is, virtuous acts, like charity, are of a purely spiritual essence. As such, they are universal. Where there are no virtuous acts of spiritual essence, there is only a partial or distorted knowledge of both the self and the world outside the self.

In addition to setting aside delusions of a separate self, disconnected from others and God, the spiritual seeker must find an authentic Spiritual Guide. Just as one needs a guide to climb to the peaks of Mount Everest, one needs a spiritual guide to ascend even further beyond the cosmos to embark upon the path to Enlightenment. The spiritual guide must (a) possess familiarity with the spiritual teachings necessary to provide guidance in climbing the cosmic mountain and (b) have received the power to initiate transmittance of God's Grace (which Taheri refers to as حلقه های رحمانیت, and which I translate as the Links of Grace as discussed throughout this book). We cannot let go of our ego by simply "trying hard." We need divine help through these Links of Grace.

Throughout time, people have likely been tapping into the same Links of Grace, but what they are called, the manner in which they are accessed, and the way the experience is interpreted are influenced by context, such as Christianity, Buddhism, or Sufism. Thirteenth-century Persian Sufi poets, like Rumi and his spiritual guru Shams, have referenced these Links in their poems, but they otherwise left no documents, books, or even glossaries that would clearly explain the Links. Taheri is the first spiritual leader who has named, explained, and demonstrated the effects of the Links of Grace. In the case of the Shared Link of Grace (see chapter 7), the transmission of God's Grace to anyone across the globe who is ready to receive it has already occurred through Taheri himself. Therefore, no spiritual guide is needed for this Link.

It is now for the spiritual seeker to walk on the path to Enlightenment through practice, which requires consistent work, because the ego cannot be completely eliminated. While modern Sufism cautions us to be gentle with and respectful of the faith and practices of another, no technique is needed in its own spiritual practice. Unlike meditation, there is no need for correct breathing and right posture. Unlike Islamic Sufism, it has no need for daily prayers, fasting, pilgrimage, or obeying the moral instructions of Islam, which bear many similarities to those of Judaism and Christianity. Moreover, spiritual virtues are not seen to have manifested through a prophet or religious books. Finally, present-day Sufism does not require the performance of Sufi songs, musical instruments, or the sacred dance, the most elaborate of which is whirling to accompany Rumi's mystical poetry.

The spiritual practice, as described in chapter 8, is simple. There is much overlap between the broader currents of modern Sufism and Taheri's practices, which require nothing more than impartial "witnessing" or being in the present moment and invoking desired Links of Grace received earlier from a qualified instructor or Taheri himself. Individuals who are attuned to the world of materialism do everything possible to escape from the "here and now," yet the entry to the spiritual path lies in experiencing the here and now, the eternal present moment.

An ideal spiritual seeker from the perspective of both Taheri and Sufism is one who

o   is aware of the imperfection of his or her inner state;

○ therefore, has a yearning to practice the virtues of nonattachment in order to break the hard crust of the ego that has covered his or her true essence;

○ has enough intelligence to realize that this world is transient and all things that they possess in reality possess them, be they wealth, property, or even a spouse;

○ has a strong enthusiasm to travel upon the path to Enlightenment;

○ is willing to know God now rather than wait for the afterlife; and

○ is aware that like a wave, which is neither apart from the ocean nor of any element other than the ocean, the spiritual seeker neither is apart from God nor has a soul that is unreflective of God.

What is the spiritual experience of Sufism?

SUFISM EMPHASIZES THE INWARD search for God through direct experience. As Nasr points out, Sufism distinguishes several states as a result of practicing the discipline of the path to the spiritual journey. One may suddenly experience an *expansion,* which brings with it indescribable joy, or a *contraction,* as if God has forsaken that person. These experiences are patterned to the rhythm of the heart: expansion and contraction.

I'll tell you my own experience. At times I'm overpowered by a sudden feeling of *contraction*, as if something within my soul is shrinking. Even my facial muscles begin to shrivel and my eyes get teary, making the spontaneous and involuntary experience complete in my whole being. The encounter that stands out most is when I silently contemplate the shimmering ocean waves under the sun on my daily summer walks in Maine. The splendor is so powerful that it penetrates my soul, as if God is whispering sweetly, not in words but through the glittering ocean, that I am already loved. The trick is to notice this and to not let any hindrance (such as petty cynicism) prevent us from experiencing the divine gift we hold within. The failure to recognize how deeply connected we are to God is the madness that first led me to write this book (see chapter 4). As Rumi reminds us in the following poem, there is no real distinction between humanity and divinity.

> *Could lover and beloved [God] ever be separate, subject to division?*
> *No, they are one and the same. I just had double vision.*
>
> ~Rumi

After a few minutes of the exhilarating encounter, I sense in my soul a feeling of *expansion,* an overwhelming joy, in the face of the beauty of the rocky coast and the surrounding nature, reminding me where I came from, what I am made of, and where I am bound to return. Nature is so perfect and orderly that to me it is the clearest evidence of great wisdom working. It lifts me up; for a moment, the walls of the ego seem to crumble, and I can experience a spiritual state associated with awe. Such is the terrain of mystics. I recognize the same piercing feeling of instant connectedness when, for example, I come across a certain phrase in a book I read or even a tiny spiderweb on my window. As Rumi explains,

> *Even the spider is not neglected by God,*
> *But is supplied with its food.*
>
> ~Rumi

For me, there is a constant contact with God. That connection affects my soul, which is what I bring to my cosmic journey. I have to continue to remember, however, that the ultimate goal of my spiritual path is embellishment of my eternal self with wisdom and virtues (see "Positive Influences on the Eternal Self" in chapter 11) in order to be worthy of Enlightenment, not the experience of joy, even if it is of a spiritual nature.

Appendix 2

Psymentology

PSYMENTOLOGY, LIKE ITS counterpart, Faradarmani (discussed in chapter 7), adheres to a philosophical position called holism (a whole that cannot be recovered from its parts). This paradigm recognizes the influences of the whole on the properties of the parts and the influences of the parts on the whole, as well as the interaction between the two forms of causation. Both the whole and the parts are necessary for the interplay to occur. An example of the influence of the whole on the parts is Faradarmani, in which the local consciousness within molecules tends to actualize their potential only when they become part of the nonlocal consciousness (the One Consciousness). An example of the influence of the parts on the whole is psymentology, in which one's vitality (شارژ) or depleted energy (دشارژ) triggered by an activating event can send positive or negative vibrations to the nonlocal consciousness (the universal consciousness in this case).

A contrasting philosophical perspective, reductionism, explains events solely in terms of the interactions between the parts without allowing the influence of the whole on the properties of the parts, and vice versa. This view works well for describing our material, but not our spiritual, makeup because it eliminates factors which are present only when the human is seen as a whole.

The underlying assumption of psymentology is that irrational perception of life events, no matter how subtle (such as "I'm a failure"), can create powerful forms of hidden energy, which, in turn, can cause biochemical reactions that attack the body at the cellular level, producing everything from indigestion to cardiac arrest, and a multitude of things in between. It is difficult to reverse the effects of irrational perception once it has taken physical form. Taheri's certified "connectors" know that we are meant to be whole and perfect in the "now." This "knowing" is also very powerful, capable of producing energy that can heal even at a distance, hence complementing individuals' own efforts in avoiding negative thoughts.

As with Faradarmani, the spiritual seeker becomes connected to the One Consciousness via certified "connectors." After the bond between the cellular-level consciousness (شعور جزء) and the One Consciousness (شعور کل) is established, the individual automatically undergoes a scanning stage by the Divine Intelligence (هوشمندی) to detect any mental and emotional disorders that may have led to the feeling of being emotionally depleted. Once scanned and diagnosed, the affected cells begin correcting themselves to their original state and the individual's mental health is restored, experiencing less apathy (دشارژ) and more vitality (شارژ).

The role of the five senses

THE FIVE SENSES THAT convey sensory information to the brain (touch, hearing, sight, smell, and taste) are highly instrumental in creating positive and negative feelings in our day-to-day living. These qualities of experience arising from sense perceptions are often referred to as qualia, a philosophical jargon for subjective sensations. For example, the aroma of chocolate and its nutty taste are sense perceptions, but the pleasure that many of us get from eating chocolate is an instance of positive qualia, creating an uplifting mood. The feeling that comes from smelling a rotten egg, looking at a car crash, or eating a bland meal, on the other hand, is an instance of negative qualia having the potential to make us gloomy and dreary.

Spectrum of responses to activating events

A CHAIN OF FEELING-TONE relations (measured in terms of pleasantness and unpleasantness) begins with an activating event (حادثه بیرونی), whether that's induced by external stimuli or by reflecting on the state of our own mind. The event can be a complimentary or offensive remark, a memory, or a creative idea—none of which has the power in and of itself to create a particular quality of energy, "hidden energy" (انرژی پنهان), measured in terms of emotional drainage or cheeriness. The main cause of unhappiness is never the situation, which is always neutral, but the way we perceive and interpret the situation has an effect.

The way we perceive and interpret life events is largely constrained by our personality blueprint. An irrational perception of an offensive remark, for example, would be to make a judgment: "She shouldn't have said that, which goes to show you how unappreciative she is of all the things I've done for her." Such a judgment would likely cause stress, which then leads to a feeling of fatigue; this has the potential to cause the blood vessels to constrict, leading to headache pain, high blood pressure, or even stroke. A more rational perception of the offensive remark may be acceptance of "what is." That is, (a) the recognition that all the necessary antecedent conditions were met for the remark to occur, (b) the Awareness that we are manifestations of the same singular consciousness, (c) the realization that we are all fallible human beings, and (d) that this too will pass. Now, we're vibrating in harmony with our soul's highest emotions. We discover renewed energy and sparkling clarity, rather than giving power to our ego's life-draining emotions.

Let me share a personal example. When I submitted this book to several publishers, I received a few rejections in a row. This activating event began getting me down. I wondered if I would ever be able to get my message out to my readers. Then I reminded myself that I wrote the book with no outcome in mind—whatever becomes of this book, I'll be fine, especially since I don't rely on the proceeds for a living. The process of writing has taught me to serve the soul within, a rational belief that betrayed my ego's need to feel sorry for itself. Later on, I received contracts from two publishers and was faced with the task of selecting between them—another activating event. I followed the same rational belief by insulating myself from my ego and creating a secure zone to do the necessary self-inquiry. I decided to betray my ego's wish to accept the offer from the more famed traditional publisher, which would have allowed them to sculpt my book, if needed, to appeal to the broadest audience (most likely by removing Persian elements or dumbing down abstract concepts). Instead, I chose my current independent publisher. In addition to wanting to maintain the intellectual content and spiritual/cultural expression of my book, I liked its current publisher's capability of producing the highest-quality paperback possible—one that my readers would enjoy the feel of in their hands. I hope this quality of experience arising from the reader's sense of touch, or what is known as positive qualia, will create in you a cheery mood, if only for a second or two. The key point here is to not worry about what people think of you or your work. Don't give in to the ego, and follow your guiding soul.

In another situation, the activating event might be a blow not to the ego but to our physical body, which can not only cripple us but also affect our psychological state. The brain translates the sensory data into the language of the body—pain, as described below (see "The Causation Process of Rational and Irrational Perceptions"). However, the way it feels to have pain depends on how our "mind" or what I call the "Sacred Cognitive Dimension" interprets it. Said differently, the degree of unwanted pain that the body is reporting is a function of how the Sacred Cognitive Dimension, not the brain, interprets the pain. And how it interprets the pain depends, among other elements, on the maturity level of our personality blueprint, which contains the ego. Awareness of the pain is not necessarily entailed by our experiencing the pain. If we have pain but don't become reflectively aware of it, we may experience no pain, as is the case with hypnosis, which can suppress the brain's perception of pain. A rational response to the activating event that caused physical pain may be to acknowledge the pain without letting it induce stress by appealing to the divine Links of Grace. When we are on the path to Enlightenment, nothing outside of us can affect us deeply or for very long. We no longer seek nor expect a pain-free existence, for we know that nothing real can be threatened and death is of no significance. Through surrender to "what is" and resisting the "if only" agendas for happiness, we will always be at peace at our core, no matter whether we are in pain or not.

Surrendering to "what is" looks like a passive state, but in reality, it is an act of far greater power than fighting, defending, or simply hanging on. Complaining, self-pity, blaming, anger, or discontent do not serve as a foundation for vitality, energy, or enthusiasm. They invariably carry a negative charge. Instead of blaming the external world for our dissatisfaction with life events, we can take action to change the situation, speak out without making ourselves into a victim, or remove ourselves from the situation— all while accepting it and remembering that the primary cause of unhappiness is our thoughts, not the situation itself. A situation is defined by the meaning we give to it. Some people can survive war without hassle, while others get extremely annoyed by simple things. It is all about perspective. Even in the face of the most seemingly challenging event (such as a global pandemic or war), if we become aligned with and surrender to it, a space will be created for something new and good to emerge. That's when life brings a positive energy vibration that suddenly starts working for us rather than against us.

In short, the spectrum of responses to activating events is a function of how well we are able to tame our egoic thoughts and recognize ourself in one another, among other things—and that corresponds largely to the developmental level of our personality blueprint (بلوغ نفس) which creates the conditions for the feeling to occur. Personally, I've found that when I am being true to myself, communicating my feelings wholeheartedly with others, making rational choices in my everyday life, helping someone, staying positive, having self-confidence, engaging in learning and discovery, avoiding reminiscing about painful childhood memories, making use of the Links of Grace, or listening to my Divine Guide, I am more able to tame my egoic thoughts in response to a broad range of activating events. This helps me stay energized throughout the day.

The sources of depletion and renewal of energy

THE SOURCES THAT ULTIMATELY power the level of our energy are not measurable because they are not physical but, as noted above, have the capacity to either drain or charge us. The degree to which they can drain or charge us depends on the developmental level of our inborn personality blueprint—the primordial, undifferentiated template discussed in chapter 11.

Contained within the personality blueprint, are positive traits, such as enthusiasm and wonder that perennially emit positive energies as well as traits that only occasionally send positive energies (کوتاه مدت), such as compassion for victims of a crime. Also held within our personality blueprint is our ego—the destructive potentiality whose key objective is to separate us from others. Here, again, there are egos that tend to generate perennial negative energies such as arrogance, and those that create occasional negative energies, such as pretentiousness. The ego's fictitious stories that create arrogance, in particular, if denounced, will have the most dreadful downward effect on the energy level of the individual.

Neither form of qualitative experience—depletion or renewal of energy—has a physiological basis; hence the term "hidden energy." The rejuvenating feeling some get from eating chocolate doesn't come from the taste buds in the tongue signaling to the brain. The invigorating experience of seeing a beautiful sunset by some exceeds the sensory process of photons hitting the retina. The heavy feeling of envy associated with seeing the neighbor's superior lawn has no roots in physiological processes. Taheri is also unwavering in his view that neither of these two forms of energy has its root in the dark energy that causes the expansion of the universe.

Importantly, Taheri makes it clear that the subjective experiences associated with activating life events, while they are not internal constructs of the brain, do not flow from the One Consciousness—a deeper, more sacred place inseparable from our natural state of interconnectedness. Instead, we perceive these experiences because their dynamisms impinge on the sense organs. Heat, cold, and other senses detected by organs of our sensibilities are not absolutely real—they are effects not perceived as distinct from their causes. Every effect is subject to change, and every change is perishable. The One Consciousness is absolutely real and continually exists. It is the inevitable Awareness intended to bring fulfillment. The feelings emerging from the One Consciousness are glimpses of our inner self that do not have opposites because they are not part of the dualistic world. It is the experience of being at one with the universe, which only occurs when we silence the mind. While walking in nature has many benefits, the highs we feel during our walk (positive qualia) can quickly turn into pain. The joy we derive from some secondary source, which is based on the accumulated wisdom of our personality blueprint, is never very deep. It is only a pale reflection of the overwhelming feeling of joy, love, vibrant peace, flash of insight, or fleeting moment of Awareness that gives us a taste of Enlightenment beyond the polar opposites of everything worldly. This is a subtle but important difference that is rarely appreciated. We can augment our sense of calmness by spending more time in nature, for example, but calmness in and of itself is neither the higher goal nor the deep state of being we're after.

The Causation Process of Rational and Irrational Perceptions

A ROUTINE EVERYDAY EVENT, such as reading an email, leads to the creation of a certain interpretation, understanding, or creative insight that did not exist before. The email doesn't have an inherent power to create those immediate effects or to necessarily entail a certain holistic outcome. Any outcome, as noted earlier, can be attributed to the individual reading the written text. That individual, in this context, is our unique personality blueprint (نفس) that we are born with, or the "driver" of the vehicle of our cognitive, physical, and psychological dimensions.

Once the five senses (touch, hearing, sight, smell, and taste) convey sensory information triggered by an activating event to the brain, the brain transmits that information to the Sacred Cognitive Dimension (کالبد ذهن), commonly referred to as the "mind." To determine how to interpret the incoming sensory information, the Sacred Cognitive Dimension first and foremost relies on the "driver's" wishes (اراده). To honor the "driver's" wishes, the Sacred Cognitive Dimension uses its own archival data from previous lives as well as information from active life (such as personal experiences, context, health, and knowledge of universal and spiritual laws). Note that the brain, unlike the popular belief, is incapable of perceiving and making decisions. Now, if the information from the archival and active sources is well-conceived, the Sacred Cognitive Dimension will make rational interpretations of events. If, however, the information is ill-perceived, it is likely to make irrational interpretations, some of which may result in dire consequences.

Once the interpretation of the activating event made by the Sacred Cognitive Dimension, which occurs instantaneously in our "hidden state," is complete, it is sent to the "physical state." First it goes to the psychological department (کالبد روانی), where it is assessed. The psychological dimension translates the interpretation received as either positive feelings (such as joy, hopefulness, calmness), which puts the individual in a positive frame of mind (فاز مثبت), or it translates the interpretation as negative feelings (such as anger, sadness, hatred), which places the person in a negative frame of mind (فاز منفی). Each of these frames of mind is capable of creating positive or negative vibrations that can impact not only the individual's own emotions, such as vibrational depression (افسردگی تشعشعاتی), but also those of others.

Upon receipt of this mental information from the psychological

271

department, the brain translates the feelings into electrochemical language, which then gets transmitted to the physiological department (کالبد جسمی) to act accordingly.[93] For example, our face may now turn red, our mouth may get dry, our heart may beat quickly, or we may start shaking or perspiring. If the feeling of depression continues, its effect may be seen on the physical body as well creating what Taheri calls "physical depression" (افسردگی جسمی)—an ideal condition for blockage of incoming positive vibrations as well as the flow of life force energy (نیروی کیهانی) known as prana and qi.

A similar process takes place when we read for information, for example. The Sacred Cognitive Dimension analyzes the new information we read, archives it, and then sends it to the brain to be remembered (bypassing the psychological dimension). Now, we can access the information anytime we wish.[94] In either case—a life event or new information gleaned through reading—the interpretation can be rational, arising from the Sacred Cognitive Dimension's higher level of maturity, or it can be irrational or distorted, arising from its underdeveloped level of maturity.

Depending on the rationality or irrationality of our interpretation, the effect can be a positive feeling (such as joy or a spiritual insight) or a negative feeling (such as stress or fear). Joy and spiritual insight generate positive energy, leading to liveliness. Stress and fear, on the other hand, induce negative energy, resulting in drainage of energy. Liveliness sends positive vibrations to the world and contributes to our physical well-being and longevity, whereas lethargy sends negative vibrations to the world and bestows physical unhealthiness upon us, accelerating our aging process.

Guarding our vitality against an internal element: the ego

BY NOW, WE KNOW that identification with the negative ego imprisons us to our attachments to the physical world, which, in turn, results in the creation of negative states of mind, such as greed and fear—an ideal condition for compulsive extraction and consumption of our vitality, energy, and mental resources (دشارژ). Ultimately, these forms of energy determine the degree to which our physical well-being becomes affected. Moreover, they are capable of sending negative vibrations to others, thereby discharging their level of energy as well.

Insofar as we fail to recognize and deliberately tame our ego, it tends to mold our irrational interpretations of the events in the world around us. We cannot let go of our egos by simply "trying hard." We also need divine help through the Links of Grace (see chapter 7). A combination of self-knowledge and the Links of Grace would lead to a more "bulletproof" existence in a bipolar world, as would avoiding individuals with certain egos, such as arrogance, that create perennial negative energies. The effect of being in the presence of people expressing high frequencies of positive energy is to feel harmony with the universe fulfilling a common objective. Now the higher spiritual energy of harmony begins to work. The right people magically appear, the right materials show up giving us the information we've been wanting, and we see beauty in everything. Science, philosophy, and even religion can't inspire such dramatic changes in our perceptual world. It is up to us.

There is always time for us to recognize our ego for what it is, assume deliberate control of it, and ultimately adjust our behavior so that it is in harmony with our own values and standards. We have a choice to not let our ego confine us to the culture-bound notions of self-worth (having a Ferrari, entertaining lavishly, or using a prestigious publisher). As I've explained in chapter 11 (see discussion of "The Eternal Soul"), there are "stations" along the road to Enlightenment where we stop to contemplate our lessons learned. There, we decide whether we want our personality blue-prints to be continually corrected by assimilation of their ego to the soul or we want to give in to their false self by choosing to be outwardly rich and inwardly poor.

When I choose to assimilate my ego to the soul so that I can retain my enthusiasm and vitality in all of my work, many people may become inspired by that work from distances not discernible by our senses. I wholeheartedly believe that when I'm in a positive frame of mind (such as perpetual state of gratitude, avoiding distraction by the demands of the ego, and feeling an affinity to all of life in the universe), I'm utilizing the power of the creative Source to impact the consciousness of potentially thousands of people.

Every improvement in a single person (such as offering a silent blessing to beggars rather than judging them as lazy, or residing within inner peace regardless of anything external) improves the world at large for everyone. Even if the world is at war, we have the choice of either keeping our inner peace or plummeting into anxiety and stress, indicative of the ego being involved in our opinions and creating destructive energy. Feeling inner peace isn't an indication that we're callus or indifferent to events, such as the economy taking a nosedive, climate change, or a war raging some-where on the planet and killing innocent people, but rather a way of becoming an instrument of peace. Moreover, while we cherish all fellow humans and yearn to ease their suffering, we realize that the ache of everyone on Earth is relatively small, compared to the joy of eternity.

The subtle spiritual vibrations of inner peace, oneness, and positivity can help harmonize the forces of the universe that get out of balance when we live from excessive ego. They can indeed counterbalance the collective negativity of perhaps thousands of people. No one to convert. No goals to accomplish. Nothing more than tapping into the Source of everything, the One Consciousness, and staying connected to the eternal part of us that originated in infinity. The negativity of the entire human population who live with anger, hatred, and despair would likely self-destruct, were it not for these counteracting effects of positive vibrations.

Chapter Summaries and Questions to Ponder

I N T H I S S E C T I O N, I've provided summaries of each chapter and related questions to ponder. This may help you connect the content of the book to your life.

INTRODUCTION

I begin by sharing my motivation for writing this book and describing why we must defuse the highly negative energy afflicting our world today. To do this, we must begin with ourselves. I allude to the secrets revealed in the book, which are based on the teachings of Mohammad Ali Taheri, an Iranian spiritual leader who escaped death in Iran in the spring of 2020 and now lives in Canada. I also touch on how the application of Taheri's essential teachings has affected my own life. I explain how heartfelt change requires cultivation of enthusiasm for bringing the light of our true essence, the One Consciousness, into the world. Indeed, that is where our real power to begin living in unity lies. Finally, I express my hope that the book will inspire readers to use its spiritual principles to begin to heal the collective human experience.

○ How would you cultivate enthusiasm for bringing the light of your true essence into the world?

CHAPTER 1: Claiming My Life

In this chapter, I share vignettes from my life growing up in Tehran, where I was destined to get married at barely fifteen years old to my much older cousin. I describe my yearning to become educated in America, the ensuing obstacles that threatened my tantalizing dream, and my defiance of the reality in which I was trapped. I describe the power of enthusiasm and focused thought in helping me push onward and claim the privilege of self-directed movement, recognized as a male-only prerogative in Iran. The terms *enthusiasm* and *focused thought* acquire a much greater meaning in chapter 7, when I introduce the concept of the spiritual Law of Enthusiasm, a divine Facilitator that rewards us for our passion with insights, solutions, and people who can help us at just the right time. I also explain that as a young woman, I did not want to adopt a victim identity by blaming my family and culture for my circumstances. Later, in chapter 10, I explain what I now know—that victim identity is an ego challenge that can get in the way of our seeking Enlightenment.

○ Have you ever felt insights that have arrived suddenly from an unknown source, as if someone was guiding your creation? What was your level of enthusiasm and curiosity for what you were creating? Would you have manifested with no expectations of praise, fame, or money, or was the outcome relevant? Did you enjoy the process?

o How do you avoid letting social and mainstream media pummel you with a continual barrage of anger and angst, which only serves to amplify victim identity?

CHAPTER 2: Overcoming Obstacles in America

Readers learn that my American dream did come true. I give credit to my "guardian angels" (friends and strangers) for helping me hold on to that dream when I was on the brink of losing it. At one point I faced possible deportation to Iran, which would have meant a life of intellectual emptiness, all because I had run out of money and had no place to stay. There was another painful disappointment to overcome as well: at age twenty-three, I was tricked by my family into taking full responsibility for my mother under the pretext of a family reunion. My readers can experience the power of "forgiveness" as I describe my story of achieving my American dream through the transformative power of God's grace. Even as a young woman, without any formal spiritual guidance, I sensed that by forgiving my family, I could come to grips with my hurt and angry feelings and prevent them from controlling me. This way, I became invulnerable to my life challenges. In chapters 7 and 8, I call this forgiveness "acceptance of what is" and "surrendering to God" through inner strength, or the One Consciousness, which remains unaffected by the circumstances around us.

o Who were your "guardian angels," caring people—extended family, friends, or strangers who offered opportunities and shelter from the storm at just the right times?

o Have you experienced the power of forgiveness to help you

become invulnerable to your life challenges? What helped you accept "what is"?

o How would you use the power of enthusiasm and focused thoughts to help you defy the reality in which you are trapped?

o Would you characterize yourself as someone with a victim identity; that is, someone who tends to blame their parents, friends, coworkers, culture, or society for their circumstances?

o Do women everywhere have a better chance of finding happiness by living within traditional boundaries, or by defying the rules of their society, which may also cost them dearly?

CHAPTER 3: Seeking Spiritual Community

In 2019, seeking to delve more deeply into my relationship with God, I attempted to return to my original faith and joined a Jewish spiritual community. In this chapter, I share my experiences attending services at a local temple, as well as meetings of its Torah study group. As it turned out, I did not find what I had hoped to at the temple and study group. While I admired my fellow Jews' commitment to serving their community, it seemed as if they had created a rift between themselves and God. They were focused on the cultural aspects of what they perceived as myths in the Torah, not on their spiritual dimension. I later learned that many Jews became disillusioned about God in the aftermath of the Holocaust. Many questions began to surface in my mind: Could God be intrinsically fair and yet not intervene in the brutal victimization of Jews by the Nazis? Deep inside, aren't we all one? This part of my story reveals the importance of wrestling with the inner self, others, and even God in search of "who we truly are."

o   Have you ever wrestled with God? If yes, how?

o   What is your understanding of God? What is the source of that understanding?

o   Could God be intrinsically fair and yet not intervene in crises? If yes, how?

o   Do you want to delve more deeply into your relationship with God? If yes, why?

o   Would God send you to hell if you don't believe in Him? Why not?

CHAPTER 4: Lifting up Humanity

I further describe how, in the midst of my more recent searching and questioning, God offered direction, as He has throughout my life. At a casual luncheon I hosted in my home, a friend introduced me to teachings of Taheri, which are rooted in the mystical tradition of Sufism. A key insight of Taheri's is that our thoughts are often marred by a fundamental flaw, the ego. The good news is that it is possible to quiet egoic thoughts and thereby minimize the ego's control on our journey toward a deeper spiritual life. That opportunity is afforded to all of us through what Taheri says are God-given gifts. I call them Links of Grace. These gifts are available to all without exception. I also explain that this book is not a translation or a condensation of Taheri's teachings but rather my interpretation of his teachings on humanity's collective consciousness, which I call the One Consciousness, and my connecting of the dots to construct my own gestalt. I discuss how we can apply Taheri's teachings in our daily lives for the betterment of ourselves and our world.

o Why is it important that you minimize the ego's control on your own journey toward a deeper spiritual life?

o Spirituality is a broad concept with room for many perspectives. What does it mean to you?

o What are some signs of spiritual awakening that you may want to watch for?

CHAPTER 5: What Is the One Consciousness?

I define the One Consciousness and explain that in our innermost essence, we are each an expression of it. The timeless, shared consciousness is not detectable by our senses or through thinking. Indeed, experiencing it requires letting go of thoughts. Out of One Consciousness springs not only divine Awareness but also compassion, a creative spark, and love. When connection with the One Consciousness becomes a natural state of being, we are able to recognize the divine essence in others and align ourselves with whatever happens, rather than try to resist it. This chapter ends with the notion that we emit either positive or negative vibrations through our thoughts, words, and actions, and, in turn, the universe responds. The reader leaves this chapter with a closer view of a universe that is unfathomably deep, mysterious, and sacred.

o Why is the One Consciousness one of the most mysterious subjects before humanity?

o The One Consciousness doesn't have a dictionary definition; it has attributes instead. What are they?

o What gives evidence of our oneness?

CHAPTER 6: Connectivity of the One Consciousness

Here I present a new, integrative theory of the One Consciousness. I show the dynamic relationship between the One Consciousness and Taheri's other key concepts, namely God, the Divine Intelligence, Laws of the Universe, Awareness, and Enlightenment. The chapter explains how I created this thematic whole by first spotlighting Taheri's concept of humanity's collective consciousness, an idea that resonates deeply with me and that, in my mind, is most in need of attention today. I then culled Taheri's other ideas by carefully finding and following thematic threads as I read through nearly 2,250 pages of his transcribed lecture notes. This chapter also features an original graphic representation of the connection between threads, which I believe illuminates for readers the inherent unity of the collective consciousness. This way of perceiving the One Consciousness is not only reasonable to my thinking mind, but has transformed me spiritually in ways I couldn't have imagined earlier in my life. In sharing my journey with readers, I hope my liberating experience becomes a part of their experience as well.

o   Think about the original illustration in the book showing a new integrative theory of the One Consciousness with the concepts of God, Divine Intelligence, Laws of the Universe, Consciousness Fields, Awareness, and Enlightenment. How do you understand the relationships among these entities? What would your spiritual paradigm look like if you were to select different topics from this book and construct your own theory? Play around with your own visual representation.

o   What is a divine power you've never seen but that you've experienced, a power that gives but doesn't judge?

o   Why has the word "God" lost its true meaning after being misused for so long?

o   How would you become privy to more and more divine Awareness where guidance, possibilities, and love are infinite?

o   What does "nonattachment" mean to you? What are you holding on to most in your life? Can you name the egos that drive those attachments?

CHAPTER 7: Influencing Elements on the One Consciousness

This chapter describes the thematic relationships among three elements that influence the One Consciousness: Presence or stillness, which is a prerequisite for connecting with the One Consciousness; Facilitators, or spiritual "guides," which help us to, among other things, achieve the state of Presence; and Inhibitors, which are habits or ways that prevent us from reaching Presence. The Facilitators include, prominently, the divine Law of Enthusiasm and the Links of Grace. The Inhibitors, the effects of which can be minimized by using the Links of Grace, are either egoic or random thoughts, both of which we stumble on repeatedly on the pathway to Presence. These thoughts are to be distinguished from focused thoughts, which spring from enthusiasm and are used to accomplish goals and solve problems for the good of humanity. The chapter concludes with an explanation of how the powerful Links of Grace are activated and thereby create an opening through which Awareness flows.

o   What are the Links of Grace and how do they work?

o   We've all heard the proverb "Ask and you shall receive." What is it that opens the door to receive love and guidance when you ask? Can you reach Enlightenment on your own?

o   How would you settle down the ego that separates you from others and open the door to the higher realms? Could you connect with the divine resource that resides within you if you didn't slip out of your ego? Why not? Why yes?

CHAPTER 8: Connecting with the One Consciousness

As I share my personal experiences in developing a spiritual practice, readers learn practical ways to connect with their true selves, the One Consciousness, without any tools, techniques, or effort. This way, positive outcomes can only be attributed to divine grace. Witnessing mind and body sensations without any judgment, expectations, or interpretations sets the stage for activation of the divine Links of Grace and connection with the One Consciousness. Readers learn that the extent to which they can control their ego and surrender to the present moment using the divine Links of Grace is an indication of their success in connecting with their own essence. Once we are infused with the One Consciousness, a flow of divine energy helps us in miraculous ways and true compassion for others becomes possible. True compassion goes beyond empathy and charity toward others. We experience it when we go a step beyond and feel the eternal bond of the One Consciousness that we share with those less fortunate. The path to Enlightenment is thus both our gift to the world and our main purpose for living.

o   Were you able to use the "Shared Link of Grace" as a divine resource to connect with your own deepest self, the One Consciousness? If yes, what changes have you noticed in your daily experiences? If not, what obstacles did you encounter?

o   Turning off the mind's chatter, dropping the ego, embracing the present, and accepting "what is" isn't easy to achieve on one's own, no matter how many books one reads, workshops one attends, or videos one watches. What is Taheri's roadmap for achieving Presence, the entry point to Enlightenment?

o   Can you see the similarities between focused thoughts when you are attuned to what you are doing and zero thoughts when you are engaged in your spiritual practice?

CHAPTER 9: My Path to Enlightenment

I speak to readers from my heart and with great compassion. I reveal how I changed profoundly as a result of experiencing a deeper connection with the One Consciousness and how this transformation put me on the path to Enlightenment, my destiny. As we walk the path toward Enlightenment, we are given the free will to either give in to the temptations of egoic thought or gain Awareness that is transferable to the next life. Using authentic personal stories, I help readers perceive how to stay on the path toward Enlightenment by experiencing oneness with others and the universe, seeing God's presence everywhere, perceiving their life's purpose, and knowing who they truly are. As they incorporate these practices into their lives, readers will achieve a deeper level of spirituality, as well as fuller attentiveness to their own creations. These creations are unobstructed by the ego and thus capable of lifting up humanity. If an egoic thought gets in the way, readers are now more likely to witness it and realize that they are not that thought but rather the one who is aware of it.

o   How do you define Enlightenment?

o   How do you see your major obstacle in pursuing Enlightenment?

o   What is a life, in the end, if all you leave behind is a story?

o   Can you think of a personal story when you experienced oneness with yourself, others, God, or the universe?

o   Have you been able to open a place inside yourself to connect with a divine resource?

o   Everyone wants to be happy, yet often we have very little idea of what brings about genuine happiness. What are the causes and conditions that bring it about? How would you align your actions with your aspirations for happiness?

CHAPTER 10: Controlling Thoughts and Exploiting the Links of Grace

A key requirement for our journey to Enlightenment is the gradual dissolution of our egoic tendencies, which trap us into behaviors that separate us from each other. In this chapter, I describe specifically how readers can control such tendencies, including stereotyping and acquiring victim identity, and offer a number of examples from my own experience. Readers also learn about the Shared Link of Grace, which is available to anyone and which can quell egoic tendencies through Presence and witnessing the egoic mind in action. However, exploiting the Links of Grace goes beyond neutralizing the negative charges of the ego. The Links also empower the mind to create through focused thought, always against the backdrop of our natural connectedness to our true essence. When a creation is inspired by the inner being and aligned with what the universe wants, the creation contains an essence that touches everyone. This way, we become a source of positive, uplifting energy for all people.

o   Think about your past experiences and how your ego showed up in terms of emotions, such as anxiety, fear, anger, or insecurity. What did your ego tell you? Are there certain circumstances in which your ego is most likely to step in? What are some things you could do to give your ego a little attention (or not) without allowing it to control your life?

o   Write down your rebuttals of the ego to remind yourself the next time you are in a conflict in a relationship, or your enthusiasm is blocked, or you feel that past hurts and resentments are clouding your perception or your ability to make good choices.

o   How would you maintain your energy, vitality, and optimal functioning knowing that people's emotional struggles are rooted in their identification with the ego?

CHAPTER 11: Our Origin and Destination

Avoiding the temptation of egoic thoughts requires an understanding of how these thoughts originated. That is the main purpose of this chapter. The mainstream thinking that evolution occurred by chance precludes our conception of ourselves as One Consciousness, guided by the Divine Intelligence. In Taheri's view, human experience includes both the secular and the sacred. The secular, or human, side of us has evolved over billions of years. It is confined within space and time. The sacred, or divine, side of us is the eternal One Consciousness. It is timeless and energizes the secular self toward Enlightenment. Once *Homo sapiens* were created through evolution, with physical bodies that contained both cognitive and emotional dimensions, it was time to imbue them with the One Consciousness and the "personality blueprint," or clean slate, which included the ego, with which we now have an unavoidable relationship. When we die, our bodies return to Earth and our emotions vanish, but the part of us that is the One Consciousness continues beyond space and time toward Enlightenment and union with God.

o   Why shouldn't you fear your own death or the loss of someone close to you?

o   What are the key aspects of our eternal self, and how do they interact?

o   In what ways can you use your eternal self's compass to make better choices even when your human needs are calling you to an earthly desire?

o   Do you think individual lives can impact the eternal self?

o   How would you make the journey out of this land toward the light of your divine soul when you can't understand where you are going?

IN CLOSING: Remember Who You Are

The final section pulls together and interweaves some of the key ideas in the book. Readers will see and celebrate how hearts that were divided and possibly broken can become whole again. They'll recognize the signs of a changed heart and know that they can be shattered by life, yet still be whole with the universe. They'll remember the beauty of their unbreakable wholeness before they act on egoic impulses. Readers will also be reminded of how they can find balance between their secular selves (which solve problems and serve humanity) and their sacred selves (which access the One Consciousness, where there is direct connection to the Divine). If readers experience inner transformation, however fleeting, and understand (a) that all people are an indivisible whole in a way we cannot comprehend, (b) that even our smallest action can generate positive or negative energy throughout the universe, and (c) that we, in our own essence, are infinitely vast, then the information in this book will go beyond mere words and abstract concepts. Readers will recognize who they truly are and, in the process, contribute to the healing of this ailing world, where the boundaries of love, harmony, and even civility are being strenuously tested in families and other communities large and small.

o   What do you think should happen for a change in human consciousness to occur?

o   If unconsciousness seems inevitable, what can avert it?

o   What is your vision for a broader spiritual contribution to the world and beyond?

o   How would you share the magic of your spiritual transformation and awakening in the hope that it would amplify positive change in the world through the themes outlined in this book?

Appendix 1: Key Concepts of Sufism Shared with This Book

Appendix 1 provides a brief history and the essential principles of modern Sufism. This book is compatible with the path that Sufism has made possible for those of us who want to take advantage of the here and now through abandoning our ego (which tricks us into disconnecting from ourselves, from one another, from nature, and from God) and surrendering to the beloved God while we are still in the human state. When we recognize that love, which rises above the differences that divide us, is a core attribute of God, we begin to view with tolerance even things that we looked upon with contempt. As this vision develops, it occupies every moment of our life. We see our own image in others, and we see God's manifestations in nature. These valuable Sufi lessons expressed in rich mystical poetry are very much alive today, especially among the well-educated who are becoming aware of the spiritual crisis in the current world. The bitterness that exists today between and within nations is due primarily to the lack of love, which has been buried, but not lost, in the human soul.

o   What is the relevance of Sufi principles to you? Explain why.

o   How does Sufism appeal to people's capacity for compassion?

o   How has this book affected your prior understanding of Sufism?

o   Why does Sufism's account of spirituality transcend religious, national, and geographical boundaries?

Appendix 2: Psymentology

Appendix 2 gives a brief account of Taheri's concept of "psymentology," which focuses on correcting the underlying causes of mental and emotional disorders, such as feelings of despair, apathy, and hopelessness, which tend to sap vital energy. It does this by redirecting the positive and negative energies of the eternal self such that they work together in tandem. Our particular limitations are of no account in this process. We are only the channel through which the Links of Grace work. All that is essential is to have an impartial witnessing mind. Apart from that, we may hold any views on religion, or none. God could scarcely have made it simpler, and yet it seldom fails to work when given a fair trial. Once emotional disorders have been diagnosed by the Divine Intelligence, body cells begin correcting themselves by maximizing the feeling of liveliness and minimizing energy drain during the day.

o How do the five senses create positive and negative qualia? What is their source?

o Think of an activating event in your life which led to emotional drainage or cheeriness. What would be a rational way to interpret the event? What would be an irrational way to interpret the event?

o Describe the causation process for our positive or negative feelings.

Farsi Equivalents of Key Concepts in This Book

A

Ability to carry out an action: توان بالفعل
Absence of tools in spiritual practice: دنیای بی ابزاری
Activating events: حوادث بیرونی

Adam (a symbolic figure in the unipolar world): نفس واحد
Adjacent universes: جهانهای مجاور
Appearance: واقعیت

Arduous path to Enlightenment marked by intervals of destruction and resumption: کوی خرابات
Astral body: کالبد اختری
Attribute: صفت
Automatically: مداوم
Awareness: آگاهی

B

Being naturally rooted in the state of One Consciousness: شناور
Big Bang: مهبانگ
Bipolar world: جهان دو قطبی
Blessing: برکت
Brain cognition (which is capable of storing information): ذهن ماده

293

C

Cellular-level consciousness: شعور جزء
Collective cognition: ذهن جمعی
Collectively: جمعی
Complementary medicine: فرادرمانی

Connection: اتصال
Consciousness: شعور
Consciousness fields: میدانهای شعوری
Consecutive worlds: جهانهای متوالی
Constant I: من ثابت
Crossroad between any two worlds: برزخ
Cycle of lives: انا لله وانا الیه راجعون (چرخه جهان دو قطبی)

D

Divine Guide: روح هادی
Divine Intelligence: هوشمندی
Divine qualities: تجلیات
Duality: تضاد بنیادی

E

Egoic thoughts (e.g., seeking power): تیک های شخصیتی
Enlightenment: کمال
Enthusiasm: اشتیاق
Eternal self: آدم

F

Facilitators: شبکه مثبت
Feeling of emotional depletion: دشارژ
Feeling of emotional recharge or renewal: شارژ
Fields of consciousness: میدانهای شعوری
Fundamental particles (smallest particles of an atom): ذرات بنیادی
Fundamental vibrations: ارتعاشات بنیادی

G

God willing: انشاالله

God's deliverer (Divine Intelligence): کارگزار الهی

God's determination: اراده الهی

God's reflection: وجه الله

God's soul (containing Awareness originated from the One
  Consciousness): روح الله

Gratitude belongs only to God: الحمدالله

H

Hardware: سخت افزار

Heaven: جنتی

Hidden energy: انرژی پنهان

Hidden state: حیات تاریک

Holistic perspective on physical, cognitive, psychological, and
  other dimensions: کل نگری

Human being (our form in this earthly world): انسان

I

Illusionary: مجاز

Individual granting the Complementary Medicine Link of Grace:
  فرادرمانگر

Individual having inclination against Enlightenment:
  من ضد کمال (شیطان)

Individual having inclination toward Enlightenment: من کمال جو

Individual seeking the Complementary Medicine Link of Grace:
  فرادرمانگیر

Individually: فردی

Indivisible (whole): فردانیت

Inhibitors: شبکه منفی

Irrational perception: بینش غلط

J

Judgment Day: قیامت

L

Life force energy (*prana, qi*): نیروی کیهانی
Links of Grace: حلقه های رحمانیت
Local consciousness: شعور جزء
Lord of the worlds: رب العالمین

M

Master (someone who attends to both the "realm of love" and
    "realm of the mind"): رند
Matter: ماده
Mind: کالبد ذهن
Multitudinous (motion, space, etc.): کثرت در کیهان

N

Negative axis of being: محور وجودی منفی
Negative frame of mind (allowing negative vibrations to get in):
    فاز منفی
Nonjudgmental individuals: افراد بدون پیش داوری
Nothingness: عدم, هیچ

O

One and only: واحدیت
One Consciousness: شعور کل

P

Parallel universes: جهانهای موازی
Path that separates us from each other and from the universe:
    راه کثرت
Perception: بینش
Personality blueprint: نفس

Physical depression: افسردگی جسمی

Physical state: حیات روشن

Physiological dimension: کالبد جسمی

Positive axis of being: محور وجودی مثبت

Positive frame of mind (blocking negative vibrations from getting in): فاز مثبت

Potential: توان بالقوه

Pre–Big Bang supermassive black hole: سیاهچاله کیهانی

Presence: حس حضور

Programmed in our original software or nature: من برنامه ریزی شده (شخصیت اولیه)

Protective Layer: لایه محافظ

Psychological dimension: کالبد روانی

Psymentology: ذهن - روان شناسی

Q

Qualitative (not measurable, like love): کیفیت

Quantitative (measurable, like numbers): کمیت

R

Rational perception: بینش صحیح

Reality (who we truly are, the One Consciousness): حقیقت

Realm of love (beyond thoughts): پله عشق

Realm of the mind (external manifestations): پله عقل

Retreat to let the One Consciousness reveal itself: حذف من

Reward for enthusiasm: مزد اشتیاق

S

Sacred Cognitive Dimension: کالبد ذهن (ذهن حیات)

Sacred walk to oneness: راه وحدت

Self-changing impossibility (primary trait): من برنامه ریزی شده

Self-changing potentiality (secondary trait): من برنامه پذیر

Self-obsession: خود شیفتگی

Shared Link of Grace: حلقه عام

Software: نرم افزار

Software that gives us survival instinct, among others: نهاد

Software that gives us tendencies for good and bad and the free
  will to choose between them: فطرت

Software that overrides all genetic and environmental makeup: بنیاد

Soul: روح

Space: فضا

Spaceless: فرامکان

Spirituality: معنویت

Spirituality is beyond religion: معنویت فرادینی است

Split-second union or "glance": نظر

T

Time: زمان

Timeless: فرازمان

U

Union with God: وحدت (ازدواج نفس وروح الله در جهنم)

Unipolar world: جهان یک قطبی

Unity in the universe: وحدت در کیهان

Universal mysticism (Erfan-e Halgheh): عرفان حلقه

Unseen and unseen: غیب الغیوب

V

Variable I: من متحرک

Vibrational depression: افسردگی تشعشعاتی

Vice: شر

Virtue: خیر

W

Wishes of the personality blueprint: اراده

Witness: شاهد

Recommended Reading

Abbott, Edwin. A. Flatland: *A Romance of Many Dimensions* (Illustrated). Prabhat Books, 2008.

Chubb, Tanaaz. *The Power of Positive Energy: Everything You Need to Awaken Your Soul, Raise Your Vibration, and Manifest an Inspired Life*. Adams Media, Massachusetts, 2017.

Dalai Lama and Kamalashila. *Stages of Meditation: The Buddhist Classic on Training the Mind*. Shambhala, Boulder, 2019.

Davies, Oliver. *Meister Eckhart Selected Writings*. Penguin Books, 1994.

Davis, Andrew and Clayton Philip. *How I Found God in Everyone and Everywhere: An Anthology of Spiritual Memoirs*. Monkfish Book Publishing Company, New York, 2018.

Delia, Lalah. *Vibrate Higher Daily: Live Your Power*. Harper One, New York, 2019.

Dennett, Daniel C. *Consciousness Explained*. Little, Brown and Company, New York, 1991.

Dyer, Wayne. *The Power of Intention: Learning to Co-Create Your World Your Way*. Hay House, Inc. New York, 2004.

Eisenstein, Charles. *The More Beautiful World Our Hearts Know Is Possible*. North Atlantic Books, Berkeley, 2013.

Emerson, Ralph Waldo. *Nature and Other Essays*. Dover Publications, Inc., New York, 2009.

Emerson, Ralph Waldo. *The Most Important Essays by Ralph*

Waldo Emerson. Studium Publishing, 2018.

Goldstein, Joseph. *One Dharma: The Emerging Western Buddhism*. Harper Collins, 2002.

Gray, Kyle. *Raise Your Vibration: 111 Practices to Increase Your Spiritual Connection*. Hay House UK Ltd, 2016.

Horgan, John. *Mind-Body Problems: Science, Subjectivity & Who We Really Are*. Abridged E-book edition, 2018.

Huxley, Aldous. *The Perennial Philosophy: An Interpretation of Great Mystics, East and West*. Harper Perennial, New York, 2012.

Inayat Khan, Hazrat. *The Unity of Religious Ideals*. Sufi Order Publications, New York, 1979.

Kabat-Zinn, Jon. *Coming to Our Senses: Healing Ourselves and the World Through Mindfulness*. Hyperion, New York, 2005.

Kastrup, Bernardo. *Brief Peeks Beyond: Critical Essays on Metaphysics, Neuroscience, Free Will, Skepticism, and Culture*. iff Books, Winchester, UK, 2015.

Kastrup, Bernardo. *Decoding Jung's Metaphysics*. iff Books, Winchester, UK, 2021.

Kastrup, Bernardo. *Decoding Schopenhauer's Metaphysics*. iff Books, Winchester, UK, 2020.

Kellough, Constance. *The How to Inner Peace: A Guide to a New Way of Living*, Namaste, 2021.

Lanza, Robert and Matej Pavsic. *The Grand Biocentric Design: How Life Creates Reality*. BenBella Books, Texas, 2020.

Masri, Ziad. *Reality Unveiled: The Hidden Keys of Existence That*

Will Transform Your Life (and the World). Awakened Media LLC, 2017.

McDowell, Alice. *Dance of Light: Christian, Sufi, and Zen Wisdom for Today's Spiritual Seeker*. Wisdom Editions, Minneapolis, 2022.

Menon, Sangeetha. *The Beyond Experience: Consciousness in Bhagavad Gita*. Bluejay Books, New Delhi, 2007.

Moezzi, Melody. *The Rumi Prescription: How an Ancient Mystic Poet Changed My Modern Manic Life*. Penguin Random House LLC, 2020.

Myss, Caroline. *Anatomy of the Spirit: The Seven Stages of Power and Healing*. Harmony Books, New York, 2017.

Nasr, Seyyed Hossein. *The Garden of Truth: The Vision and Promise of Sufism, Islam's Mystical Tradition*. Harper Collins Publishers, New York, 2007.

Osho. *Awareness: The Key to Living in Balance*. St. Martin's Griffin, New York, 2001.

Prabhavananda, Swami and Christopher Isherwood. *The Song of God: Bhagavad Gita*. Hollywood, Vedanta Press, 1944.

Pollan, Michael. *How to Change Your Mind: What the New Science of Psychedelics Teaches Us about Consciousness, Dying, Addiction, Depression, and Transcendence*. Penguin Press, 2018.

Rahman, Imam Jamal. *Sacred Laughter of the Sufis: Awakening the Soul with the Mulla's Comic Teaching Stories and Other Islamic Wisdom*. Skylight Paths Publishing, Vermont, 2014.

Rawat, Prem. *Hear Yourself: How to Find Peace in a Noisy World*. Harper One, New York, 2021.

Roger, Derek. *Enlightened Living: A Book of Being.* Austin Macauley Publishers, London, 2019.

Singer, Michael A. *The Untethered Soul: The Journey Beyond Yourself.* New Harbinger Publications, Inc., 2007.

Snyder, Kimberly. *You Are More Than You Think You Are: Practical Enlightenment for Everyday Life.* Hay House, New York, 2022.

Taheri, Mohammad Ali. *Halgeh (Interuniversal) Mysticism.* Interuniversal Press, 2006.

Taheri, Mohammad Ali. *The Human Worldview.* Interuniversal Press, 2010.

Taylor, Jill Bolte. *My Stroke of Insight: A Brain Scientist's Personal Journey.* Viking, New York, 2006.

Tolle, Eckhart. *A New Earth: Awakening to Your Life's Purpose.* Penguin Books, New York, 2005.

Tolle, Eckhart. *Stillness Speaks.* New World Library, California, 2003.

Tolle, Eckhart. *The Power of Now: A Guide to Spiritual Enlightenment.* Namaste Publishing, Vancouver, Canada, 1999.

Tyson, Neil deGrasse. *Astrophysics for People in a Hurry.* W.W. Norton, New York, 2017.

Walsh, Neale Donald. *Conversations with God: An Uncommon Dialogue,* Book 1. G. P. Putnam's Sons Publishers, New York, 1996.

Walsh, Neale Donald. *Conversations with God: Living in the World with Honesty, Courage, & Love,* Book 2. Hampton Roads Publishing Company, Inc., Charlottesville, Virginia, 1997.

White, S., Sabatini, J., Park, B.J., Chen, J., Bernstein, J., and Li, M. (2021. The 2018 Oral Reading Fluency Study (NCES 2021-025). U.S. Department of Education. Washington, DC: Institute of Education Sciences, National Center for Education Statistics.

White, Sheida. *Taking Off from Tehran: An Iranian Immigrant's Memoir of Leaving Behind Gender Expectations and Succeeding in America.* Wise Ink, Minneapolis, 2022.

Whitman, Walt. *Leaves of Grass.* Pandora's Box Classics, 2004.

Yogananda, Paramahanasa. *Autobiography of a Yogi.* Self-Realization Fellowship, Los Angeles, 2007.

Endnotes

1   In his book *The Power of Now*, Eckhart Tolle says that there are parts of the Bible that use symbolism in ways that no one has understood. Here are a few: The quote "Then I saw a new heaven and a new earth, for the first heaven and the first Earth had passed away" represents the moment we attain complete consciousness. The phrase "the light of the world," which is used to describe Jesus, suggests that Jesus is simply a man who reached Enlightenment, or, perhaps more accurately, was born Enlightened and manifested in a spiritual being having a human experience. The quote "Jesus never relinquished his body and ascended to heaven with it" is another symbolism intended to show how important the body is to one's journey to Enlightenment and that transformation happens inside the body, not outside of it.

2   Months after my realization that my spiritual belonging did not lie with the Torah study group, I learned that there are other schools of thought with roots in Jewish mysticism that make deeper interpretations of the Torah, in ways that are more in line with the teachings of Taheri. This Jewish tradition teaches the recognition of God, the purpose of creation, and the afterlife. Specifically, it teaches that there is a piece of God in our bodies (the Soul) which never dies. The profound reality of our soul

imbued with God's breath cannot be eradicated by the accident of bodily death. Not only were we created by God, but the root of our existence is here and now with God. Our divine soul has the faculties with which God functions as the Creator, including kindness and knowing. In the same way that an already divine reality exists within our bodies, there is a degree of our physical body in the soul. The body is a tangible form that preserves and reflects the soul within it. It becomes the temple of the divine soul, so to speak. There is thus a connection between the body, which returns to dust, and the divine soul, which yearns to reconnect with its Source. We have existence in all realms of being, from the spiritual (sacred) to the physical (secular), from microcosm to macrocosm, and from subjective revelation to objective knowing. The Torah also says that in hell, the soul undergoes cleansing of its egoic thoughts before it enters heaven. It is these egoic thoughts' assertion of their separate existence that distances us from God more than anything else. (For more discussion, see *Perceiving Our Destination* in chapter 11).

3   There are far too many different schools of belief, and they are all loaded with their own jargon and special concepts. The amount of discrepancy is, for me at least, mind-boggling. Frankly, I don't care that much about keeping track of all the ways one philosophy, religion, denomination, or sect differs in its orthodoxy from the others. To me, it's all One.

4   Spirituality (معنویت) is a broad concept with room for many perspectives. In the context of this book, it includes a sense of connection to our inner self, the One Consciousness, as a way of resisting the constant temptations of the ego, a key component of separation from others. Knowing that our lives have significance

that originates from a web of relationship and existence that is in perfect unity helps us to transcend shallow understandings of matter and ascend into Enlightenment, the ultimate purpose of our creation. In this view, we don't necessarily become good by trying to do good things or being kind, but rather by finding and allowing the goodness that is already within us to emerge. In other words, spirituality includes but goes beyond "helping people around us who are suffering" to include "deep work on ourselves"; that is, to discover the ultimate nature of who we are and to carry that Awareness in our journey, which started from the source of all existence, the One Consciousness. Humanity and love will naturally and automatically follow when we experience oneness with others and the universe, resulting in a happier society. Spiritualism not only goes beyond ordinary morality, it goes beyond religion (معنویت فرادینی است) for many.

5   The word *consciousness* remains at once the most familiar and most mysterious aspect of our lives. Perhaps the only widely agreed-upon notion about the topic is the intuition that it exists. In the context of this book, the term *consciousness* should not be confused with (a) the word *conscience*, a human concept whereby we distinguish right from wrong; (b) human cognition and introspection that allow reflection upon our own thoughts and experiences; (c) raising political or social consciousness; (d) regaining consciousness after fainting or entering an altered state of consciousness caused by medication; (e) "being conscious," the basic sensory awareness we have of changes in our environment, which is easy to measure experimentally; or (f) any other state of consciousness that emerges from the operations of the brain.

6   By "not being subject to dualities that characterize our

bipolar world," I mean that there is no opposition or contrast, such as good and bad, cold and warm, or real and illusory.

7   Reductionists and materialists, on the other hand, hold the position that while consciousness may exist, it can be fully understood as being created by matter (the brain), allowing some time for evolution to work its magic. In other words, they say that the brain emits consciousness. Their inability to explain how consciousness emerges from matter is known as the "hard problem of consciousness," a phrase coined by David Chambers. In reality, there is no "hard problem" of consciousness to begin with if we don't conceptualize a universe outside consciousness and then postulate that consciousness was somehow generated by that same universe. Consciousness is the sole reality that is independent, beyond being. Without this shared assumption, people starting from different assumptions talk past each other to no good effect.

8   The word "experience," in the context of this book, has both a superior and an inferior meaning, depending on context. The superior meaning refers to direct perception of God in an act of Awareness. The inferior meaning is the "experience" induced naturally when we feel God's force postulating through our bodies. What suddenly triggers this experience in me is sometimes reading a certain phrase related to God, seeing a sunrise, or simply observing the orderliness of nature—all of which bring indescribable joy and tears (see discussion of "qualia" in Appendix 2, "Psymentology"). While the highest form of this kind, I'm not imagining it to be some special divine favor, the experience of union, or the experience of purely spiritual Awareness of God. I'm far from being perfectly selfless or Enlightened.

Still, neither one of the above experiences, superior and inferior, has relevance to the theatrical and ritualistic techniques used to generate high emotional appeal in some organized religions. This type of emotional experience tends to become an end in itself instead of a means to the eternal self's ultimate union with God through such inquiries as "Who am I?" "Where do I stand in relation to the universe and its Creator?" and "What must I do to come to my final end?"

While religion-prompted emotional experience may lead to a great good, it is often not gratuitous. That's because the contact between the eternal self and God is not direct but is mediated through religious authorities, who may either not have deep understanding of what their prophets actually said or be tempted to use their power for individual satisfaction.

9   A puzzle in discussions of consciousness is the conflict between epistemology (knowledge) and phenomenology (the subjective experience of consciousness). While the nearest empirical validation for the nature of consciousness is *experience*, Taheri has taken a serious turn to validate first-person experience by third-person consensus in his current studies.

10   Another useful analogy for the silent Awareness I call the One Consciousness is this: Imagine the One Consciousness as a stage in a theatre, which is in darkness except for the area illuminated by spotlight. In that moment, we become fully aware of what is in that spotlight (a bit of Awareness emanating from the One Consciousness), but the other parts don't go away or become less important. All that is required would be to move that spotlight for more to come into focus. For example, Beethoven's creative idea for composing his famous Fifth Symphony likely came to him at the moment where the spotlight was.

11   Traditional theories have confused *reality* (حقیقت) with its *appearance* (واقعیت). Moreover, they have confused reality's *qualitative* nature (کیفیت) with its *quantitative* descriptions (کمیت) such as matter and energy. Due to these confusions, some traditional scientists conclude that consciousness doesn't have stand-alone reality and can be explained in terms of the chemistry of the brain. This view ignores the fact that consciousness is *qualitative* in nature. It is *nonphysical* and thereby outside the workings of the brain. At the end, there is only One Consciousness. Everything else is the *appearance* of it.

12   The infinite must include all possibilities, including the possibility of evil. What is called evil is the result of our separation from the collective consciousness by clinging to our attachments to the material world. Our veils of imperfection (our egoic thoughts with which we usually identify ourselves and our existence) can be removed largely with God's help (see discussion of "Links of Grace" in Chapter 7).

13   There is no empirical universe outside consciousness itself. Symbolically speaking, consciousness is beyond the waves of the ocean—the living beings and inanimate objects—that conceal the steady and still water underneath the ocean—i.e., the One Consciousness. Because of the disturbance created by the waves, such as our egoic thoughts and associated emotions, we have the impression of separateness from each other and from the rest of the universe.

14   The seeming nothingness or emptiness of space seethes with unimaginable power that can penetrate in zero time, no

matter the distance, to help us perceive a fundamental oneness rather than individual entities separated by space.

15   I've found that connecting with the One Consciousness gives me the highest and most enduring level of spiritedness and joy without any of the side effects (such as boredom) associated with the repeated pleasures of the physical world (like having a favorite meal four nights in a row).

16   We are never so lacking in free will and so enslaved by desire as when we are in romantic love. It is the love that can break our heart and subject us to polarities of pain and joy. Buddha said we can make ourselves immune to heartbreak by detaching ourselves from desire, but without desire we become inhuman, according to Taheri. The divine love is transcending, yet containing, the romantic love. The divine connection we feel for *everyone* may resonate with a single person's secular characteristics (such as intellect, spirituality, emotions, or physical looks) in ways we don't understand, leading to a strong attraction and desire for intimacy. Sextual expression of love that doesn't cause hurt to anyone is the result of an exquisitely complex process which fuels all life.

17   As human beings, we all have egos. It is very much part of our primal "personality blueprint," which is present from birth. But the ego is a relative, not an absolute concept—meaning that it has both positive and negative aspects. What matters is how we handle it. As long as we are in control of our ego, it may work for us. A positive ego can mean, for example, a healthy sense of self-pride, a quiet sense of jealousy that motivates us to do better, or resilience when things go wrong. The ego becomes an issue when it starts controlling us, which, unfortunately, is most of the time. It is this

sense of the ego and the inability to distinguish it from reality that I refer to when I use the word "ego" (تیک های شخصیتی) throughout this book. An example of such ego is over-estimating our smartness, which can make people, especially those who cherish objectivity and humility, lose trust and respect for us. Other examples include focusing on the outcome rather than on the process and underestimating the effort and skill required to achieve goals.

Knowing the higher meaning of existence can change our perspective as to where we draw the line between the positive and negative ego. If we want to reach Enlightenment, then we go beyond our ego by relinquishing the need to control, to be approved, and to judge—the kind of things the ego is doing all the time. By taking some time to recognize the ego—the ideas that we construct about who we are—we can begin to shed some of its levels. For example, we can begin by not becoming self-absorbed, not trying to acquire evidence of our importance, and not dividing people into winners and losers. In doing so, we activate the power of oneness by transcending the ego. My mystical intuition tells me that without the ego, there can be no willpower; without willpower, no character.

18   Still, the love we feel for one another in this earthly world, especially the intense love of a man for a woman or of a woman for a man (in the romantic sense, not merely sexual attraction), is a key factor that brings us closer to divine love. It is the testing ground for the growth of spirituality. Such a love is a gift from God to us, which grows rather than diminishes as time goes on. This assertion does not negate the possibility of detachment from such a love for the love of God, which is the highest level. All other forms of love are reflections, albeit sometimes faint ones, of

this supreme love, which eventually liberates us from not only this world but also the next.

19   Consistent with this idea, English poet, John Donne, writes: "Any man's death diminishes me, because I am involved in mankind; and therefore, never send to know for whom the bell tolls; it tolls for thee [you]," suggesting that when a funeral bell tolls for another person's death, it marks the death of a part of us.

20   "Timeless" (فرازمان) means that there is no past or future. Nothing has a duration, whether it is in millionths of a second or billions of years. In other words, time has no independent existence on its own. Events can still be distinguished by the distance between them in the remaining dimensions, but all such events are occurring at a single instant. Time is programed into our software, so that, for example, we can keep appointments with relative ease in this universe. Broadly speaking, time is a tool our mind uses to weave information together into a coherent experience and to perceive changes in our universe.

21   "Spaceless" (فرامکان) means that there are no dimensions in which objects exist and move. Events can still be distinguished by the distance between them in the time dimension, but all such events are occurring at a single point in space. For example, if we cross a football field at lightspeed, the space would be barely the size of a period at the end of this sentence. Therefore, like time, space has no independent existence on its own. Again, it is part of the software program for the universe so that we can accomplish essential functions, such as searching for our cell phone in the right places. Time and space are often referred to as "space-time"

because they are related in the sense that motion in space affects passage of time.

It is conceivable to have no dimensions. In that case, events in reality would be seen as having no difference between them. Everything happens all at once and in the same place. That is, without space-time, everything would overlap and become indistinguishable from one another. Indeed, the whole world would become one indivisible whole without space-time.

22   The motion of electrons around the nucleus of atoms requires some clarification. The Bohr model suggests that electrons move around the nucleus in a fixed orbit as particles. However, one interpretation of the Schrodinger equation, the basis of quantum theory, is that an electron is not a particle orbiting the nucleus. The electron looks like a cloud of multidimensional wavelike oscillation that could be characterized as wavelet. In this cloud model, the electron is located throughout the cloud-like region around the nucleus.

23   A more technical description of the "dancing" electrons around atoms by some recent studies would be that material objects are composed of discrete packets of energy, characterized as fundamental particles, all of which are endlessly vibrating in different modes. These packets exchange energies and mutually constrain each other's movements. Under special conditions, the vibrations form a synchronized pattern, creating the effect of solidity. Using this description, my fingers processing words on my keyboard, are thought to be made up of molecules each of which is a vibrating bundle of individually vibrating atoms. These atoms include a vibrating bundle of individually vibrating nucleons enshrouded by multi-layered vibrating clouds in which are nested

individually vibrating electron clouds. Each nucleon is a vibrating bundle of quarks. Each quark is itself a vibrating packet of energy. The movements of all these bundles of packets of energy are orchestrated by energy exchanges facilitated by bosons, yet another kind of vibrating packet of energy. In short, according to these studies, fundamental particles are vibrating packets of pure energy, each of which is seemingly everywhere and nowhere simultaneously. Under special conditions, the boson vibrations form a synchronized pattern, creating the effect of energy fields, including electromagnetic fields.

24 The existence of Earth will not continue indefinitely. Eventually, the Sun will consume all of its fusible hydrogen. After it does so, it will then fuse heavier atoms into even heavier atoms. In the course of doing so, it will expand in physical volume to the point that it consumes all the inner planets including Earth.

25 The term "consciousness" in the context of this book applies not only to the universe that started nearly fourteen billion years ago and that we think of as the ongoing Big Bang, but potentially to other universes currently unknown to us and to the quiescent sea of consciousness that may lie between those universes. In other words, consciousness is everywhere, including areas we have not thought of. Some refer to "consciousness" as the "cosmos," which comes from the Greek word *kosmos*, meaning "order." While consciousness is assumed to be the same across all other possible universes, it would likely entail different constraints (such as time and space) outside our own universe. Therefore, there would likely be different laws of those universes.

26 "Nonlocal" is a term used by some to represent a

world-view that argues the reality of an interconnected universal field of relationships. It is closely related to the view presented in this book that there is a pervasive collective consciousness that conveys meaning. Individual forms, like our physical bodies, arise from this singular consciousness; thereby, they have a secondary status. However, while individual forms have a secondary status within the nonlocal paradigm, they each have a "local consciousness," a channel through which all interpretations are developed.

27   Taheri's online classes, which began in the spring of 2021, followed a different format. This book was slightly refined in light of those online classes, in which I participated, but no substantive changes were required to Taheri's original 2,250 pages of lecture notes in Farsi transcribed over a decade ago.

28   My statement that "everything that exists is the manifestation of God" is not to be confused with the position held by *pantheists,* who posit that God is the world and the world in its totality is God. What my statement asserts is not that God is the world, but that the world originates from and belongs to God. Said differently, the One Consciousness is the one and only fundamental, and every event in reality is an entailed effect of consciousness activity. Using Taheri's analogy, the reality of God is not affected by His "image" (his manifestations) in the mirror. That is, no change would occur to God if the mirror were to be broken. Creation is thereby seen as myriads of reflections of the divine qualities (تجلیات) in compassion and mercy. Furthermore, the relation of the world to God is not based solely on a temporal event called "at the beginning . . ." Creation is renewed at every instant, making possible our and the cosmos's continuous existence, in the

same way that each breath we take rejuvenates the continuation of our life.

29   The unipolar world refers to a world that has no time, space, or opposites.

30   The phrase "چرخه ی انا لله وانا اليه راجعون" means "We originated from God, and to Him we shall return."

31   By free will, I mean our capacity to make a conscious choice among competing options. For example, the other day I chose to politely end a text messaging session with someone I know well rather than extend an unpleasant exchange, which I had characterized as having an inappropriate tone and being judgmental. I asserted my free will based on what I know and have experience of about myself and about that individual, not factors that unfold without my personal awareness, control, or experience. The path my decision took was not predetermined. It constituted a free decision among several available paths.

Other times, my choice is not as straightforward, requiring negotiation with my ego. I allow myself to accommodate to my ego and enjoy the pleasure of something I like (dark chocolate, for example) or a "sinful" thought that isn't good for me, so long as I know when to stop and not feed a craving. Socrates once said, "True freedom means not being enslaved by your appetites." Resisting appetites and temptations is not an easy endeavor. It requires determination and sufficient free will, which God has given us so that we won't be puppets of our ego. In addition to constraints created by our ego, there are cultural, legal, economic, educational, and political constraints influencing our free will. And, for factors we have the least control over, such as physical, intellectual, and emotional limitations, the range of free will is even smaller. To ease these constraints and take responsibility for myself (rather than assigning my fate to my genes, my childhood environment, or divine plan), I try to rise above the earthly world and see it from the perspective of eternity.

Speaking of eternity, I thank Adam and Eve, the mythical names we've given to represent the first man and woman. Their act of eating the forbidden fruit of the tree of knowledge may not have been original sin, but rather a blessing. In being the first to make a wrong choice, they created the possibility of making any choice at all.

32   According to Taheri, *fundamental vibrations* (ارتعاشات بنیادی) initiate the movement of *fundamental particles* (ذرات بنیادی), beginning with the smallest particle, known as quarks, all the way to molecules. The pervasive energy of the fundamental vibrations is different in character from the energy of the fundamental particles in the material universe. We, humans, are made up of fundamental particles that make up the physical universe, but our consciousness is embedded into the fabric of the universe's fundamental vibrations, originated from the One Consciousness. This entity (the subject of chapter 5) is the origin of everything there is, albeit not in the realms of matter, energy, time, or space that are accessible to our knowing. Something more than simply "wonders of evolution" was required to (a) bring into being a cell with the inborn capability of transformation and to (b) direct that one-celled entity to achieve transformation into a fully functioning bug.

Extending the metaphor of the ocean to this context, the surface waves symbolize the entire physical universe. As we go deeper, the movements subside. Where there is no current at all lies the silent Awareness, consciousness, that which knows the story of the universe from the very beginning. Riding within the big ocean waves are inanimate objects creating the coarsest disturbance in the ocean. They likely have no consciousness, defined crudely here as having a sense of being an individual physical entity separate from (and unable to react to) the world that stimulates it, although inanimate objects are *within* cosmic consciousness. At the other extreme are the finest and tiniest ocean waves, representing human beings. They have the highest consciousness capable of both perceptual and abstract representation (that is, the way things interact with one another), although it varies by individuals. Animals and plants, which have moderate and low consciousness, respectively, fall between humans and inanimate objects. Animals are capable of perceptual (but not abstract) representation, and plants can only react to stimuli, as in the case of flowers turning to follow the sun.

It is indeed likely that these variations in consciousness relate to *free will*, accessible through humans' unique ability to engage in *self-reflection*, so that we can achieve something beyond the reach of the rest of nature and report experiential states—all resulting from humans' ability to engage in conceptual thinking and abstract reasoning. In short, there is a continuum of levels of being, ranging from zero in inanimate nature to subtle levels in plants and animals, to higher levels in mankind.

The ability to separate ourselves from our own objective experiences (self-reflection) is what gives meaning to life, according to Carl Jung. I'd take Jung's statement a step further by saying that self-reflection allows us to recognize our ego, which constantly produces stories about our past and what the future might be (such as becoming mentally paralyzed, being alone, change, getting old, or the unknown). Failure to recognize the ego leads us to bitterness, regret, and inability to accept "what is," which eventually results in fear and anxiety. This forces us away from the One Consciousness, in which resides life's profound meaning. In contrast, by reflecting upon and quieting our egoic tendencies, we increase access to the One Consciousness, the matrix of all existence. Notice the association of the One Consciousness with self-reflection, an aspect of the brain. We may say that the One Consciousness is self-luminous, and we are the reflecting body.

Without suggesting that dogs, for example, are devoid of inner experience, we can assume they probably lack the self-reflective introspection that allows humans to express their experiences, apply moral judgments, and grow spiritually. While each of the three entities (humans, animals, plants) has its own level of consciousness, they each play a role in the physical universe and the conscious substrate that contains it. For example, if we think of the entire kingdom of plants as being a single entity, some people may have awareness of being connected to plants, and they are likely to respond accordingly.

In short, while the universe is embedded in consciousness, this doesn't mean that every entity in the universe has acquired the same *degree* of consciousness. Additionally, the ocean waves symbolize not only our own universe, but other potential universes—namely, adjacent universes (جهانهای مجاور) and parallel universes (جهانهای موازی)—whose properties, if they exist, are a mystery to us at this time. Eventually all waves (small or large, within or across universes) will collapse such that they are no longer a distinguishable feature of the One Consciousness. That is, we begin and end with the One Consciousness.

33   The word "field" in the term "consciousness fields" simply implies that consciousness traverses in vast unseen pathways. Each of these pathways has an influence throughout the physical universe, which is within the substrate of overall consciousness. While

we cannot change the causal constraints described by the laws of the universe (see discussion of "Laws of the Universe" in chapter 6), we do have the power within those constraints to impact events through a vast array of consciousness fields using methods not yet explained by science (see "Links of Grace" in chapter 7).

34   In 1687, for example, Isaac Newton discovered the physical Law of Motion, which is governed by three principles, the first being that objects in a state of uniform motion will remain in that state unless an external force acts on them. For example, if no forces act on a ball rolling across a flat surface, it will continue to roll at constant speed forever without change in direction—a departure from a previous understanding that objects need to be constantly pushed if they are to be kept in motion. Of course, if a force does act on the ball (for example, if the ball is thrown), it would make the speed of the ball faster in proportion to the force of the hand. To figure out the path of the ball, one would need to know its *position*, its *speed*, and the *forces* acting on it. Spacecraft, for example, use this principle to maintain their orientation.

35   There is a slowly developing acceptance by reductionists of the need to move beyond describing matter alone. What exposed their weak proposition was partly their failure to provide a means of explaining how consciousness emerges into our Awareness from the interaction of neural activities in the brain alone. Neural activity is an externally observable effect of consciousness, and not its cause. Life affords a much richer milieu in which the processes of both science and spirituality can be understood, studied, and validated, each using their own governing principles and methodologies.

36   The power and beauty of the universal (physical) laws is that they apply everywhere. For example, if you land on another planet with a healthy alien civilization, they will be exposed to the same laws that we are on Earth. However, consciousness might entail different constraints outside our own universe. The descriptions of those constraints (such as time or location dependency) would be the laws of those universes, and may not be the same as the laws in our universe.

37   As I wrote these words, the song "Hero" by Mariah Carey popped into my mind in a flash. In it she sings, "There's an answer if you reach into your soul. . . . It's a long road when you face the world alone, but you'll finally see the truth, that a hero lies in you." The "soul" in the context of this book would refer to God's Soul (روح الله), discussed earlier, and the "truth" to its Awareness, the current topic. Such coincidences are referred to as *synchronicity* by Swiss psychotherapist Carl Jung. I see these seemingly insignificant events as being orchestrated in harmony and am not surprised when the perfect person appears or when information arrives unexpectedly in different forms giving me the information I need. I accept the idea that there are no accidents in a universe that has an invisible consciousness at its Source. These events, which are somehow associated but have no scientific explanations, defy our conception of space and time, and can be meaningful. Their meaning seems to rest on spiritual laws, which Jung calls *archetypes*.

I think of the similarity in meaning evoked by coinciding events that occur instantaneously across space as a "wink" from the divine reassuring me that I am on the right path (for example, a song popping into my head that captured the essence of my thoughts with startling specificity). This equivalence of meaning between our own state of consciousness (perhaps achieved through presence) and the world around us is suggestive of a universal unity, the One Consciousness, that underlies both the inner state and the physical world itself. Allow me to belabor this a bit more for clarity. The concept of synchronicity suggests that we relate to the physical world (and it relates to us) not only according to the physical principles of causality (such as a flash of light from a bolt of lightning, which we understand by observing the regularities of nature's behavior), but also spontaneously according to an unseen underlying principle. The physical principles of causality are just approximations of this underlying principle. In other words, what we do observe are the results of the action of an underlying principle that, in and of itself, remains invisible to us. Because the universal laws are approximations of this underlying principle, they necessarily allow for ambiguity. These ambiguities differ from the scientific concept of "randomness," where there is no clue as to what will happen next.

Perhaps it is in recognition of these meaningful ambiguities that many handmade Persian carpets contain a deliberate mistake made in the execution of the pattern. Jung's concept of synchronicity takes these "chance" events as meaning something more than mere chance. Unlike the Copenhagen interpretation, where the act of observation causes a transformation to occur, in synchronicity, the seemingly isolated events, which occur at the same moment of observation, convey a common meaning to the observer. The observer does not make this happen by observing. They simply uncover a meaning not entailed by material cause, but rather implied by the simultaneous occurrence of the events.

38   Once we have known divine Awareness through connecting with the consciousness that we all share regardless of our religious beliefs or lack thereof, being alert (هوشیار) can become

an enduring by-product. Even when our thoughts are still, we are alert. Taheri reminds us that we must be alert in every ordinary activity. Even when we are resting, we're a watcher. We may forget and get involved in some emotion, such as anger or fear, resulting from egoic thoughts. We should remember to run back to our center of watching. Life changes its quality, and everything, even walking, will be done consciously, rather than as a robotic movement. Alert witnessing or alert presence must not be situational. Moreover, Taheri tells us that we need to understand how our witnessing relates to the broader understanding of the nature of reality, including Enlightenment.

Psychedelic drugs, such as LSD and psilocybin (the active compound found in "magic mushrooms"), alter the natural state of mind to create a sense of mystical experience, often in the form of ego-dissolution (that is, diminished sense of self as distinct individuals) accompanied by bliss and a growing sense of oneness. So does a massive hemorrhage flooding and shutting down the left hemisphere of the brain, and so does witnessing discussed in this book. While qualitatively different—*changing* the mind through drugs, *shutting down* the mind through hemorrhage, and *transcending* the mind through witnessing—in all three cases, one's thinking and, consequently, one's judgment and ego are quieted.

Egos, as noted throughout this book, are mental constructs that perform certain tasks on our behalf. Chief among these is maintaining the boundary between self and the other by means of attachments to wealth, education, and the rest. It is only when these boundaries fade, as they seem to do under the influence of psychedelics, massive stroke, and alert witnessing, that we can perceive the boundaries of our earthly bodies dissolving and melting into something much larger than anything we can imagine—a web of universal interconnectedness. Instead of the constant chattering of the brain that attaches us to the egoic details of our life, there is a growing sense of alert presence, euphoria, and unity. These experiences mean that we are capable of tapping into a blissful state of being amidst the normal chaos of our life—an alternate reality, another plane of existence, a higher dimension, a glimpse behind the veil of *maya* (the Hindu term for the illusion of reality), a deep sense of connectedness to the One Consciousness.

For me, alert witnessing, coupled with the help of divine intervention, is a small price to pay in exchange for these lavish and enduring gifts, with none of the potential side effects associated with psychedelics or massive stroke. Ineffability is a hallmark of the spiritual experience of connecting with this unitive, non-dual consciousness. So, allow me to put into words this mystical experience as faithfully as I can recount it. None of what I say here is a function of swallowing a chemical substance or brain hemorrhage, nor is it independently verifiable by scientific methods (at least not yet).

To review, witnessing, followed by activation of the divine Links of Grace (discussed in chapter 7), entails melting of our thoughts and thereby freedom from the tyranny of our egos, which burden us with attachments to objects, feelings, people, and, importantly, our conceptual mind—all leading to the fear of dying and anything else life can throw at us.

When thoughts and egos are out of the way and we have achieved a level of detachment from our desires, Awareness reveals something waiting to be discovered. This something, the hallmark of my mystical experience, may be (a) a sense of merging into a larger totality away from a bounded self and connectedness to all beings and the environment; (b) a wonder-filled universe and worldly beauty; (c) placidity in the hard-won order of my brain as a result of containment of the ego, which feeds on the rigidity of the mind, so that I can be open to new experiences and insights; (d) the presence of God everywhere; (e) knowledge of life's purpose; (f) conviction that love, unattributable to any individual but God, is everything; (g) a sense that every moment exists in perfect isolation, because the sequencing of events requires intellectual connection that the mind no longer performs; (h) the softening of lines of any kind that set distinctions, dualities, and hierarchies, such as self and other; or (i) a touch of eternity—the ultimate reality that goes all the way back to the pure consciousness that caused the bipolar universe to fall into time, space, and other dimensions.

The effects of the ego-transcending Awareness gleaned from my spiritual practice are enduring because I stay motivated and mindful that I am part of an eternal structure from which I cannot be separated. In my everyday life, I feel I'm noticeably more present to the moment and less inclined to worry about what's next. I reflect about death, infinity, and how fortunate it is to be alive in my little patch of cosmic real estate. I'm also surprised by how little it takes for waves of love for God to wash over me and make me tear up, unexpectedly, all at once. Witnessing has become a "default" or sustained state of consciousness, shaping my everyday life in profound ways by awakening compassion, gratitude, and wonder that are hidden in plain sight, the magical beauty into which I'm born and to which my physical body will return at the end of this life.

The mindset and prior spiritual knowledge that one brings along may affect the psychedelic experience, or lack thereof. A relative of mine who had taken "magic mushroom" in his youth recalled in vivid detail his experience as magnification of all sensory perceptions. He clearly relished the opportunity to relive that blissful experience for me. I heard a similar story from a friend who took LSD in graduate school to boost his self-confidence.

While traces of these experiences may have remained accessible, they didn't seem to have the numinous quality of arousing divine experience or bringing either one of them closer to a belief in a cosmic form of consciousness. A psychedelic experience by itself may not prepare one for a spiritual life. The effects of psychedelic experience, whether they prove durable or evanescent, might depend, in addition to the mindset and prior spiritual knowledge gleaned perhaps from reading, on whether or not there is recollection and reinforcement of the mystical experience in daily living.

In short, three qualitatively different mechanisms (*changing* the mind through psychedelic drugs, *shutting down* the mind through brain hemorrhage, and *transcending* the mind through alert witnessing) are capable of producing similar mystical experiences: a sense of unity, eternity, ego dissolution, and so on. These direct experiences are *attributes* of our collective consciousness, which is indifferent to humans' morality, religion, or belief system. This observation is perfectly in line with Sufi's key message, and by extension with the philosophy of this book: Using different paths, human beings can have direct personal experience of God—their only purpose on this earth. Note that God is essentially our collective consciousness (explained in chapter 6). In our essence, we are all part of this collective consciousness, and our only purpose on this earth is to recognize and sustain that Awareness.

The specific path we choose must be conducive to our own spiritual life and to the many exigencies that are required just to survive. The benefits of each path can only be answered by the one who has undertaken the experience, not by onlookers. People view the world from the unique perspective of their individual experiences. Sometimes these experiences are being ground down by the "wheel of life" (چرخه جهان دو قطبی), and sometimes they are on top. That's to be expected.

39   In my earlier days, I prized fashion and tended to buy my designer apparel from Saks Fifth Avenue and Neiman Marcus. I've spent my fair share of money and time engaging in consumerism—long enough to learn that it doesn't offer lasting pleasures. While I still partake, I recognize its limited gratification.

40   While the label "nothingness" is used in both Taheri's teachings and Buddhism (a philosophy founded by the Buddha, a Hindu, more than 2,500 years ago), it is interpreted differently by the two philosophies. The teachings of Taheri are rooted in his own divine revelations, with striking similarity to the revelations expressed in poetry by Persian mystics, in prose by the Western mystics described in Huxley's *The Perennial Philosophy: An Interpretation of Great Mystics, East and West*, and in epic story by the five-thousand-year-old *Bhagavad Gita*.

The mystics' idea is that the singular God has imbued His soul into us. As such, the concept of God as the expression of "nothingness" in Taheri's teachings takes on a whole different meaning than the concept of "nothingness" as viewed by mainline Buddhism. Having God's Soul (روح الله) at the heart of our being necessarily implies that there is an *eternal self*. It also implies that *ego* is the eternal self's most formidable obstacle to *Enlightenment*, subsequent *union with God*, access to the treasure box of Awareness, and eventually reconnection with the One Consciousness—i.e., nothingness.

The notions of God, eternal self, ego, union with God, treasure box of Awareness, and reconnection of the eternal self with the One Consciousness are, to my incomplete knowledge, irrelevant to the mainline Buddhist's notion of "nothingness." The path to Enlightenment (Nirvana) in Buddhism is through *meditation* (calming the mind through objects of concentration, such as the breath, a mantra, a mental note, or a visual image) and development of *morality*, which means avoidance of harmful actions: three of body (killing, stealing, sexual misconduct), four of speech (lying, harsh words, gossip, and useless talk), and three of mind (covetousness, ill will, and wrong view).

Meditation and ethical living are said to free individuals from suffering in a world full of pain perpetuated by attachments. These fundamental elements have remained the same, despite being reinvigorated over the centuries by various schools of Buddhism. Buddhism is thus a pragmatic philosophy which questioned the established tenets of ancient Indian thoughts that began with the *Bhagavad Gita*, instead paying allegiance to freeing the mind from suffering by encouraging meditation and engendering morality.

In Taheri's teaching, morality naturally and automatically follows, like a shadow, when we harmonize ourselves with God and His creations, rather than being externally imposed. We have the potential (توان بالقوه) to do that using the assistance of the "gardener," the Divine Intelligence, to supply us with "water" and "soil," the Links of Grace. When we do align ourselves with God (akin to the One Consciousness), we perceive, experience, and emulate His qualities, such as compassion and forgiveness. When we move away from the confines of philosophical statements and enter into the world of *direct experience* with the One Consciousness, reaching across the boundaries of nationality, language, religion, and culture naturally follows without having to cultivate compassionate acts through effort. Awareness that is already there has been awakened, and when good comes on its own accord, it has a grace, a simplicity, a humbleness. It doesn't ask for reward because it is its own reward.

There appears to be, nonetheless, some common ground between the two philosophies when it comes to the notion of "nothingness," including the belief that we are connected to an absolute truth by an unbreakable bond.

41   Heisenberg's Uncertainty Principle is a limit on our power to observe. Specifically, it says that it is impossible to design an apparatus to determine the position and speed of an electron without at the same time interfering with its pattern. The claim that the act of observation perturbs the process of being observed, has created a growing confusion in the question of how electrons (without which, matter at all scales, including the water we drink and the smartphone we use, wouldn't exist) really behave. Heisenberg's Uncertainty Principle goes against our intuition—namely that the physical properties of an object (such as the shape and position of electrons of which my teacup is made) should have the same values even when the object is not being observed.

Schrodinger's equation in 1926 presumed that fundamental particles were "point particles." Using his mathematical equation, Schrodinger was able to describe the likelihood of finding an electron in a certain position around the nucleus: where the wave function is most dense. He made no ontological interpretation of the wave function. This became the basis of what would come to be known as Quantum Physics. Subsequent research led many physicists to characterize an electron as more like a cloud than a particle. Schrodinger's equation makes no comment on the human observer or consciousness.

However, the *Copenhagen Interpretation*, posed by Bohr in the 1920s, says that an observer's eyes (presumably a human's consciousness) can bring precision to the position and velocity of quantum particles like electrons, which otherwise exist in a blurred state (that is, exist in all their possible states at once). Bohr's interpretation, if valid, has direct implications for everyday experiences which involve large number of particles moving very slowly. For example, there is some uncertainty about the particles that make up what's underneath our feet until those particles are observed by us. In other words, simple everyday activities, like standing face-to-face with an object that appears independent of us, could find a connection that no microscope could find—an effortless, unseen mechanism of astonishing intricacy, bordering on magic. Essentially, it suggests that what is observed is real; all else (time, space, matter) is a product of the imagination, lending some of the authority of science to speculations.

It is worth noting that the question about the position and velocity of an electron becomes relevant only if we consider Bohr's characterization of an electron as a *particle* moving around the nucleus in a fixed orbit (rather than a cloud of oscillating energy characterized by a wavelet). Moreover, Bohr's concept of "observation"—the idea that the behavior of all objects is inextricably linked to the presence of an "observer," and that there is no reality out there that is independent of our observation—has been regarded as a major feature of the Copenhagen Interpretation. An objection to this claim is that ontologically, events occur at specific regions in the space-time continuum. We do not "will" them into existence by observing them. In plain language, his critiques considered Bohr as being flat wrong.

Recent experiments cited by Bernardo Kastrup appear to have given some credibility to a particular interpretation of quantum physics—namely that when observed by a person, or even to a lesser extent by an animal and a plant (but not an inanimate object like an electronic detector), the position of electrons in the physical world becomes precise and thereby known. Some (including Deepak Chopra) have taken this claim to mean that quantum physics proves consciousness. Still, others (Einstein among them) have argued that the mathematics of quantum physics simply doesn't provide proof for consciousness. Einstein's EPR Paradox, as clarified by the work of John Bell, requires looking outside the bounds of reductionism to find an explanation for an observed "hidden variable" that characterizes photon entanglement without numerical representation and has yet to be discovered.

Consistent with the conclusion of an observed, real-world event that falls outside the descriptive power of both quantum physics and reductionism, Taheri says that fundamental particles, of which the electron is one of eighteen, are not the only things that exist in the universe. Events in the universe are not simply the cumulative effects of the interactions between fundamental particles. Taheri goes on to assert, however, that there is a myriad of seemingly disjointed fields of consciousness within an otherwise integrated universal consciousness, each consisting of indivisible potentialities. In other words, consciousness is embedded into the fabric of the universe. Taheri's strategy of critically examining direct *experiential* evidence and logically reasoning upon it may be viewed as an admissible aspect of scientific endeavor if we don't define scientific endeavor in the strict sense of reductionism.

That universal consciousness exists and is everywhere is a fundamental axiom that is shared by the philosophies of both Taheri and Kastrup. Furthermore, in both philosophies, the deep interconnection within humanity is a logical conclusion drawn from observations of reality as seen from the perspective of the fundamental axiom.

42 Answers to questions about the origin of consciousness, the universe itself, and life in the universe are generally not sought by theorists, perhaps because they believe the answers are unneeded for their theories to make sense. The same is true about answers

to questions about afterlife, such as "Is there any individuality left after death?"

43   Within the universe, dualities give rise to *motion*, which, in turn, produces *space*. Space then determines *gravity*, which *time* counts on. In other words, without space, there would have been neither gravity nor time—suggesting that space and time are fused together. Time, in succession, relies on *waves*, which in dense mediums create *matter* and in less dense mediums create *energy*. All these elements are subordinate to the *fundamental vibrations*, beyond which there can't be any vibrations, because they are outside the realms of matter and energy, and thereby inexplicable. Yet this perceived "nothingness" outside the realms of matter and energy is the origin of consciousness in which existence is in perfect unity.

44   In addition to acknowledging the interdependency of the "realm of love" and the "realm of the mind," we acknowledge that the path toward Enlightenment is arduous (کوی خرابات), requiring step-wise progression marked by intervals of destruction and resumption. With each destruction (death), there is a distinct possibility for a higher renewal (birth) than before. This preparation will continue indefinitely until such time that our egoic and frivolous thoughts disappear completely and we get access to the treasure box of Awareness, Enlightenment.

45   Taheri's spiritual path has unique characteristics, some of which are ethereal, such as the "Links of Grace" and "glance." The uniqueness of his approach doesn't suggest that it has a monopoly on truth. Respect for others' approaches, whatever they may be, is a key spiritual message of this book and its poetic attempts. It is a virtue that naturally and automatically springs from the heart

when a person begins to see himself or herself in others as a result of practicing connection with the One Consciousness.

It is beyond the scope of my knowledge to describe, much less judge, other spiritual approaches. I was reminded of my naivete when in an email conversation with a dear friend who has extensive meditative experience, I said "Unlike meditation that focuses the mind on mantra, breath work, or other techniques, the Links of Grace require freeing the mind and no technique because connection with the One Consciousness is attained by divine grace in less than a blink of an eye." "Meditation is not what you think," he replied and then proceeded to eloquently explain what his type of meditation practice is asking to open to, to feel, and to know.

Each spiritual path thus gives us fresh lenses with which to come to know ourselves across the span of cultures and of time. I like to think that the view through all lenses is the same—that we are connected to an absolute truth by an unbreakable bond.

One thing that my friend and I immediately agreed on is that our respective spiritual practices are not for those who are unenthused and avoid the longing of their hearts for an experience with the One Consciousness—whispering that we are seamlessly embedded in the web of life, and that within that web there is an invisible essence that allows the potential for Awareness to transform ignorance into wisdom. If the unenthused did engage in either of our spiritual practices, they would be fighting with themselves, thinking it is nonsense or waste of time. Being caught up in their resisting and objecting, they might never settle into the "witness seat" to explore the interior landscape of their body, in which it looks empty, not realizing that at the same time, nothing important is left undone.

46   To elaborate on the concept of cellular-level "local

consciousness" (شعور جزء), everything is made up of the vibrating energy of consciousness. A single cell is a living organism in its own right nested within a functional organ (such as a heart or an eye), which too is a living organism in its own right. It contains all the individual cells nested within it. A human body is an even bigger living organism and has all the smaller organs nested within it. In other words, consciousness lies throughout a living organism within the sea of universal consciousness mediated by the Divine Intelligence (هوشمندی).

While consciousness lies within each living organism, our consciousness is different from the consciousness of animals and plants. The pattern of vibration in the human consciousness is more intricate than that in an animal consciousness, which is in turn more intricate than that in a tree consciousness. Inanimate objects, such as a rock, don't have consciousness, but are still nested within the sea of universal consciousness. In disembodied souls (that is, souls whose physical bodies cease to be self-preserving), consciousness is still there, but little or none of its vibrational activity is occurring in the dimensions of material space-time. It's out there, but we are not usually aware of it—in the same way that the One Consciousness is out there but obfuscated from our local consciousness, unless we try to make an effort to connect with it through the facilitative functions of the Links of Grace.

47   The coordinating function of the Divine Intelligence is through the "Sacred Cognitive Dimension" (کالبد ذهن), which is directly in charge of cellular management.

48   Materialism holds the position that everything in the universe, including humans, consists of matter ruled by physical forces. God didn't design us, natural selection did, they claim. And

when we die, that's the end of us. They say that the prospects for transcendent meaning (that is, meaning beyond the contentment one can achieve in this world) is an illusion. That doesn't mean, materialists say, that there is no morality; natural selection made us selfish, but it also made us compassionate and concerned with fairness because these tendencies helped us see that our well-being depends on the well-being of all humans and all nature.

49   Connection may take place at a designated time between the seeker (فرادرمانگیر) and connector (فرادرمانگر) with or without the *physical* presence of the connector, that is, from near or far. For example, in a live Zoom class, students may either practice connection in the presence of their instructor, or be told to take a witness seat on their own at a designated time (for example, at the top of an odd hour during a twenty-four-hour cycle). They will then receive the Link from their certified instructor from anywhere in the world, regardless of the local time zone.

50   In addition to vibrations, the working of the consciousness may be experienced as بیرون ریزی or what I call "disclosure," whereby symptoms associated with illnesses experienced in the past are temporarily disclosed. For example, the pain experienced as a result of a leg broken in an accident six years earlier is temporarily disclosed from the conscious memory. This is a blessing in disguise in that, when we unveil past health conditions, they can be absolved by paving the way for the Links of Grace to do their job.

51   Psychic acts involving *telepathy* (whereby people's thoughts are read with or without their consent), *precognition* (seeing the future), *séance* (contact with the dead through the agency

of a medium), and the like are tempting, especially for the novice, given people's general fascination with mystery. Even if real and reliable, such acts are not necessary for knowledge and love of God and Enlightenment. The Sufis regard these acts of psychic powers (which may come, unsought, as a byproduct of spiritual contemplation) as "veils" intervening between the eternal self and God, leaving the eternal self empty. If attended to, the psychic powers they develop may set up insurmountable obstacles in the way of Enlightenment, because they lack the understanding of the underlying conditions of the "miraculous" symptoms they have displayed. Worse, they may become a standing temptation to vanity and deceit, either for profit or to show off. For someone who has enthusiasm for Enlightenment, the path in the direction of inner height and spiritual knowledge, paved with God's Links of Grace, is much sweeter and more rewarding.

52   The Links of Grace are mediated by the Divine Intelligence. Thus, the information about our "hardware" (body), which consists of physical, psychological, cognitive, and other dimensions is already within the cosmic "software." As such, the information can be instantly traced and acted upon when we use a "glance" expressing our desire for a specific Link (or field of consciousness) to be activated and then simply take the witness seat. We can experience the connection from any distance in a flash because consciousness lacks space and time.

The "instructor/connector" is required initially for a Link to be formed, as described earlier. Using a metaphor, imagine there is an electrical company in your hometown that generates electricity. Now imagine that despite having a sound home electrical system, the electrical company cannot supply electricity to your home because no technician is available to wire your home's electrical system to the company's source of electricity.

Analogously, despite the availability of the Links of Grace for all people, you cannot tap into the One Consciousness because no "instructor/connector" is available to make the connection between you, the spiritual seeker and the Divine Intelligence. In other words, the Link hasn't been made active. Once the three-way spiritual connection is made, the Link (consciousness field) becomes active, and the "instructor/connector' is no longer needed for that specific Link in the same way that once the technician has wired your home's electrical system to the company's source of energy, the technician is no longer needed for your specific home. The spiritual seeker can now use the Link any time they wish to make connection with the One Consciousness, in the same way that you can go to any room and turn on the light.

The Shared Link of Grace (also discussed in this chapter) works the same way, except that no instructor is needed. That is, the initial connection has already been granted by Taheri as the "connector" and so it is not necessary to contact Taheri to ask for connection to this collection of Links, I call the Shared Link as a grace offered by God through Taheri for everyone. All the seeker needs to do is impartially witness following a "glance" toward this Shared Link.

Since his release from prison nearly two years ago, Taheri has been teaching online courses to Farsi-speaking students from around the world. As of this writing, his lecture notes are being translated into English to be used by trained instructors. Interested English-speaking spiritual seekers may go to the following website (https://cosmointel.com) for updates.

53   For these rare individuals, answers to their extraordinary yearning for grasping life's philosophy (e.g., "Who am I? Why am

I here? Where did I come from? What is my destination?") may require years of sustained enthusiasm. When they do come as revelations or divine rations, they are transferable to the individuals' certified instructors and students. Instructors and students don't need to go through the same process. All they need is nonjudgmental witnessing.

54   Experiencing physical sensations is not obligatory for connection with the One Consciousness and subsequently for healing to take place, because the connection itself is outside space and time. We simply experience its effects.

55   Historically, according to Taheri, this type of healing was called a "miracle," but from Taheri's perspective, it is not complicated once we perceive the reality behind the scene. Taheri is also clear that this healing is not to replace traditional medical therapy, but rather to complement it.

56   As someone who has been granted several Links of Grace by my certified instructor, Maryam, I can help an individual in trouble by calling on selected Links of Grace—essentially by "praying"—with or without their consent, depending on the Link. However, because I am not a certified instructor, the recipient of the Link will not get to keep the Link indefinitely. It is temporary. Interestingly, the action of helping others by sharing the Links that I've benefited from creates a context for my own further growth toward Enlightenment, according to Taheri.

57   Connection with the One Consciousness may occur individually (فردی), collectively (جمعی), or automatically (مداوم). The latter results in the greatest enthusiasm for connecting with

our deepest being (نهادینه). When our axis of being (محور وجودی) is aligned with the One Consciousness, we may even feel the vibrations emanating from it through our senses. With that comes the joy of connectedness with all of God's creations.

58 Also contributing to reduced longevity is physical energy derived from overeating.

59 The space-time continuum is a "frame of reference" that we use to differentiate unique events. Events are distinguished by their locations in each of their four dimensions—i.e., one dimension of time and three dimensions of space (length, width, and depth). In Newtonian physics, this frame of reference is absolutely rigid—meaning that space itself does not expand or shrink as we move through it, and the flow of time's rate remains fixed. What Einstein discovered was that all the dimensions (not just time) of the space-time frame of reference must be flexible to accommodate the fact that the speed of light is a universal constant. In the world of Einstein, the dimensions of space change their size, curve, or flex depending on the situation. Similarly, time slows down as we move, and passes very slowly as we approach the speed of light. Everything else must flex, because the speed of light never flexes.

60 We spend over 99 percent of our lives making decisions, reasoning, solving problems, or struggling to balance competing values and desires. For these, we need focused thoughts. But focused thoughts reflect only one aspect of our total reality. Complementing our focused thoughts are the *qualitative* experiences of everyday life, such as the feeling associated with watching a sunset. They represent the other aspect of our total reality.

61   What appears at first as a concept in the mind (a form) may become a divine reality, which further informs the theory that began with the mind, with whose help we can delve even deeper in the spiritual aspects of external reality. From this point of view, we can say that all our dimensions, including the psychological, emotional, imaginative, and intellectual, have the capacity to help us perceive the spiritual reality, and vice versa. Science has been an ally in the spiritual cause, helping us develop concepts that can lead to the sublime experience of contemplation.

62   Divine Awareness includes perceptions of life's purpose, Enlightenment, Presence, oneness, our origin, and our destination (see chapter 6 for more details).

63   The nature of spiritual experience is highly individualized based on context and what the person brings to the experience, such as their level of "alert presence" (awareness of their own awareness). Further, consciousness is necessarily ambiguous because it is not mediated through perception by the senses or conceptualization, so the experience is not self-evident and may require interpretation. We can never know with certainty if other human beings are experiencing their inner self, and if they do, what the nature of that experience is.

64   I create *gaps* not only in the steady stream of random thoughts during my spiritual practice, but in all situations as best as I can. If, for example, I'm angry, I watch my anger. In that very moment, I can become detached from it. The gap can only occur in the now. Going into my childhood for an explanation won't help because the anger is no longer there. I cannot go back and undo what my family or my society have done or not done. I can

simply not identify with the anger. It is so with greed, overeating, pride, and everything else that the mind is capable of.

The whole methodology of Taheri can be reduced to one word: witnessing. Using it, my center remains untouched. The moment I am centered (that is, I've cut all identities that I'm not, such as my family, my body, my mind), I have a distance from my periphery that is bound to be touched by everything that happens, including praise. And when my actions are born out of Awareness, Divine Intelligence helps me with insights, vitality, solutions, certainty, and creativity. Witnessing brings a new quality into my everyday actions.

Two years ago, I would have been different. But now I try to act only from the silence of my innermost center where no one can penetrate; then I start enjoying whatever happens on the surface. If I'm eating, for example, I'm enjoying it. My body, mind, and soul are in tune. There is also harmony in all three layers of my being when I walk, shop, brush my teeth, peel an orange, or cook. They all become luminous acts.

I'm not new in this bipolar universe. I've lived on many Earths. I am even older than the sun. My eternal self carries the essential experiences of all these lives. My form belongs to this life created by the Big Bang. It has been trained in the universities and by the societies in which I've lived. I don't want to repeat the same old patterns—being preoccupied solely with my periphery. I exist on two planes, the plane of the center and the plane of the periphery—a dance between the sacred and the secular. I need the inner silence to come back rejuvenated in order to participate joyously in everyday life. And out of these polarities, a balance is born so that I never become lopsided.

65   If you start feeling frustrated for not achieving longer

Presence (that is, watching yourself from within), then you cannot come back to the Awareness that you were practicing. There is no need to feel repentance. Accept it as natural. It happens to me and every spiritual seeker I've met. The moment you remember you are unaware, simply come back. Gradually, you may have "alert presence" for a fraction of a second, a whole second, and even more. There is no hurry. You have an eternity at your disposal. Awareness grows slowly. Bring it to each act.

66   Containing the ego, even to the extent of obscuring its output to our lucid Awareness, is of course necessary, but we do this primarily by learning to recognize the ego and understand that it often provides incomplete information. This way, we create an opening to dismiss it.

67   In addition to our Sacred Cognitive Dimension (ذهن حیات) and the brain cognition (ذهن ماده), there is a collective cognition (ذهن جمعی), which reflects a collective form of intelligence.

68   The movements of the solar system include the orbiting of the moon in a curling movement around the planet Earth and on its axis every 27 days; the orbiting of the planet Earth every 24 hours on its axis and every 365 days around the sun; and the tilting of the planet Earth on its axis at an angle of 23 degrees to create the seasons as it makes its yearly journey around the sun. Smooth operation of these elements in the universe with highly complex orbiting motions for fourteen billion years without any collisions with anything bound to them by gravity in the solar system requires an intelligent "architect." The architect's highest ingenuity comes later in designing human beings, where each body part is in perfect ratio to the rest and their cells regenerate themselves

every single day without any prompting. The planet Earth and the human body are marvels of engineering. The thought that the universe's highly orderly and intricate manifestations occurred by chance doesn't compute.

69   Each star in the sky is a sun like our own, but incredibly far away from Earth. Our sun is just one of a billion stars in our own Milky Way—one galaxy among hundreds of billions of galaxies. The closest stars are four "light years" away (each light year is the distance that light travels in one Earth year or six trillion miles). Since our galaxy is about eighty thousand light years wide, stars still in our galaxy can be thousands of light years away. Some of these stars are much larger than our own sun. On average, each star has at least one planet orbiting it. Imagine standing on an inhabitable planet within one of these stars' orbits. You'd see our own sun as a tiny star in the sky. The universe is such a vast expanse of space, and still expanding outward!

70   I use the term "prayer," but not in the traditional sense of asking God to bring me happiness and prosperity or observing any kind of ritual or fasting. God doesn't serve as the "complaint department." I use the term "prayer" instead within a different context—one that requires not a temple or a church or a mosque, but the soul and nothing more. My soul lays itself open to the immanent God within. I ask nothing, but leave myself in the arms of God without wasting time in any desire, except to want God to direct me to the right path. I praise God's creation—the universe. But praise is easy. My prayer goes beyond praise to show gratitude for God's wonderous kindness to all humans in offering His Links of Grace so that we can experience oneness.

One way I show that gratitude is to help evoke, through my

writing, the awakening of my readers to the One Consciousness that resides within each of them. Most importantly, I seek help in withdrawing egoic thoughts, which have been conditioned to create suffering in humans for thousands of years. The latter prayer gets to the heart of "who I am" uncoupled from the act of bowing, kneeling, or singing. There is nothing wrong with these ways of showing humility and joyful thanks, so long as they are not seen as absolving the practitioner of any obligation that binds them to others, and granted they are performed with good intentions and deep understanding of the inner meaning of the prayer. Outwardly worshipping and making the various movements of the prayers while inwardly being completely engrossed in one's business affairs is not the kind of prayer through which the individual ascends in their journey to God.

71   Indeed, everything in the universe is unique—in the same way that every fingerprint is unique. Even two atoms of the same chemical element (such as two atoms of *sodium* from table salt, or two atoms of *gold* in a wedding ring, or two *carbon* atoms found in the cells of any growing living thing, including our own bodies) are not perfectly identical. They are distinguished by the number of neutrons within their nucleus, the speed with which their electrons travel, and other factors. Since all matter in the universe, whether it is living or not, is composed of chemical elements, and since the atoms that form the chemical elements are not identical, we can see then why nothing in the universe is identical.

72   The protective layer, while permanent for those who have been granted its associated Link of Grace by a certified instructor, is only effective when used for purposes that bring us closer to Enlightenment, such as (a) relinquishing self-centeredness and a

sense of separation from others; (b) coming to the realization that we are all one; and (c) studying to acquire a deeper understanding of Enlightenment, putting it to practice, and sharing it with others without fear of being misidentified by some as being "superstitious" or "out of touch with reality." Once we start engaging in anti-Enlightenment activities, such as gossiping, ridiculing, being disrespectful toward those with differing political or religious views, reading others' thoughts by means of telepathy, or anticipating events through precognition, we are no longer protected by the layer from potential inhibitors.

73   According to the Torah, grieving for the dead doesn't mean feeling sad. It is not about the living. Instead, it is about showing empathy for the wrenching change that the soul of the departed person is going through, which is most intense in its first seven days. At the end of seven days, it has begun to settle into its new experience. At the end of thirty days, the soul has made another step into settling. If one starts grieving beyond this period, it is no longer for the experience of the deceased person, but rather feeling sorry for oneself.

74   The start of the expansion of the universe is believed to be the beginning of *time* as we know it. Like motion, gravity can affect time. Time moves slower near gravitational force. One millionth of a second of our time represents thousands of years in the pre–Big Bang supermassive black hole with immense gravity unconstrained by the elements of time and space. If, at that time, we were to stand outside the universe—outside both space and time—to lift our arm, it would take thousands of years, because lifting the arm requires time. Similarly, a clock on Earth ticks a tiny bit slower than a clock on the moon. So time is relative,

meaning it is a function of various factors, one of which is gravity, as noted above. Another factor that affects time is speed. Time passes at different rates depending upon how fast objects are moving. The faster the speed, the faster time goes. Thus, to travel in time without aging along on the way, we would need to travel near light speed. But then, nothing that weighs anything can attain the speed of light—a minor snag!

75   Some physicists further elaborate that in the instants immediately after the Big Bang, the volume of the entire material universe was smaller than the volume of a present-day atom. That volume is expanding, and is currently billions of light-years in extent. The ultimate conclusion of that expansion is unknown to science and is probably inaccessible via the theoretical tools presently available. The constraints on the motions of the universe and everything in it are characterized by universal Laws of the Universe.

76   Some physicists claim that the location of Earth within the space-time continuum is akin to a single point on a circle, meaning no point on the circle has any claim compared to all the others as being the center. Also, given that the circle is continuously expanding (as we believe the space-time continuum to be expanding), from any point on the circle, the rest of the circle appears to be expanding away from us. This creates the illusion that we are at the center. However, an observer at any other point on the circle experiences the same illusion.

77   It remains largely a mystery why dark energy is dominating the rate of expansion of our universe billions of years after the Big Bang. Less of a question mark is the fact that dark energy is inherent to the fabric of *space* itself, occupying roughly 68 percent

of the universe. When dark energy gets swallowed by what is called a *black hole* within the universe, it gets transformed into *dark matter*, which occupies 27 percent of the universe. The rest, everything observed with all our instruments, adds up to less than 5 percent of the universe. Black holes are regions in space where gravity is so strong that no light can escape it. There are millions of black holes in the Milky Way alone. These black holes are different from the pre–Big Bang supermassive black hole unconstrained by the elements of time and space, which created the universe with an unimaginable density.

78   Dark energy, according to Taheri, is expanding the universe into its eventual death, in accordance with the Universal Law of birth and death, which applies to everything, including the universe itself. The universe was born with the Big Bang. With this birth, it became multitudinous (کثرت در کیهان), beginning with dualities that led to motion, space, gravity, time, waves, and the rest.

The mechanism through which this invisible dark energy expands the universe is to apply pressure to its edge using the massive energy it contains, and in so doing to thin and soften the hard edge of the universe. This is when, over a very long timescale (billions of years), the temperature reaches -460 degrees Fahrenheit. This "absolute zero" temperature is too cold to support the movements of any matter in the universe, from galaxies and stars to atoms and subatomic particles. Even space and time dimensions dissipate. This Big Chill is called the "entropic exhaustion of the universe." In time, Taheri extrapolates, the death of the universe will lead to the creation of another supermassive black hole (سیاهچاله کیهانی) where matter is in its absolute unity (وحدت در کیهان).

Unity in the center of the black hole means that all subatomic particles (such as electrons) are indistinguishable from each other due to the extreme gravity. This compacted matter with infinite density eventually transforms into intense heat, causing the black hole to explode with unimaginable force, thereby releasing the matter to give birth to another universe with new stars and planets. This stellar process repeats itself endlessly, with the universe (a) becoming extremely cold at its death, (b) transforming into a unified embryotic state within a supermassive black hole, and (c) being born again as a result of another big explosion. It is in this sense that the physical universe is simply an *appearance* embedded in reality. The universe's physical phenomena, including nature and our bodies, is an appearance that will eventually dissolve after death, and all its matter will be reduced to an absolute unity of nuclei in embryotic state.

Dark energy is not to be confused with Consciousness. Consciousness, which is embedded into the fabric of the universe's fundamental vibrations, is an unappreciated absolute truth, which plays a significant role in our path toward Enlightenment. Consciousness does not have entropy or uncertainty because it never stops working. This constraint within consciousness that compels it to create the cosmos in a variety of configurations as effectively as possible drives evolution within the Big Bang. The emerging cosmic particles from consciousness tell us that there is a bedrock connection between the cosmos and us. The essence of our universe—and billions of speculative universes—is also our own essence, the One Consciousness, central to any true understanding of reality.

What we, as human beings, experience is the echo of the universe's experiences of physical death, unification, and rebirth. Our bodily forms become less distinct in the next adjacent (مجاور) world; the One Consciousness traces itself back to its original, irreducible essence where there is no form or grounds for the separation between people or entities; and we are reborn like a perennial flower that always blooms. I see my death no more final than the autumn decay of my purple clematis vines in Maine, the roots of which remain unaffected and ready to sprout new life in the following spring.

79   Even though a Greek named Eratosthenes, who lived about two hundred years before Christ, had figured out that Earth was a sphere and even calculated its circumference, there was resistance to the idea. In early 1600, Galileo, an Italian astronomer, was prosecuted by the Roman Catholic Church for supporting the idea that Earth was a globe. His discoveries undermined traditional ideas about flat world.

80   Our personality blueprint is accompanied by two categories of traits, according to Taheri. The first category is the "self-changing impossibility," a set of firm traits that are controlled by three key software. The first software (فطرت) gives us inclinations toward Enlightenment (من کمال جو) and against Enlightenment (من ضد کمال) as well as the free will to choose between the two. The second software (نهاد) gives us survival instinct, and the third software (بنیاد) overrides all genetic and environmental makeup, an example of which is no identical twins having the same personality. None of these traits are within our control.

The "self-changing potentiality" (من برنامه پذیر) is a secondary set of traits that, unlike the primary traits discussed above, isn't inborn. It is programmed during our lifetime in this physical world, primarily in childhood. It is based on environmental factors, such as information gained and lessons learned. This potentiality and the ensuring temperaments with which we normally identify, though extremely powerful, do not have to be succumbed to.

People can and do refuse to identify themselves with what would be too easy and natural for them to be.

Knowledge of our primary traits that precludes any interference on our part (self-changing impossibility), works in tandem with knowledge of our secondary traits that allow intervention ("self-changing potentiality"), to determine our unique overall personality. This self-knowledge allows us to reflect on sources of difficulty when faced with life events, shift gears if needed, and with the facilitative functioning of the Links of Grace create a better balance between our primary and secondary traits. Sometimes crisis alone is sufficient to make a person forget to be his or her customary self. Transcendence of our personality and idiosyncrasies and attendance to our inner self so that at every moment we know who we are in relation to the universe and beyond, is the aim of spiritual practice.

81 God's Soul, which has emerged from the One Consciousness and with which we are imbued may be what religions mean when they say that we were created in the "image of God." It probably doesn't mean, as some have suggested, that our physical bodies look alike, but rather that our essence is the same.

82 When I talk about expanding upon the wisdom and memories we brought from previous lives through our Sacred Cognitive Dimension, I'm not referring to our ordinary memory, the warehouse filled with opaque memories of everyday experiences, such as our gender, bodies, and the rest, which are often about the world of separation. Instead, I'm referring to the memories associated with our inner reality, our true identity.

83 Literally becoming one or merging with God is impossible

because we are the image of God, in the same way that an image of us in the mirror cannot be combined with us, the owner of our image. However, we may have union with God, the One Consciousness.

84   This unification refers to the "marriage" of the higher elements of the personality blueprint and God's Soul (see chapter 6 discussion of "God") in hell.

85   These "limbo" periods (برزخ) are places between death and rebirth where the eternal self is free to contemplate the wrongdoing of its former life. Once the eternal self leaves a limbo period, the door to the previous world is closed and the eternal self, which is embodied (merged in a different lifeform on its journey), can improve. Here, the eternal self and the body intermingle to benefit from each other's wisdom while retaining their relative independence.

86   At some point, however, the concept of "sooner or later" would no longer exist as a continuum or a flow the way we experience time in our current world of relativity. Instead, we'd be experiencing ourselves in the eternal moment of "now."

87   I draw a subtle distinction between (a) divine revelations received and directly expressed through poetry, speech, or written text by rare and Enlightened people like the ancient Persian Sufi poets, Meister Eckhart and Taheri, and (b) divine Awareness or insights that are perceived by every inspired person directly from connection with the One Consciousness.

Divine revelations of Enlightened people are simply the record of the immediate experience of those who are pure enough to be able to see God and transfer informational content that falls upon every aspect of life to others. Whatever an Enlightened man or woman does, ordinary people will follow their example. Such revelations can be acted upon without resort to any kind of religious faith. There must, however, be faith in the genuineness of the revelations, which the spiritual seekers can verify for themselves if they are prepared to fulfill the necessary conditions. By divine Awareness or divine insight, however, I mean information that comes directly into the mind of ordinary people (often specific to their own immediate needs). Neither revelation nor Awareness/insight is a result of the evidence of the senses or rational reflection on such evidence.

The striking consistency of the mystical revelations throughout ages in both West and East (see Huxley's The Perennial Philosophy) and the concepts recorded in the Bhagavad Gita over five thousand years ago excludes the possibility that the revelations could all be wrong. The records left make it abundantly clear that all were attempting to describe the same indescribable facts, which are viable in the present day.

88   These traits that accompany our personality dimension, and which have been preserved from the previous bipolar world, enter the fetus of an unborn baby. The fetus could be in Africa, Japan, or Spain. Because the personality blueprint doesn't know its new world, but can recognize vibrations, its selection of the fetus is based on one with similar vibrations. These distinctive personality traits are different from our genes inherited from our parents or acquired from their training. That is why no identical twins have the same personality traits. Using myself as an example, the blueprint of my original personality traits, which included enthusiasm as discussed in the opening pages of this book, came to this world

from a previous bipolar world. It merged with a fetus, "the physical me," which carried the biological characteristics (including the emotional responses to my experience of the world) inherited from my parents living in Tehran. In this sense, enthusiasm is a permanent aspect of my original personality blueprint, which has the capability to transport itself from one world to another.

89   The Divine Guide (روح هادی), our inborn moral compass—which shows us the path toward Enlightenment as we incarnate into a new body—complements (not contradicts) the view that moral codes are developed through the ability to self-reflect in the process of evolution. Hunter-gatherers seeing other hunter-gatherers as their own equivalent likely led to the survival of the human species. In both views—Divine Guide and biological evolution—our moral sensitivities' strength and the particular form they take vary depending on the pool of wisdom that we have accumulated over our incarnations in various physical forms or states, and the intervals in between. Adolf Hitler, for example, didn't apply his own moral judgment and went along with his ego (which regarded the ultimate good as existing, not in eternity) to commit one of the worst crimes in history of the world. Mahatma Gandhi, on the other hand, surrendered his ego by employing nonviolent resistance, leading to successful independence from British rule.

Regarding this book's subject matter, morality is framed in a way that aligns us with our own true self, God, others, and nature. In this view, we find and allow the goodness that is already within us to emerge. Not wanting to harm other people, animals, and ecosystems follows automatically and naturally. This is not to say that actions are not needed in certain contexts. The Holocaust occurred because the Nazis were crazed against the Jews beyond all reason. The world had to make them stop. Morality is thus not a cut-and-dried decision.

90　The more one teaches or writes about the divine Awareness, the more one becomes a master of the knowledge that one transmits and ultimately gets carried in the cosmic journey.

91　Suppressing our own ego, as noted throughout the book, is not helpful because disidentification with the ego creates a strong resistance as the fictitious person is so familiar. Connecting with the One Consciousness facilitated by the Links of Grace is our primary hope for abstention from the ego and thus virtuous actions.

92　Mysticism is sometimes defined, in a derogatory and false sense, as mere belief in ghosts and other phenomena, such as giving up worldly pursuits, or spending long periods of time in seclusion.

93　We have a dimension in our primal "hidden state" (حیات تاریک) called "astral body" (کالبد اختری), which is capable of communicating information from the Sacred Cognitive Dimension to body cells directly and swiftly, bypassing the brain. This way, the body is alerted and ready to react quickly to the incoming information from the brain, rather than waiting for the brain to translate it into electrochemical language. This phenomenon reminds me of my dance competition days when I would commit each movement, say spinning, to memory through weeks and years of practice. Once in "muscle memory," I could reproduce those movements without thought when competing, and, instead, "feel" the music and express it through movement.

94   Note that the brain also has cognition (ذهن ماده) that is capable of storing information. Together with the Sacred Cognitive Dimension (ذهن حيات), they form a broader cognitive dimension.